# Bullying Among Prisoners

Bullying in prisons can have severe consequences, both for those directly involved and for the prison regime as a whole, yet the subject has been curiously neglected in literature. In 1993 the Prison Service introduced their first anti-bullying strategy and since then there has been a great deal of research on the subject. *Bullying Among Prisoners* summarises this research and seeks to answer some important questions.

*Bullying Among Prisoners* identifies problems in defining and measuring bullying, and proposes guidelines on how research in this field should be conducted. The book covers

- what bullying is
- how and why it occurs
- the effects of bullying
- practical strategies for preventing bullying.

By outlining a series of interventions that can be employed to address bullying, this book will be an invaluable resource for all those working directly with the perpetrators and victims of bullying, not only in prisons but also in secure hospitals.

**Jane L. Ireland** is a chartered forensic psychologist and a member of the International Society for Research into Aggression. She has published many journal articles in the area of bullying among prisoners.

# Bullying Among Prisoners

## Evidence, Research and Intervention Strategies

Jane L. Ireland

Brunner-Routledge
Taylor & Francis Group
HOVE AND NEW YORK

First published 2002 by Brunner-Routledge
27 Church Road, Hove, East Sussex BN3 2FA

Simultaneously published in the USA and Canada
by Brunner-Routledge
29 West 35th Street, New York, NY 10001

*Brunner-Routledge is an imprint of the Taylor & Francis Group*

© 2002 Jane Ireland

Typeset in Times by Keystroke, Jacaranda Lodge, Wolverhampton
Printed and bound in Great Britain by Biddles Ltd, Guildford and King's Lynn
Paperback cover design by Sandra Heath

*British Library Cataloguing in Publication Data*
A catalogue record for this book is available from the British Library

*Library of Congress Cataloging in Publication Data*

ISBN 1–58391–186–3 (hbk)
ISBN 1–58391–187–1 (pbk)

## Dedication

To the memory of my nanny, Irene Foxwell. Without her encouragement this book would never have been written.

# Contents

# Figures

# Tables

# Foreword

The aim of the Criminal Justice System is to protect the public by preventing crime. The Statement of Purpose of the Prison Service reads that prisoners are to be kept secure throughout the time that they have been committed by the courts, to be treated with humanity and helped to lead useful and law-abiding lives in prison and on release. In essence this means that everything possible must be done to prevent prisoners re-offending on release.

Nothing undermines the smooth running of a custodial establishment, and so its ability to satisfy the Statement of Purpose and achieve the Aim, more than a climate of fear – fear amongst staff about their treatment by management and other staff members, or fear that they may be assaulted by prisoners; fear amongst prisoners that they may be assaulted by staff, or not be protected from being assaulted by other prisoners; fear amongst those who work at or visit an establishment about how they will be treated. These may sound like extremes that could never happen in the United Kingdom in 2001.

But, only very recently, a further three Prison Service senior officers and officers were sentenced to long terms of imprisonment for ill-treating prisoners in Wormwood Scrubs. Furthermore, the officers had compounded their offence by alleging that they themselves had been assaulted by the prisoner, to which assault they had merely responded. They were clearly acting on the unspoken assumption that stories told by staff would be believed because they were staff, and that stories told by prisoners would not be believed because they were prisoners. Fear among the prisoners that their allegations are unlikely to be believed is itself a form of bullying because of the mental pressure that it exerts on prisoners. The fact that the courts believed the prisoner and not the staff is of great significance, not just because we are now in what has been described as the Human Rights era, but because it sent an important signal to those who might be tempted to act in the same way. That sentences for abusing prisoners in this way have now been passed makes the publication of Dr Jane Ireland's important book particularly timely, because not only does she catalogue ways in which bullying may manifest itself, but also how it can – and must – be identified and eliminated.

As part of a thematic review of suicide and its prevention in prisons, *Suicide is Everyone's Concern* (HM Inspectorate 1999), I introduced what I called the 'healthy prison concept' as a way of describing what I should like to find in terms of the treatment of prisoners and the conditions in which they are held in custody. There are four aspects to this

1  everyone should feel and be safe – staff, prisoners, those who work in prisons and those who visit them
2  everyone should be treated with respect as a fellow human being
3  prisoners should be enabled to improve themselves through access to purposeful activity
4  prisoners should be enabled to maintain contact with their families and prepare for release.

Of these conditions safety is paramount. Unless staff feel safe when delivering treatment, and prisoners feel safe in prison – in their cells, while moving around and when attending activities – nothing can happen. The importance of everyone feeling themselves to be safe cannot be over-estimated, something that is, unfortunately, overlooked by too many middle and senior managers. There can be no worse example of poor management than turning a blind eye to bullying, as happened for far too long at Wormwood Scrubs.

As Dr Ireland says, bullying is a specific form of aggression that is difficult to define, and it takes many forms. It can be both direct and indirect and is by no means confined to physical abuse. Verbal bullying is often focused on some form of difference between the abuser and the abused, such as cultural diversity, mental disorder or disability. Cultural diversity is not just between black and white but between people from different towns and cities or different parts of towns or cities. It can take the form of inexorable pressure based on debt, often related to drugs, which can be meted out not only on an individual but also on his or her family. It can take the form of staff denying access to activities, or making subjective reports that result in unnecessary moves between institutions or delayed release on parole or tariff. Its manifestations are endless, but they all point to one overriding implication – that is, if a custodial institution is to run smoothly and deliver the outcomes expected of it, immediate intervention by management is absolutely essential to eliminate bullying.

This is where Dr Ireland's book is so particularly useful. Rightly she devotes much detailed attention to intervention, including the need to take full account of the perception of the victim. I have to admit to a deep hatred for what is called the cult of 'managerialism' when applied to dealing with people – the idea that everything can be directed on paper, by means of endless written instructions, targets and performance indicators, and by measuring the quantity of process. It is a dangerous and fallacious practice, particularly in the hands of those who are responsible for the well-being of other people. That well-being can only be ensured by constant, hands-on supervision by responsible and accountable managers. They in turn must be backed up by supportive and responsive senior management who will, if necessary, take swift action to remove identified wrongdoers, thus reinforcing the ethos that bullying, of whatever kind, simply will not be tolerated. This is also why it is so important that senior management does not adopt a bullying style in dealing with subordinates.

Sadly, swift action does not happen in the Prison Service today, whose management is obsessed with exact compliance with rules, budgets and targets and which is unable to provide full, purposeful and active working days for all prisoners, designed to challenge offending or anti-social behaviour, or tackle educational, work skill or medical deficiencies. Management is so involved in the minutiae of the bureaucratic process that it is unable spend as much time as it should where it should, i.e. on the landings ensuring that prisoners are being properly and humanely cared for. Failing to oversee is a form of neglect, and neglect is a form of institutional bullying. All concerned should read Dr Ireland's book if they doubt the veracity of this.

Bullying takes place everywhere, in homes, schools and workplaces. That is not to condone it but to confirm that the motivations behind bullying can be complex, as Dr Ireland says, and not always easy to determine. But, wherever it remains unchecked, it undermines human relationships as well as the smooth running of establishments. After reading *Bullying Among Prisoners* there can no longer be any excuse for protested ignorance about this.

But Dr Ireland also invites examination of another sad fact, all too often forgotten when considering bullies, that the vast majority of them have themselves been bullied, and are meting out to others what has been meted out to them. These are what she calls bully/victims. It is essential that part of any attempt to challenge bullies includes an examination of their past, to try to determine the circumstances in which they experienced being bullied. Prisons are now required to have in place 'anti-bullying strategies'. Strategy is the wrong word to use, but what this implies is that every prison is required to have programmes in place for challenging any identified bully, and separating them from other prisoners while this takes place. A significant part of any offending behaviour programme is devoted to the victim. This is more difficult when the perpetrator has also been a victim, but it is important that any work done does not ignore the point.

I therefore warmly commend Dr Ireland's book. It results from careful observation and research but is essentially practical in its message. No custodial institution can afford to turn a blind eye to bullying. No member of staff of such an institution can afford to ignore the results of unchecked bullying because of the climate of fear that can result. If what Dr Ireland preaches is put into practice, every prison – which means every prisoner and member of staff – should feel safe. Then our prisons will be healthy and work with prisoners can be carried out to ensure that the public will be better protected.

Sir David Ramsbotham<br>
Her Majesty's Chief Inspector of Prisons 1995–2001

# Preface

My interest in bullying research started in 1994 when I was trying to decide what topic to address for my undergraduate dissertation in psychology. I'm not really sure where my idea of studying 'bullying among prisoners' came from, but when I started my literature review I quickly discovered, to my amazement, that it was an area of research that had received little attention. Indeed, I could only find a grand total of three studies, two of which were unpublished. Ironically, it was this lack of research that got me interested in the research field as a whole.

When the negative effects that bullying can have on its victims (and on prison regimes) are considered, it is astounding that research has been so minimal. No one who has had contact with victims can fail to be moved by the situation in which they find themselves – away from family and friends in an unfriendly environment, targeted by aggressive peers and offered little means of escape. This in itself should be impetus enough to conduct more research into this area.

Since about 1996 there has been a drastic increase in the number of studies focusing on bullying among prisoners, and prisons are now able to draw from this body of research to develop specific prison-based anti-bullying strategies. The research field is also evolving, away from merely describing the nature and extent of bullying to looking at why it occurs, the different groups who are involved, and so on. Anti-bullying strategies are evolving in conjunction with the literature and this has been particularly evident in the UK Prison Service, a service that appears to be leading the way in terms of developing such strategies. Consequently, for those interested in bullying research this is proving to be an exciting time.

The reason for this book was a simple one. To date no books have been written on this subject and I wanted to write one that brought together the research that has been done so far, and one which made some practical recommendations on how to manage bullying in secure settings. In doing so I hope that the book proves useful to researchers, academics, students, managers and practitioners alike. When I first thought of putting the book together I had intended to include only one chapter on intervention strategies. As I started writing, however, I realised how little focus had been given to dealing with bullying in secure settings. In view of how difficult bullying can be to manage this is perhaps not surprising. Indeed, as I highlight in Chapter 4, bullying is a product of both the individual and the environment and impacting on both is a difficult task. This is not to say that it should not be attempted, rather that the focus of strategies should be different, namely away from eradicating it completely (an unobtainable goal) towards reducing it through preventative measures and appropriate responses to it when it occurs. Thus, I felt that a single chapter did not do this area justice and decided to include two – one on preventative approaches and one on reactive approaches.

What will be evident from the book is how much research is needed into this area. I hope that the research field continues to develop and that the publication of this book will encourage researchers to move away from addressing those areas that are becoming 'over-researched' (e.g. the nature and extent of bullying), and move towards areas which will add to our knowledge about bullying and help the development of effective intervention strategies.

# Acknowledgements

I would like to thank all those who encouraged and inspired me to write this book, especially the prisoners who have participated in the research that I have conducted over the years. Without their contribution, researching this area would be impossible. Thanks are also extended to my friends and colleagues (there are too many to name but you know who you are), to my family, particularly my mum, nan, Carol and Tracey, and to David who has been forced to live and breath *Bullying Among Prisoners* for the past year.

Special thanks are reserved for Katie Bailey, Mike Jennings, Martha Blom-Cooper, Dr Jon Sutton, Professor John Archer and Dr Mike Eslea who each reviewed individual chapters for me, particularly to John and Mike who also looked at the original proposal and supervised my PhD. An acknowledgements page would not be complete, however, without a special mention for John Archer, who encouraged and inspired me to do a PhD in this area in the first place and who also had the 'pleasure' of supervising my undergraduate dissertation on bullying.

## Permissions for the use of copyright material

Throughout the book a number of quotes have been used from other sources and I am grateful to the publishers, authors and editors for allowing them to be reproduced here. They are as follows.

Academic Press, for quotes from Geen (1998: © *Human Aggression, Theories, Research and Implications for Social Policy*), in Chapter 1, from Connell and Farrington (1996: © *Journal of Adolescence*), in Chapters 2 and 4, and from Ireland (2002d: © *Journal of Adolescence*), in Chapter 2. Permission to reproduce the quotes from the *Journal of Adolescence* was obtained from Ann Hagell, Editor.

American Psychological Association, for quotes from Davis (1983: © *Journal of Personality and Social Psychology*) and Toch (1992: © *Living in Prison: the Ecology of Survival*), in Chapters 5 and 6 respectively.

Carol H. Ammons, Senior Editor, *Psychological Reports*, for a quote from Ramanaiah and Deniston (1993: © *Psychological Reports*), in Chapter 5.

British Psychological Society, for quotes from Beck (1995: © *Issues in Criminological and Legal Psychology*), in Chapters 4 and 7, quotes from Sutton, Smith and Swettenham (1999b: © *British Journal of Developmental Psychology*), Ireland (2001c: © *Legal and Criminological Psychology*), in Chapter 5, and Livingston (1997: © *Issues in Criminological and Legal Psychology*), in Chapter 6.

Brunner-Routledge, for a quote from Smith and Sharpe (1994: © *School Bullying: Insights and Perspectives*), in Chapter 4, from Randall (1997: © *Adult Bullying: Perpetrators and Victims*), in Chapter 1, and from Gilbert (1994: © *Male Violence*), in Chapter 4.

Canadian Criminal Justice Association, for a quote from Cooley (1993: © *Canadian Journal of Criminology*), in Chapter 1.

Elsevier Science Ltd, for a quote from Farrington and Nuttall (1980: © *Journal of Criminal Justice*), in Chapter 4.

Heldref Publications, for a quote from Rigby and Slee (1993: © *Journal of Social Psychology*), in Chapter 4.

Her Majesty's Stationery Office (Crown Copyright), for quotes from Beck and Ireland (1997: © *Inside Psychology: The Journal of Prison Service Psychology*), Marshall (1993: © *Inside Psychology: The Journal of Prison Service Psychology*), O'Donnell and Edgar (1996a: © *The Extent and Dynamics of Victimisation in Prisons*), O'Donnell and Edgar (1996b: © *Research Findings, Home Office Research and Statistics Directorate*) and O'Donnell & Edgar (1997: © *Prison Service Journal*), in Chapters 2, 5, 6, 7 and 8 respectively. Permission for quotes from O'Donnell and Edgar (1996a, 1996b and 1997) was also obtained from Dr Kimmett Edgar.

Lawrence Erlbaum Associates Inc, for a quote from Salmivalli (1998: © *Journal of Research on Adolescence*), in Chapter 5.

Joe Levenson, Prison Reform Trust for a quote from Levenson (2000: Beating the bullies? The prison service's anti-bullying strategy), in Chapter 1.

Oxford University Press, for a quote from Liebling (1995: © *The British Journal of Criminology*), in Chapter 6.

Plenum Publishing Group, for a quote from Björkqvist (1994: © *Sex Roles*), in Chapter 2.

Taylor and Francis Ltd: Overseas Publishers Association, for a quote from Connell and Farrington (1997: © *Psychology, Crime and Law*), in Chapter 2.

Jane Whitaker, Editor, *Human Givens: The Mental Health Journal*, for a quote from Smith (1994: © *The Therapist*), in Chapter 1.

John Wiley and Sons Ltd, for a quote from Ireland (2001a: © *Aggressive Behavior*), in Chapter 5, from Björkqvist, Österman and Lagerspetz (1994b: © *Aggressive Behavior*), in Chapter 3, and from Smith (2002: © *Children and Society*), in Chapter 1.

Ellen Wilson Fielding, Editor, *Federal Probation*, for a quote from Nacci, Teitelbaum and Prather (1977: © *Federal Probation*), in Chapter 4.

University of Chicago Press, for a quote from Ellis, Grasmick and Gilman (1974: © *American Journal of Sociology*), in Chapter 1.

Permissions were also obtained from John Wiley & Sons Ltd for the interview schedule presented in Table 2.1, from Academic Press for the questionnaire schedule presented in Table 2.2, and from Governor David Thomas, HMYOI Lancaster Farms for the Bullying Incident Report presented in Table 2.4 and for the guidelines presented in Figure 8.2. I am particularly indebted to D. Lockwood for quotes recorded from prisoners in his 1980 book *Prison Sexual Violence*. A number of these quotes appear in Chapter 6. Unfortunately this book is now out of print and I was unable, after a number of attempts, to locate the author and request permission to reproduce them here. I have still included the quotes since they add greatly to the text and credit for this is reserved solely for D. Lockwood.

# Chapter 1

# Bullying in prison: the research field to date

## Why study bullying among prisoners?

The issue of bullying among prisoners is an important one. According to Levenson

> Many prisoners are assaulted, regularly threatened or harassed. The physical safety of some prisoners, especially sex offenders, can only be achieved by segregating them for their own protection. Violence and bullying are endemic in most prisons and young offender institutions.
>
> (Levenson 2000: 1)

By studying bullying among prisoners our knowledge and understanding of this type of behaviour can be increased, the victims of bullying protected and the security of the prison improved (Connell and Farrington 1996). There are also implications for classifying offenders in terms of need and risk assessment (Connell and Farrington 1996): if bullies and victims can be reliably identified then this will undoubtedly inform any such assessment. The effects of bullying on the prison as a whole can be varied and include an increase in the level of suicide, self-harm, stress, drug use, drug trading, escapes, absconds, failures to return from home leave, prisoner complaints, assaults, prisoners requesting transfers or to be placed under the protection of staff, and increased levels of damage to prison property (Home Office Prison Service 1999). Levenson (2000) argued that bullying also reduces the likelihood that prison staff will be able to work productively with prisoners to help them to address their offending behaviour and prepare them for release.

The types of bullying that prisoners are subjected to can be severe and include physical abuse, ranging from 'slaps', punches and the deliberate burning of victims with cigarettes, to batteries being placed in socks and used as weapons with which to 'beat' someone. Bullying also includes cold water being poured over bedding or excrement placed in it, or prisoners being forced to become the 'personal servants' of the bully. 'Practical jokes' or 'horseplay' are common, for example victims are thrown into cold baths, have their eyebrows shaved and/or their hair cut (Brookes 1993). Livingston and co-workers (1994) also report bullies name-calling, making threats, spreading rumours, deliberately ignoring or frightening others, and forcing prisoners to cause trouble. Brookes and colleagues (1994) report instances where victims have deliberately been given smaller helpings of food, have had property stolen from their cells and glass placed into their soap. Incidents of sexual abuse have also been reported including masturbating another prisoner or shaving a prisoner's pubic hair whilst the victim was tied to a bed (McGurk and McDougall 1986).

The effects of such actions on the victims cannot be underestimated. The following account comes from a woman who wrote the following on the back of a questionnaire addressing bullying.

> When I first came in I gave out tobacco and rizlas to people who asked me. I found I was short at the end of the week. This last week I refused and my life has been made hell. I've been continually harassed for my canteen day and night, usually by the hardcore people I shared the dormitory with: if not them they have been getting other people to ask me on their behalf and when I refuse abuse me verbally and lie about me. When in the dormitory I made the mistake of saying I was gay and have been ostracised by the very couple who have been sleeping together in bed! I have come off my medication to get out of here – not sleeping much, around three hours per night. I just want to be left alone to serve my time and leave prison never to return. I cannot relate well to people and need medication: going through hell yet I have tried very hard to fit in and appear normal. I don't want to cause trouble but it's very difficult not to retaliate verbally and I feel like I'm near to cracking up.

Another account comes from a male young offender who wrote the following letter to prison officers in January 2000.

> I have been getting bullied off lads on this unit for about eight weeks. They have been saying things like 'I shagged your mum' and betting lads on the wing half an ounce of tobacco that they wouldn't be able to batter me. Nearly all the lads on the unit have been taking this offer up and having a go at me. Every day for the past eight weeks they

have been getting on my case by calling my mum names and saying to other lads that I have been calling their mum things like 'fat slag' etc. They have done this so that the other lads will batter me. They have told me that I had better string myself up because they are never going to leave me alone. One of the lads is in court on the same day as me, and in the same court. He told me that he's going to batter me there and I think that he would. PS. I'm really scared what might happen now when I go to court with him and what he might do. Even if he doesn't do it at court he might do it at reception. I don't want anything like that to happen.

## Defining aggression

Before presenting a definition of bullying, it is worth focusing briefly on aggression research in general, particularly the different types of aggression and how these may relate to a discussion of bullying. Geen argues that the term 'aggression' is not a scientific one and is 'taken from everyday English and used to describe a number of functionally different behaviours that have in common the infliction of harm upon another person' (1998: 1). A number of different varieties of aggression have been suggested (Dodge 1991). One of the most useful distinctions between these, and one which may prove relevant to a discussion of bullying behaviour, is the notion of reactive and proactive aggression (Dodge 1991). There is compelling evidence that supports the validity of the distinction between these two types of aggression (Dodge and Coie 1987). Reactive aggression occurs when an individual overreacts to minor provocations. In such a situation the individual is generally viewed as short-tempered and volatile. Reactive aggression has also been referred to as 'angry aggression' and can be described as a fear-motivated response (Weisfeld 1994), one that includes defensive postures in response to threats. Proactive aggression involves more planning on the part of the perpetrator and is used instrumentally to obtain a goal through bullying, dominating or coercing others (Dodge 1991).

Another useful distinction between types of aggression is that of direct and indirect aggression. Direct aggression includes the most observable forms such as physical or verbal abuse, forms in which the identity of the aggressor is known. Indirect aggression is subtle and includes spreading rumours, and ostracising or gossiping about an individual. It represents a form in which the aggressor may remain unidentified (Lagerspetz *et al.* 1988). Björkqvist and colleagues (1992a) conceptualise styles of inter-personal aggression as falling along a continuum of development, with direct forms of aggression used at an early age to be largely replaced during adolescence and adulthood by indirect aggression.

## What is bullying and how does it relate to aggression?

Aggressive relationships between individuals can be categorised into two distinct types: 'symmetrical' or 'high-conflict' relationships in which each member aggresses towards and is victimised by the other member, and 'asymmetrical' or 'low-conflict' relationships in which one member adopts the role of aggressor and the other the role of victim (Perry *et al.* 1992). Bullying represents the latter category of aggressive relationship (Olweus 1996) and is a distinct form of aggression that can either be direct or indirect in nature (Rivers and Smith 1994). It can also be described as a proactive form of aggression in which an individual manipulates and dominates others in order to obtain a goal, whether this is material or social. It can also include an element of planning and organisation on the part of the perpetrator, thus fitting the definition of proactive aggression. I would suggest, however, that particularly in a prison environment, not all bullying is highly organised and some can represent a 'reaction' to being bullied. Individuals who fall into the bully/victim category (i.e. those who report both 'bullying others' and 'being bullied') may be reacting to their own victimisation by aggressing towards others. The provocation in this situation is their attempted victimisation by others. It may not necessarily matter if the intended victim of the bully/victim is someone who has aggressed towards them – the fact that they are showing some form of aggression towards others suggests that they are attempting to assert and maintain their dominance (Ireland 1999a), and in this way avoid being labelled as a 'victim', thus preventing any future victimisation (Connell and Farrington 1996). In this situation the reaction of the bully/victim could be conceptualised as a fear or defensive response.

Thus, I would argue that bullying behaviour is not necessarily proactive, but can also include elements of reactive aggression depending on the motivation of the aggressor and the social constraints of the environment in which it takes place. It would seem that 'pure' bullies, namely those who only bully others and are not victims themselves, are more likely to represent proactive aggressors, whereas bully/victims are more likely to represent reactive aggressors. Dodge (1991), however, argues that the distinction between reactive and proactive aggression is only a relative one and it is possible for reactive aggression to contain proactive elements and vice versa. This can be related to bullying behaviour as follows: although bully/victims may be displaying reactive aggression there may also be a proactive goal, namely a way of communicating to the rest of their peer group that they will not readily submit to being bullied and are thus not targets for future victimisation.

As a specific form of aggression, bullying has proven difficult to define (see Chapter 2 where I discuss definitional issues in more detail). In a review of the literature Farrington (1993) reported that there was widespread agreement among researchers that in order for a behaviour to be classed as bullying it must represent a repeated and unprovoked act of aggression that includes physical, verbal or psychological attack, an imbalance of power and an intention to cause fear or harm to the victim. This definition has not been applied, however, by all researchers and there does not appear to be any *universally* accepted definition of bullying (Farrington 1993). Randall, for example, describes bullying much more simply as 'the aggressive behaviour arising from the deliberate intent to cause physical or psychological distress to others' (1997: 4), with Smith describing it as a 'systematic abuse of power' (1994: 12), stating that it is most likely to occur in social groups where there are clear power relationships, and low supervision. Power relationships are present in any social group 'by virtue of strength or size or ability, force of personality, sheer numbers, or recognised hierarchy' (Smith 1994: 12), and this power can be abused. Smith further argues that the exact definition of what constitutes abuse depends on the social and cultural context: if the abuse is systematic then 'bullying' is a valid term by which to describe it.

There are also problems in devising a definition that encapsulates the whole range of direct and indirect aggressive behaviours considered representative of bullying. In one of the first studies that I conducted, for example, I used a behavioural checklist with prisoners that described a total of thirty-three discrete behaviours indicative of bullying others, twenty-four relating to direct aggression and nine to indirect (Ireland 1999a). These behaviours included stealing prisoners' tobacco, starting fights, trying to turn prisoners against one another, calling prisoners names, and intimidating and threatening prisoners. Attempting to include all of these behaviours into one narrow and overly specific definition is virtually impossible.

Despite a lack of agreement regarding the specific criteria applied to bullying, two criteria are now widely used by researchers, namely that in order for a behaviour to be classed as bullying it must include repetition of the aggressive act and involve an imbalance of power (Smith and Brain 2000). Again, although these criteria are widely applied, this does not mean that they are universally accepted (Smith and Brain 2000), with some researchers preferring to use much broader definitions that make no reference to these elements.

However, bullying has only recently been recognised as a distinct form of aggression in academic studies and this could explain the lack of a standard definition of bullying. Indeed, Birkett comments that

> Bullying is not new: for centuries children have been persistently calling each other names, stealing each other's toys, and sending former friends to Coventry. But the recognition of bullying as a distinct phenomenon, to be analysed and academicised, is relatively recent.
>
> (Birkett 1998: 24)

Attempts to define bullying have been hindered by an apparent 'hierarchy' of bullying behaviours ranging from 'least damaging', to 'most damaging', with verbal methods of bullying being seen as least damaging and physical methods as most damaging. Such a view is captured by a father whose 17-year-old son was accused of 'bullying a schoolgirl to death' who said 'you know how kids are . . . they never physically hurt her. They just called her names – Fatty and Smelly, and things like that' (Birkett 1998: 32).

It is also important to note that the term 'bullying' is not one that is universally used. Smith describes it as an English term that 'appears to have originated in the sixteenth century from the middle Dutch word "boele", meaning lover: this became "fine fellow" and "blusterer" and eventually its present meaning' (2002: in press). Interestingly Smith (2002) notes how the original more positive meaning of the word is retained in the phrase 'bully for you' indicating an expression of 'approval at a daring action'. Other cultures have used other terms to convey an action similar to bullying – the Scandinavian term is 'mobbing', the Dutch 'pesten' and the Japanese 'ijime' (Smith 2002). None of these terms, however, are exactly equivalent to bullying. Smith and Brain (2000) describe how evidence for the existence of bullying has been found in sixteen European countries, the United States, Canada, Japan, Australia and New Zealand, with indications of similar behaviour reported in the developing world.

Most of the research into bullying has been limited to the study of children in a school environment. By comparison little research has addressed bullying among adults and, according to Randall, 'Bullying is still seen as a problem for children in schools and most people never suspect the range, severity and depth of misery created every day, nearly everywhere, by the bullying of adults by adults' (1997: vii). Researchers do recognise that bullying can occur among adults in many settings such as the workplace, prisons, old people's homes and family homes (Smith and Brain 2000).

The majority of work conducted among adults has focused on the workplace and was pioneered by Adams (1992). Since 1992 there has been a substantial amount of work published in this area that has led to the recognition that bullying at work is a major occupational stressor (Hoel *et al.* 1999). It has been suggested that the bullying that takes place between adults can be particularly subtle and is often rationalised by the aggressor. Adams (1997) describes a range of aggressive practices that the adult bully may engage in at work including repeatedly telling someone off or criticising them, using offensive language, over-monitoring their performance, withholding information that is essential for the victim to complete the task, intercepting or listening to telephone calls, interfering with mail, changing desk and office arrangements, preventing the victim from attending training or taking leave without adequate explanation, and setting the victim up to fail by delegating to them impossible tasks to complete with impossible deadlines.

Different terms to describe bullying tend to be used for different settings. In the workplace terms such as trauma, mistreatment, harassment, abuse, and tyranny have been used interchangeably to describe inappropriate and abusive behaviours between adults. The term bullying has also been used but its use has been restricted to research conducted in the United Kingdom and Ireland (Hoel *et al.* 1999). In the family home the term abuse tends to be used more than bullying, particularly when describing the parent–child relationship (Smith and Brain 2000), although the term bullying could also characterise abusive relationships between partners. In a prison setting, the majority of research has used the term bullying to describe the abusive behaviours that occur between prisoners. There have been some variations on the exact use of this term with some researchers using phrases such as 'bullying behaviour' and 'behaviours *indicative* of bullying'. The term bullying, however, in whatever format, is one that is readily utilised by both prisoners and staff to describe the aggression that can occur between prisoners. Smith (2002) makes the important point that the term bullying is one that can be applied to any social situation from which a victim feels unable to readily remove themselves. Such an argument can be readily applied to a secure environment such as a prison.

## What research has been done into prison bullying?

Much of the research that addresses bullying within prisons has been confined to the United Kingdom with the exception of Connell and Farrington (1996, 1997) who addressed bullying among young offenders at an open-custody facility in Canada. Indeed, studies conducted outside the United Kingdom have rarely referred to the concept of bullying. This is not surprising when it is considered that bullying is primarily an English term (Smith 2002). Research has been conducted outside the United Kingdom addressing issues related to bullying in prison, but this has concentrated on concepts of violence (e.g. McCorkle 1992). There is undoubtedly a degree of overlap between violence and bullying, for example Olweus (1996) argued that violence can take place without bullying, just as bullying can take place without violence. The best examples of forms of bullying which do not constitute violence would be indirect bullying and theft-related bullying (Ireland 2000a). Both of these latter forms of aggression have been included in prison-based definitions of bullying.

Researchers outside the United Kingdom have tended to concentrate on direct assaults between male prisoners, particularly sexual assault (e.g. Sagarin 1976; Donaldson 1984; Ruchkin et al. 1998). This latter area of research has not been focused on by researchers in the United Kingdom, with sexual assault often included as one of a range of aggressive behaviours that may occur between prisoners (e.g. Ireland 1999a). The majority of research outside the United Kingdom has also concentrated on the perpetrators of aggression (Wright 1991), and on 'uncovering the relationship between violence in prison and variables such as population density, prisoner transiency, age or the relationship between violent offenders and violence in prison' (Cooley 1993: 480). This is in contrast to research conducted in the United Kingdom (and to a lesser extent Canada) that has focused less on why the aggression occurs and more on assessing the nature and the extent of the problem, identifying who is involved and the consequences of the abuse for its victims.

Researchers outside the United Kingdom have also operationalised very different terms and definitions to describe a range of abusive relationships that may occur between prisoners. Wright (1991), for example, focused on 'violent and/or victimised' prisoners with violent prisoners representing those who had been charged with an assault on an inmate or a staff member, and victimised prisoners those who had attempted suicide or had inflicted an injury on themselves. Fuller and Orsagh (1977) also used the terms 'violence and victimisation' with no definition of what this referred to. Shields and Simourd (1991) referred to 'predatory behaviour', describing predatory prisoners as those who actively sought exploitative relationships with other prisoners and who would force them to engage in various acts. Mutchnick and Fawcett (1990) addressed 'violence' among incarcerated juvenile offenders, and broadly defined it as a perceived or actual act of physical or verbal aggression. Mutchnick and Fawcett (1990) also used the term 'victimisation' and, referencing Bowker (1983), described it as an abusive 'transaction' in which a more powerful individual would obtain goods or services from a less powerful individual. Cooley (1993) used the term 'criminal victimisation' and applied the following criteria: prisoners were *not* considered to be a victim if they indicated that the prisoner who had aggressed towards them was using force equal to or lesser than the force used by them. Bartollas and co-workers (1974) focused on behaviours indicative of (sexually) exploiting others, or being exploited, describing the perpetrators of sexual aggression as 'booty-bandits'. Ellis and colleagues focused on the 'aggressive transgressions' of prisoners defined as 'any behavior proscribed by prison rules that harms or injures another person' (1974: 18). Finally, Johnson (1978) used the terms 'prison games' or 'peer games' to describe some of the abusive behaviours that occurred between prisoners, including incidents involving teasing and ostracising. The *range* of terms to describe aggression between prisoners is not evident in the research conducted in the United Kingdom where, with very few exceptions (e.g. O'Donnell and Edgar 1996a, 1996b), the term bullying has been systematically applied. Thus, researching aggression between prisoners within a framework of bullying is primarily an English phenomenon.

Since the focus of the current and following chapters is on *bullying* behaviours among prisoners, I will concentrate on those studies that have dealt specifically with this phenomenon, although in parts it will be necessary for me to expand the discussion to include research that has applied more general terms such as violence or victimisation.

The first study conducted into bullying among offenders was that of McGurk and McDougall (1986). Since then there have been thirty-six studies addressing bullying among prisoners. The majority of these studies have not been published in academic peer-reviewed journals, with only sixteen appearing in such publications to date. Of the remaining studies, the majority have either been presented in 'in-house' professional journals (e.g. Marshall 1993) or been completed as surveys designed solely for use within prisons (e.g. Bolt 1999). A summary of the studies conducted to date is presented in Table 1.1. The table briefly outlines the main

Table 1.1 Studies conducted into bullying among prisoners (presented in year order)

| Authors | Characteristics of the study | | | Description of study | Percentage reporting to be a bully (victim) | Percentage reporting to have seen bullying | Percentage reporting behaviours indicative of bullying others (being bullied) | Rate of bullying per 100 of prison population | Where the study was published[i] |
| | Year | Sample[a] | Method[b] | | | | | | |
| --- | --- | --- | --- | --- | --- | --- | --- | --- | --- |
| McGurk and McDougall | 1986 | 23 male YO | interview | nature and extent of bullying, terms given to bullying by prisoners | – | 61 | – | – | 3 (published in 1991) |
| Beck | 1992 | 189 male YO | questionnaire | nature and extent of bullying, exploration of definitions of bullying | 21 (29) | – | – | – | 5 |
| Brookes | 1993 | 56 adult males | interview | nature and extent of bullying, characteristics of victims | 0 (13) | 24 | – | – | 4 (part published (2) in 1996 as Brookes and Pratt) |
| Marshall | 1993 | male YO[c] | interview | operational methods employed to address bullying | – | – | – | – | 2 |
| Falshaw | 1993 | 176 male YO | questionnaire | identifying victims by their responses to bullying, comparisons between prisons | 67 (8) | – | – | – | 5 |
| Brookes, Cooper, Trivette and Willmot | 1994 | 123 adult | interview | nature and extent of bullying, characteristics of victims | 3 (8) | 15 | – | – | 4 |
| Livingston, Jones and Hussain | 1994 | 47 adult males | interview | nature and extent of bullying, effectiveness of the anti-bullying strategy | 62 (57) | 74 | – | – | 4 |

| Study | Year | Sample | Method | Aims/approaches | | | | | |
|---|---|---|---|---|---|---|---|---|---|
| | | YO | naire | | | | | | |
| Swift | 1995 | 65 male YO | interviews | nature and extent of bullying | 14 (34) | 31 | – | – | 4 |
| Connell and Farrington | 1996 | 20 male YO | interview and questionnaire | nature and extent of bullying, developing an interview schedule | 45 (25) | – | – | – | 1 |
| Ireland and Archer | 1996 | 90 adult males, 48 adult females | questionnaire | nature and extent, when and where bullying takes place, who is involved | 6 (14) | 49 | – | – | 1 |
| O'Brien | 1996 | male YO – 90 incidents of bullying | official records | analysis of suspected and actual bullying incidents recorded over a 1-year period, location of bullying, methods and motives | – | – | – | – | 4 |
| Power, Dyson and Wozniak | 1997 | 707 male YO | questionnaire | nature and extent of bullying, self-reported attitudes and behaviour | 11 (24) | 76 | – | – | 1 |
| Dyson, Power and Wozniak | 1997 | 5 male YO prisons[d] | official records | using official records to estimate bullying, problems with such records | – | – | – | 2.0–28.9 | 1 |
| Livingston and Chapman | 1997 | 92 male YO | interview | relationship between bullying and self-injurious behaviour | (45) | – | – | – | 2 |
| Willmot | 1997 | 123 adult males | interview | nature and extent of bullying, vulnerable groups | 4 (7) | – | – | – | 2 |
| Beck and Smith | 1997 | 397 male YO | behavioural checklist | prevalence of behaviours indicative of being bullied, relationship to staff ratings | – | – | (75) | – | 2 |
| Connell and Farrington | 1997 | 34 male YO | interview and peer reports | reliability and validity of different methods used to measure bullying | 35 (26)[e] | – | – | – | 1 |
| Osiowy | 1997 | 35 adult prisoners | interview and focus groups | effectiveness of anti-bullying strategy | – | – | – | – | 5 |

Table 1.1 (continued)

| Authors | Year | Characteristics of the study | | Description of study | Percentage reporting to be a bully (victim) | Percentage reporting to have seen bullying | Percentage reporting behaviours indicative of bullying others (being bullied) | Rate of bullying per 100 of prison population | Where the study was published[i] |
| | | Sample[a] | Method[b] | | | | | | |
| --- | --- | --- | --- | --- | --- | --- | --- | --- | --- |
| Biggam and Power | 1998 | 100 male YO | interview and questionnaire | social problem-solving skills of victims and psychological distress experienced by victims | – | – | – | – | 1 |
| Loucks | 1998 | 88 female adult/YO | interview and official records | nature and extent of bullying, use of official records | 11 (25) | 51 | – | 13.9 | 6 |
| Duckworth | 1998 | 24 males, 6 females[f] | questionnaire | identifying potential victims by their behaviour | 23 (23) | – | – | – | 5 |
| Mosson | 1998 | 161 female adult/YO | questionnaire | nature and extent of bullying, characteristics of those involved | (51) | – | – | – | 2 |
| Ireland[g] | 1999a | 235 male adult/YO, 74 female adult/YO | behavioural checklist | nature and extent of bullying, characteristics of groups involved, reactions to victimisation | – | – | 58 (52) | – | 1 |
| Ireland[g] | 1999b | 235 male adult/YO, 74 female adult/YO | behavioural checklist | provictim attitudes and empathy, how each relates to bullying behaviour | – | – | – | – | 1 |
| Ireland | 1999c | 404 male YO | behavioural checklist | prevalence of bullying behaviours, reactions to victimisation, intervention strategies | – | – | 61 (45) | – | 2 |
| Grant | 1999 | 210 female adult/YO | questionnaire | nature and extent of bullying, relationship with fear and precautionary behaviours | 30 (6) | 72 | – | – | 2 |

| | | | | | | | | | |
|---|---|---|---|---|---|---|---|---|---|
| | | ...males | behavioural checklist | ...response to victimisation | – | – | 55 (55) | – | 1 |
| Ireland and Ireland | 2000 | 194 adult males | behavioural checklist | nature and extent of bullying, provictim attitudes, characteristics of those involved in bullying in a maximum-security prison | – | – | – | – | 1 |
| Ireland and Hill | 2001 | 9 male YO | focus groups | focus groups with victims, bullies and those not involved in bullying to address the effectiveness of anti-bullying strategies | – | – | – | – | 2 |
| Ireland[h] | 2001a | 210 adult males, 196 females | behavioural checklist | number and type of solutions generated to hypothetical bullying incidents, comparison across groups involved in bullying | – | – | – | – | 1 |
| Ireland[h] | 2001c | 210 adult males, 196 females | behavioural checklist | personal descriptive and behavioural characteristics associated with bullying behaviour | – | – | – | – | 1 |
| Ireland[i] | 2002b | 285 adult males, 217 adult females | behavioural checklist | relationship between social self-esteem and bullying behaviour | – | – | – | – | 1 |
| Ireland[i] | 2002c | 285 adult males, 217 adult females | behavioural checklist | relationship between assertiveness and bullying behaviour | – | – | – | – | 1 |
| Ireland | 2002d | male YO – 107 incidents of bullying | official records | summary of suspected and actual incidents of bullying reported over a 14-month period, types of bullying, where they occur, who records the information | – | – | – | – | 1 |

Table 1.1 (continued)

| Authors | Year | Sample[a] | Method[b] | Description of study | Percentage reporting to be a bully (victim) | Percentage reporting to have seen bullying | Percentage reporting indicative behaviours of bullying others (being bullied) | Rate of bullying per 100 of prison population | Where the study was published[j] |
|---|---|---|---|---|---|---|---|---|---|
| | Characteristics of the study | | | | | | | | |
| Ireland | 2002e | 95 male juvenile, 196 YO | behavioural checklist & question- naire | comparison of juvenile vs. young offenders, comparison of different methods used to measure bullying | 6 (5) | 57 | 53 (45) | – | 1 |
| Ireland and Archer[h] | 2002 | 210 adult males, 196 females | behavioural checklist | consequences of responding aggressively to different types of bullying | – | – | – | – | 1 |

Notes
a  YO = young offenders.
b  See Chapter 2 for a detailed description of the specific methods employed.
c  The number of young offenders were not supplied by Marshall (1993); this study also used staff checklists to categorise 284 prisoners into six groups but it was not clear how this related to bullying.
d  The number of reports was not disclosed.
e  Based on self-reports during interviews.
f  Taken from a maximum-security youth treatment centre housing young offenders and children in care.
g  Ireland (1999a and 1999b) were papers published from an MSc project completed by the author.
h  Ireland and Archer (2002), Ireland (2001a and 2001c) were papers publishing separate results from the first phase of the same PhD thesis.
i  Ireland (2002b and 2002c) were papers publishing separate results from the second phase of the same PhD thesis.
j  1 = peer-reviewed journal, 2 = professional journal, 3 = book chapter, 4 = not published, 5 = unpublished dissertation/thesis, 6 = other publication.

characteristics of each study and provides information on the focus of the study and the findings regarding the extent of bullying.

In addition to the studies presented in Table 1.1, O'Donnell and Edgar (1996a) conducted a study into victimisation, as opposed to bullying, among a sample of male adult and young offenders. The study was entitled *The Extent and Dynamics of Victimisation in Prisons* and included some discussion of the relationship between victimisation and bullying. Results from this study were later published in two professional journals (O'Donnell and Edgar 1996b, 1997).

Although Table 1.1 has attempted to include all of the known studies addressing bullying among prisoners, undoubtedly there are a number of studies conducted solely for use within prisons that have not been made available to researchers. There is a tendency for research into bullying, if conducted by prison staff, to remain unpublished or inaccessible to outside researchers. Thus, trying to ascertain the true extent of bullying research is difficult.

In addition to the studies presented in Table 1.1 there are a total of thirteen other papers that relate to bullying among prisoners. These papers represent discussions of previous studies or reviews of the research field (e.g. Ireland *et al.* 1998, 1999; Ireland 1998a, 1999d, 1999e, 2000a, 2001b, 2002f), the Home Office Prison Service Anti-Bullying Strategies (Home Office Prison Service 1993, 1999; Levenson 2000), a paper discussing an anti-bullying awareness training package for prison staff (Ireland 2000), and one describing interventions for bullies and/or victims (Ireland 2002a). Only one of these papers has been published in a peer-reviewed journal (Ireland 2000a).

## How has the research field evolved?

As Table 1.1 shows, bullying among prisoners is an area that has only recently received the attention of researchers. Although the first study was conducted in 1986 this was not published until 1991 (in a book chapter), and there was no further research conducted until 1992. The first papers into bullying among prisoners did not appear in peer-reviewed journals until 1996 (Connell and Farrington 1996; Ireland and Archer 1996), with the first review of research appearing in 2000 (Ireland 2000a). Interest in prison bullying has steadily increased since 1996. This increase has also led to an interest in *how* bullying is measured, notably the validity and reliability of the various methods used by researchers (e.g. Dyson *et al.* 1997; Connell and Farrington 1997; Ireland 2002d), an issue that I will discuss in detail in the following chapter.

Researchers have tended to concentrate solely on samples of male young offenders, followed by studies concentrating solely on adult men, and those addressing combined samples of adults and young offenders (men and women). Women prisoners have been researched to a much lesser extent than men. This observation is not limited to bullying among prisoners, the aggressiveness of men across a range of situations has been studied to a greater extent than that of women (Björkqvist 1992). The fact that women can be aggressive has only recently been recognised by researchers, and has led researchers to describe in some detail what are now termed 'female forms of aggression' (Björkqvist and Niemelä 1992). Indeed, when I first began to research bullying behaviour among female prisoners I was told by staff at one prison that women didn't really bully each other and that perhaps I should have chosen another area to research, one that could provide interesting findings. Regardless of this, however, I published my findings in 1996 and it represented the first study that specifically addressed (adult) women prisoners (Ireland and Archer 1996). Since then there have been eleven more studies conducted with women, five addressing both adults and young offenders, five focusing on adult offenders, and one focusing on young offenders. The majority of these studies have compared the responses of women directly with those of men. The studies conducted among women have shown that women do engage in bullying behaviour to the same extent, if not more so than men. They also highlight important sex differences with regard to the types of bullying that occur, and the types of prisoners who are likely to bully and/or be bullied (see Chapters 3 and 5 where I discuss sex differences in more detail).

Recently research has also begun to compare different samples with one another. Earlier studies tended to focus on one group of offenders in isolation (i.e. young offenders *or* adults), whereas half of all studies conducted between 1999 and 2001 have compared samples of men and women directly, with some studies comparing men and women, adults and young offenders together (e.g. Ireland 1999a).

Juvenile offenders have only recently been studied as a group on their own, with researchers tending to combine young offenders (those aged between 18 and 21 years) and juveniles (those aged between 12 and 17 years) together. It is only recently that juveniles housed in prisons have been clearly distinguished from young offenders. They are now housed and managed separately which will undoubtedly encourage researchers to address juveniles as a separate group. Indeed recent research has highlighted a number of differences between juveniles and young offenders in terms of the perceived extent of bullying and the types of bullying that they experience or engage in (Ireland 2002e).

Research has also focused on the nature and the extent of the problem, and on prisoners' perceptions of the characteristics of those involved in bullying either as bullies or victims (e.g. McGurk and McDougall 1986; Brookes *et al*. 1994). This is particularly true of the earlier studies into bullying. Researchers have now begun to move away from merely describing the problem to attempting to address the actual characteristics of perpetrators and victims (see Chapter 5). These characteristics have included both descriptive characteristics such as age, offence type and sentence length, and behavioural characteristics such as the non-bullying behaviours that prisoners display towards staff and other prisoners (Ireland 2001c). The intrinsic characteristics of the perpetrators and victims of bullying have also been addressed including attitudes, empathy (Ireland 1999b), beliefs about aggression (Ireland and Archer 2002), self-esteem (Ireland 2002b), social problem-solving (Biggam and Power 1998; Ireland 2001a), assertiveness (Ireland 2002c) and psychological distress (Biggam and Power 1998).

Researchers have also started to adopt a system of classifying prisoners into one of four bully categories

- *pure bullies* those who solely report behaviours indicative of bullying others
- *pure victims* those who solely report behaviours indicative of being bullied
- *bully/victims* those who report behaviours indicative of being bullied and of bullying others
- a *not-involved group* those who report no such behaviours (Ireland 1999a).

Although this classification system is crude, it is a marked improvement on earlier studies that tended to focus on bullies and victims as two separate groups failing to adequately assess the cross-over between the two (i.e. bully/victims) and also the importance of the non-involved group. This latter group is a particularly important one to consider as bullying is not a behaviour that occurs between a few individuals in isolation from the peer group as a whole. It is very much a product of the peer group and is maintained by their reaction to it. Thus any analysis of bullying should incorporate *all* members of this peer group, regardless of their direct involvement in incidents of bullying.

Finally, it is important to recognise the different types of prison establishments that have been researched as well as the different types of prisoners surveyed. All prisons in the United Kingdom are categorised in terms of the security level that is needed to contain the prisoners, and the risk that the prisoner would pose to the general public should they escape. Prisons housing men are categorised into four groups

* maximum/exceptionally high-risk (category 'A' or 'dispersal' prisons)
* medium-high risk (category 'B')
* low-medium risk (category 'C')
* low risk (category 'D' or 'open' prisons).

Prisons housing women are categorised into two groups

* 'closed', which could in theory house prisoners equivalent to those housed in category 'A', 'B' or 'C' prisons
* 'open', which represent low security prisons roughly equivalent to category 'D' prisons.

Young offender and juvenile establishments follow the same categorisation system as women's prisons. To date there is no known research conducted within open prisons (male or female). Research has been restricted to closed prisons, with the majority of this (among men) focusing on category B and category C establishments. Only one paper has specifically addressed maximum-security (category A) male establishments (Ireland and Ireland 2000). In this study, prisoners in maximum-security establishments were found to hold more negative attitudes towards the victims of bullying and positive views towards bullies than prisoners held in other types of prisons. Other research also suggests that the type of prison under study may have a marked influence on the nature and extent of bullying reported (Ireland 2000b).[1] This is not surprising when it is considered that bullying is not a product solely of the individual but is an interaction between the individual and their environment (see Chapter 4). The importance of the environment has been recognised by school-based researchers for a number of years. Sutton and colleagues (1996), for example, describe bullying as part of the fundamental dynamic of the social world, with Mellor (quoted in Birkett 1998) arguing that we should move away from viewing bullies as 'intrinsically and irrevocably bad' and removed from the environment in which they act, instead viewing their behaviour to be a result of 'the social situation they find themselves in . . . there's nothing intrinsically wrong with them. In a different environment, they might not bully at all' (Birkett 1998: 32).

## Summary

This chapter introduced the importance of studying bullying in a prison environment in terms of the effects that bullying can have on its victims and on the prison regime as a whole. The effects on victims will be discussed in more detail in Chapter 6. The problems in defining bullying have also been introduced, highlighting how it is a complex form of aggression in which there is no single universally accepted definition, and one in which the term used to describe it differs according to the country in which it is being studied.

The focus of research in prisons has varied across countries, with work outside the United Kingdom tending not to address bullying *per se* but focusing instead on general violence and aggression. Bullying research in prisons, although limited, has begun to evolve in terms of the focus of the research and the populations studied. Whereas earlier studies focused on men and the nature and the extent of bullying, more recently researchers have focused on women and have shown more interest in the characteristics of the different groups involved in bullying and begun to acknowledge the impact of the environment on bullying. With regard to this latter issue, more research is needed across a range of prison establishments, research that would allow for direct comparisons to be made between them. At present the research conducted cannot be generalised to open prisons or maximum-security establishments. There are also problems associated with the range of methods and definitions used to measure bullying among prisoners which influences how findings are interpreted and to what extent they can be generalised. The methods and definitions used by researchers will be the focus of the following chapter.

# Chapter 2

# Defining and measuring bullying in a prison environment

## Defining bullying in a prison environment

Prison-based researchers have defined bullying in a number of ways. Beck presented prisoners with the following definition.

> We say a young person is being bullied or picked on, when another young person, or a group of people, say nasty or unpleasant things to him [sic]. It is also bullying when a young person is hit, kicked, threatened, sent nasty notes, when no-one ever talks to him [sic] and things like that. These things can happen frequently and it is difficult for the young person being bullied to defend himself [sic]. It is also bullying when a young person is teased repeatedly in a nasty way. But it is not bullying when two people of about the same strength have had the odd fight or quarrel.
>
> (Beck 1992: 15, based on Smith 1991 and Olweus 1989)

Whereas Connell and Farrington presented prisoners with the following definition.

> We say that a resident is being *bullied* when he/she is pressured, threatened, intimidated (for example for money, food or cigarettes), or made to do things against his/her will, including sexual acts. It is bullying if a resident is beaten up, hit, pushed, kicked or restrained, if no one ever talks to the resident, or when someone tries to bother him/her by saying mean or unpleasant things. These things happen to the resident often, usually by the same people or groups of people, and it is hard for the resident being bullied to defend him/herself. It is *not* bullying when two residents of about the same strength sometimes have a fight.
>
> (Connell and Farrington 1996: 91, based on Smith 1991)

Both of these definitions are derived from school-based definitions. There are problems in applying definitions developed for use within schools to the bullying that occurs within a prison, primarily because they do not take into account the special characteristics of prison environments (Ireland 2000a). For example, school-based researchers would argue that it is the repetitive nature of bullying and the fact that it is based on an asymmetrical power relationship that makes it a distinct form of aggression (Olweus 1996). It is also these two qualities, however, that have made such definitions difficult to apply to a prison, and have led prison-based researchers, such as Beck and Ireland (1997), to conclude that a broader definition of bullying needs to be applied to a prison sample. This is particularly the case for three forms of bullying specific to prisons

- 'taxing', a behaviour in which prisoners who are new to a wing or unit have goods taken off them under the pretence of 'taking for tax'
- 'initiation ceremonies', these are inflicted on prisoners when they first join a unit (McGurk and McDougall 1986)
- 'baroning', this involves goods being given to prisoners and then repayment demanded with a high rate of interest.

Each of these behaviours can occur on a single occasion, thus excluding them from school-based definitions of bullying. Beck and Ireland (1997), however, argue that behaviours do not have to be repeated to be described as bullying. This is supported by Mosson (1998) who, in a study of women prisoners, found that many of those reporting being bullied indicated that it had been a single, isolated incident. Indeed, in a prison where prisoners are regularly moved to new locations (either to or from different prisons or wings) the repetition of an aggressive act by a bully towards the same victim is often impossible. Thus, the abusive relationship that is so characteristic of bullying between individuals in a school tends to develop and be maintained over a much shorter period of time when it occurs within a prison. This does not, however, mean that the aggressive act is not bullying. Indeed, Randall (1997) argues that it is the *fear* of repeated aggression that characterises bullying, not the actual incidence. This concept of 'fear' is especially relevant to bullying in a prison: once an individual is targeted by an aggressor, unless they defend themselves adequately they risk becoming labelled as a victim by other members of their peer group (Connell and Farrington 1996). Once labelled as a victim the individual increases their chances of being victimised further by the same perpetrator or by others. The fear in this situation is not just limited to the possibility of being aggressed towards again by the same perpetrator, but it is also a fear of becoming a viable target for other aggressors in the future.

Similarly, Olweus (1996) acknowledges that not all bullying has a repetitive element and that a serious, single instance of victimisation can be regarded as bullying under special circumstances. This raises the question of what is considered a serious instance of victimisation and what is not. This concept of seriousness is especially relevant to the behaviours of taxing and initiation ceremonies. Primarily, these activities represent one-off incidents of aggression towards a prisoner when he/she is new to the environment. As these forms of victimisation are likely to happen only once within a short space of time they seem, on this criterion, to fall outside classic definitions of bullying. Both, however, could be classified as serious 'special' occurrences of bullying: taxing can be described as a serious incident of theft, and initiation ceremonies have potential long-term consequences for the victim. How a victim defends him or herself during this ceremony will decide whether or not they will be victimised in the future (Connell and Farrington 1996).

Both taxing and initiation ceremonies are reported to be common among prisoners and so embedded in their subculture that they are viewed as 'acceptable' forms of victimisation, and ones that all prisoners new to a wing or prison should expect (Connell and Farrington 1996; Marshall 1993). As new prisoners expect these behaviours to occur it could be argued that they are in a position to *fear* the possibility of being aggressed towards, thus fitting with Randall's (1997) argument that it is the fear of repeated aggression that is important in defining bullying, not the actual incidence.

Finally, baroning is a good example of an abusive behaviour that is not based on an asymmetrical power relationship. Initially, the victim enters the relationship voluntarily and therefore it is not asymmetrical. Indeed, many prisoners do not construe such an activity as bullying (Ireland and Archer 1996). Baroning is an example of extortion, however, and represents an abusive relationship that extends over a period of time and one in which the prisoner who 'barons' has ultimate control over the 'loan'. The punishments advocated for those who fail to pay their loans or 'honour their debts' include physical assaults and threats (Ireland and Archer 1996; Brookes 1993). Thus the victim is in a position to fear the occurrence of future aggression. Baroning, like the other specific types of prison aggression, represents a special form of victimisation that would also fit the criteria of bullying.

Definitions applied to prison bullying must ensure that they include *all* of the possible types of aggression that can occur. I am referring here to the distinction between direct and indirect aggression. By indirect types of aggression I am referring to all subtle types of aggression sometimes referred to as 'covert' or 'relational' by researchers. The majority of prison-based research has not recognised this distinction or the importance of measuring indirect aggression in such an environment. Consequently, examples of indirect aggression are either absent from definitions of bullying or when included reference is made only to the most salient forms, namely gossiping, ostracising, spreading rumours (Ireland and Archer 1996) or teasing (Beck 1992).

Indirect aggression has only been recognised by researchers fairly recently as a specific form of aggression (Lagerspetz *et al.* 1988; Crick and Grotpeter 1995). Due to the subtle and covert nature of this type of aggression it is more difficult to identify and recognise than its direct counterpart. It is easy to dismiss activities such as social exclusion, gossiping and playing practical jokes as a widespread form of behaviour, and therefore normalising it (Ireland 1999c). Thus, prisoners who engage in such behaviours may not recognise it as such, and may not admit to either bullying others or being bullied if it is not specified that indirect aggression can constitute bullying. This is consistent with the observation that prisoners do not perceive indirect aggression as bullying, and that they are more likely to perceive direct aggression as bullying (Ireland 2002e).

Researchers have only recently attempted to describe the many discrete types of indirect aggression that can occur between children (Owens *et al.* 2000) and adults (Björkqvist *et al.* 1994b; Campbell *et al.* 1997; Archer *et al.* 1997). Owens and colleagues (2000) described four categories of indirect aggression in a sample of teenage girls

- talking about others (e.g. spreading rumours, criticising)
- exclusionary behaviours (e.g. ostracising)
- non-verbal harassment (e.g. staring at others in a threatening way)
- indirect harassment (e.g. prank phone calls).

Campbell and co-workers (1997) attempted to distinguish between types of indirect aggression in an adult sample by separating it into indirect-expressive and indirect-instrumental aggression. The former was conceptualised as an 'anger discharge' not directed at harming another individual, and the latter as 'machiavellian acts' which used the social network to aggress towards victims, and included acts such as trying to make others dislike the victim. Campbell and co-workers (1997) suggested that indirect-expressive aggression may not be a form of aggression as it does not include any aggressive intent. Archer and colleagues (1997), however, argue that the findings of Campbell and co-workers should be treated with caution: using a similar sample they failed to find these two forms of indirect aggression, instead reporting the main and most robust distinction to be between direct and indirect aggression. Björkqvist and colleagues (1994b) also described two types of indirect aggression among adults: social manipulation and rational-appearing aggression. Social manipulation occurs when aggressors manipulate others to attack or harm the victim, for example by spreading false rumours. Rational-appearing aggression is when aggressors attempt to conceal their aggression by using behaviours that are seen as rational and almost devoid of any aggressive intent, an example of which would be judging the victim in an unjust manner (Björkqvist *et al.* 1994a). Although both types represent indirect aggression, Björkqvist and colleagues (1994b) describe rational-appearing aggression as having some direct properties as well. Evidence for both types of aggression has been found among prisoners although they have not always been recognised as such. McGurk and McDougall (1986), for example, described a specific bullying technique known as a 'kestrel' in which a cup of water is placed on the pillow of a sleeping inmate and a boot is thrown at them. Their startled response spills the water on their pillow and face. Such an act could be described as a practical joke and is consistent with definitions of rational-appearing aggression in which actions are easily rationalised by describing them as 'only a joke'.

When indirect bullying among prisoners is examined, it is found to occur to a greater extent than direct forms of bullying (e.g. Ireland 1999a). This can be related to Björkqvist and colleagues' (1994b) effect/danger ratio theory of aggression which suggests that aggressors will assess the relationship between the effect of the intended strategy and the physical, psychological or social danger involved. The aim of this exercise is to find an aggressive technique that will reap the most benefits to the aggressor at the least cost. Direct aggression is an effective strategy to attain goals, but it comes with an increased threat of returned direct aggression. Thus it is not a surprise that direct means of aggression are supplemented or substituted with indirect aggression. Indirect aggression offers the aggressor a safer means of attaining a goal, i.e. 'the more able the aggressor is at staying out of the reach of the opponent, and at assessing the opponent's retaliation resources, the better [s]he will be at avoiding counter-attack, and minimising risks' (Björkqvist 1994: 181).

Such a theory is particularly pertinent to a secure environment such as a prison. For the prisoner, direct aggression may well produce the maximum possible effect on their victim; however it also carries the highest cost in that it is more likely to be responded to by the victim and/or the prison authorities. Punishment for bullying is harsh within penal institutions, with bullies risking having days added on to their sentence, transferral from the establishment, or segregation. Indirect aggression, however, also has a damaging effect on the chosen victim, and yet is the least likely to evoke retaliation. In this way it combines a high effect on the victim with low danger for the bully. Thus it is easy to see why a prisoner may choose this form of bullying over direct forms. This highlights the importance of explicitly including indirect bullying in the definitions of bullying that are applied to prisons. Research that has failed to do so may have under-reported the extent of bullying by providing prevalence rates based solely on direct abuse.

At this point it is also worth discussing the criterion (based on school bullying) that there must be an *intention* on the part of the bully to cause fear or harm to the victim if the behaviour is to be considered bullying (Farrington 1993). Arguing that there must be an intention to cause fear or harm is based on the premise that all individuals have a degree of insight into their own behaviour and its effect on others. Although it is recognised that some incidents of bullying do involve insight on behalf of the bully and a clear intention to cause fear or harm, caution is advised in overgeneralising this assumption. This is particularly true when applying this criterion to prisoners, as it is recognised that offenders often lack insight into their actions (Blud 1999). This may apply especially to indirect bullying – when such aggression has been used it could be argued that the bully has *intended* to behave in a certain way towards a victim, but has not fully realised the impact of their actions. As we have seen, certain types of indirect aggression are often considered 'normal' since they are so widespread. Similarly, the intent in a prison environment may not be to cause fear or harm but simply to obtain material goods or status from peers. The motivations behind bullying in a prison are varied and often ingrained in the prison subculture, and it should be acknowledged that the intention of the bully is not limited to causing fear or harm. Perhaps, one of the most important criteria in determining whether or not an incident of bullying has taken place is the victim's perspective. If the victim perceives the incident to have either caused them distress or intended to cause them distress, regardless of the actual intention of the bully, then this should be recognised as an incident of possible bullying. Beck and Ireland (1997) also query the need for a behaviour to be 'unpro-voked', on the part of the victim, before it can be classified as bullying (Farrington 1993), arguing that the provocation by the victim can some-times be unintentional.

Thus, any definition of bullying applied to a prison needs to take into account the specific nature of the environment and recognise a number of the following key elements

- bullying can include a single incidence of aggression, particularly if it is severe
- the fear of repeated aggression must be acknowledged
- the imbalance of power is not always obvious and can be implied
- bullying includes both direct and indirect types of aggression
- the perception of the victim must be accounted for
- the intention of bullies may not always be acknowledged
- the motivations behind bullying can be complex
- the provocation on the part of the victim can be unintentional.

Recently, I proposed the following definition of bullying that could be applied to a prison environment.

An individual is being bullied when they are the victim of direct and/or indirect aggression happening on a weekly basis, by the same or different perpetrator(s). Single incidences of aggression can be viewed as bullying, particularly when they are severe and when the individual either believes or fears that they are at risk of future victimisation by the same perpetrator or others.

(Ireland 2002d: in press)

In view of the key elements described previously, this could perhaps be updated to

An individual is being bullied when they are the victim of direct and/or indirect aggression happening on a weekly basis, by the same or different perpetrator(s). Single incidences of aggression can be viewed as bullying, particularly when they are severe and when the individual either believes or fears that they are at risk of future victimisation by the same perpetrator or others. An incident can be considered bullying if the victim believes that they have been aggressed towards, regardless of the actual intention of the bully. It can also be bullying when the imbalance of power between the bully and his/her victim is implied and not immediately evident.

There are three areas of importance here that should be noted. First, the recognition that definitions of bullying can and should be changed in accordance with the environment in which it is being studied; second, that definitions derived from one situation (e.g. schools) cannot be readily applied to another (e.g. prisons); and third, that definitions should change in accordance with developments in the research field.

Recently researchers have argued for a more behavioural definition of bullying that can be applied to a prison environment. Although it is recognised that a fixed measurable behavioural definition is unlikely to emerge (Beck and Ireland 1997), this does have implications for how we measure bullying, and suggests that researchers should avoid attempting to apply overly strict criteria. This has led to a gradual shift in how we measure bullying, with recent studies moving away from providing a definition and avoiding use of the term bullying altogether. A description of the different methods used, along with the rationale for developing measures not bound by definitions, is presented in the following section.

## Measuring bullying: the methods used

The measures used to research bullying among prisoners have varied depending on the aims and purpose of the research. Measures have been used to assess the prevalence, frequency and nature of bullying, the times and places of risk, how bullying changes and develops over time, motivations behind bullying and the identification of those vulnerable to victimisation (Beck and Ireland 1997).

The specific types of methods used have included prisoner self-reports in the form of interviews or questionnaires (including behavioural checklists), peer reports, official records and focus groups. This section will describe and discuss each of these different methods in turn. It will conclude by describing some general problems associated with measuring bullying in prisons and by outlining a series of guidelines that researchers studying this area of aggression should follow.

### Self-reports: interviews

Prisoner self-reports represent the most common method used to measure bullying. Initially, interviews were a preferred method of prisoner self-report (e.g. McGurk and McDougall 1986; Brookes 1993), and were either structured or semi-structured in format. Prisoners would be presented with a definition of bullying by the interviewer and then asked a series of direct questions. Table 2.1 displays an example of an interview format.

Interviews are particularly useful for collecting detailed information about incidents of bullying, and can elicit information that is not often

*Table 2.1* Example of an interview schedule

**About being bullied**

1. How often have you been bullied here?
   A never
   B it has only happened once or twice
   C about once a week
   D several times a week
   E every day

2. Have other people tried to harass you by saying mean and unpleasant things to you?
3. Have you been punched, hit or pushed here?
4. Have you been beaten up here?
5. Have you been bullied in a sexual way here?
6. Have you had any of your own things taken by threat or force?
7. Have you been threatened, pressured or intimidated here?
8. If you have been bullied in any other ways, please list them here.
9. Have you been bullied by one or several people?
   A I haven't been bullied here
   B mainly by one person
   C by several people

10. If you have been bullied, where does this usually happen?
11. If you have been bullied, when does this usually happen?
12. About how many times have you been bullied in the last week?
    A none
    B once
    C twice
    D 3 or 4 times
    E 5 or more times

13. Have any staff talked to you about being bullied?
    A I haven't been bullied
    B no, they haven't talked with me about it
    C yes, they have talked to me about it

14. Were you bullied when you first came here?
15. Were you bullied in school before you came here?
16. Were you bullied when you were in custody before?

**About bullying other people**

17. How often have you bullied other people here?
18. Have you bullied one or several people?
19. About how many times have you taken part in bullying other people in the last week?
20. Have any staff talked with you about bullying other people?
21. How often did you bully others when you first came here?
22. How often did you bully others when you were in school before you came here?
23. How often did you bully others when you were in custody before?
24. Do you think people who are bullied usually deserve it?
    A I don't know
    B almost never
    C once in a while
    D often
    E almost always

25. Would you join in bullying someone who you didn't like?
    A yes
    B yes, maybe
    C I don't know
    D no, I don't think so
    E no

26. Do you think bullying is just part of the way things work in places like this?
27. How often do you think staff know about it when someone is being bullied?
28. How often do you think staff try and put a stop to it when someone is being bullied?

29. Have you told any staff that you have been bullied?
30. About how many people here do you think have been bullied in the past month?
31. How often do other residents here try and put a stop to it when they see someone being bullied?
32. What do you usually do when you see someone being bullied here?

A  nothing, it's none of my business
B  I don't do anything, but I think I should
C  I try to help in one way or another
D  it depends on the situation

33. About how many people here do you think are bullies?

Source: Connell and Farrington (1996), © Academic Press, reproduced with permission.

recorded when prisoners complete questionnaires themselves (Connell and Farrington 1996). If prisoners have questions about bullying or require clarification about certain issues or questions, the mere presence of an interviewer makes this easier. They are also more likely to admit to being a 'victim' in an individual interview as opposed to a group-administered self-report questionnaire (Connell and Farrington 1996). This is consistent with the findings of Connell and Farrington (1997) who argued that whereas school-based researchers have found that children will attempt to conceal their involvement as perpetrators of bullying, the concealment of being a victim of bullying is more of a problem in a prison. They comment on how 'bullies seemed quite happy to admit their bullying, perhaps because bullying behaviour in prisons could be a source of status among offenders' (Connell and Farrington 1997: 2).

Connell and Farrington (1997) assessed the reliability and validity of bullying data collected via reports from residents, peers and staff. Resident reports required prisoners to identify themselves as bullies, victims, neither or both during an individual interview. Peer and staff reports were obtained by presenting participants with a list of all of the residents housed in the facility at that time and asking them to identify each as a bully, victim, neither or both. This study was unique in that no research to date had attempted to measure bullying using peer reports or to directly compare a range of methods. Connell and Farrington (1997) reported significant agreement between all forms of reporting suggesting that all of these methods had some reliability. The data collected during the individual interview showed the highest validity in identifying bullies and victims, compared to the other methods. This study, however, consisted of a very small sample of offenders housed within a fairly unique secure facility, where the ratio of staff to offenders was much greater than in other penal facilities. Thus the findings reported by Connell and Farrington (1997) may not readily generalise to other facilities.

Using interviews to collect data on bullying, however, is not an ideal method. All of the research incorporating interviews has presented prisoners with a definition of bullying and/or used the term bullying throughout. This in itself, for the reasons outlined previously, poses particular problems in providing an accurate measurement of bullying. Researchers such as Dyson and colleagues (1997) have also criticised research using such methods stating that they provide only anecdotal information about the nature of bullying. Interviews are also time-intensive and only allow for relatively small samples to be assessed in any given period, although Connell and Farrington make the important point that there may be a trade-off between 'obtaining less valid data from a large sample and obtaining more valid data from a small sample' (1996: 84).

One of the main problems with interviews relates to anonymity: by conducting face-to-face interviews with prisoners, it is much harder for the interviewer to assure them of anonymity. With a topic as sensitive as bullying, being able to convince prisoners that they will not be identified is essential. This issue is important in a prison, with prisoners fearing retribution from others if they are seen to inform about bullying. Although researchers such as Connell and Farrington (1996) argue that individual interviews offer prisoners greater guarantees of anonymity than other methods, it must be noted that Connell and Farrington (1996) were comparing individual interviews with group-administered self-report questionnaires. This latter method is particularly problematic, as will be discussed in the following section.

### Self-report: questionnaires

Self-report questionnaires represent the most popular method of collecting data on bullying. They tend to focus on asking questions about the nature and extent of bullying, where and when bullying takes place, personal experiences of being bullied or bullying others, what types of prisoners tend to get bullied and why, how prisoners and staff respond to incidents of bullying and how bullying could be prevented. An example of one such questionnaire is presented in Table 2.2.

A number of the earlier questionnaires were developed from interview schedules (e.g. Ireland and Archer 1996). Using questionnaires meant that prisoners could complete them on their own, with no need for an administrator. They were easy to administrate and efficient, ensuring that a large sample could be obtained within a limited time period (Connell and Farrington 1996). A further advantage of using questionnaires is that they afford the participant greater confidentiality (Sutton and Smith 1999). Some researchers also provided prisoners with unmarked envelopes into which they could place their completed questionnaire as an extra measure of assuring them that their responses would remain anonymous (e.g. Ireland and Archer 1996). Anonymity can only be assured, however, if the self-report questionnaires are administered to prisoners on their own (usually in their cells).

Self-report questionnaires have also been subject to criticism. Early forms of questionnaires included a definition of bullying and used the term bullying throughout (e.g. Ireland and Archer 1996). Later, researchers favoured using the term bullying but without providing a definition (Power *et al.* 1997), as a way of overcoming the problems in defining bullying as outlined previously. Using the term without a definition, however, does not solve the definitional problems surrounding bullying, since it invites participants to generate their own, possibly biased, definition.

Connell and Farrington (1996) argued that group-administered self-report questionnaires were inadequate: victims were reluctant to admit to being bullied and were particularly fearful that other prisoners might see their responses in the group setting, with some prisoners finding it difficult to concentrate under the group conditions resulting in questionnaires being completed inaccurately. Connell and Farrington (1996) also highlight 'varying interpretations' of terms such as bullying as a problem with such methods. Administering questionnaires concerning a topic as sensitive as bullying in a group setting is particularly problematic, and is not an effective method of collecting data (Connell and Farrington 1996). Prisoners are reluctant to disclose incidents of being bullied for fear of being seen as a 'grass'. This was supported by Connell and Farrington (1996) who reported that victims tended to under-report when completing the questionnaire in the group setting, with three out of the ten prisoners that they surveyed informing the researchers that they were victims of bullying but had not admitted this on the questionnaire. Ireland (1999a) also argued that prisoners may be reluctant to admit to bullying others for fear of reprisals should their responses be discovered. Although these criticisms could apply to the majority of methods used to measure bullying, they are particularly pertinent to group-administered questionnaires where the chances of responses being seen by other participants are increased, regardless of the level of supervision provided by administrators. In my own experience, there were numerous instances during the collection of one data set (Ireland and Archer 1996) where,

*Table 2.2* Example of a self-report questionnaire

| ABOUT BULLYING. | 6.) When someone is being bullied do other prisoners try to help? | 9.) Have you *heard* about anybody being bullied during the past week? |
|---|---|---|

ABOUT BULLYING.
1.) To what extent do you think bullying takes place here?

0  1  2  3  4  5  6  7
Not at all                        A lot

(please circle the appropriate rating)

2.) Which sort of people get bullied here!
................................................
................................................

3.) Why do they get bullied?
................................................
................................................
................................................

4.) Describe the type of bullying that takes place in as much detail as possible?
................................................
................................................
................................................

5.) Where do they get bullied?
................................................
................................................
................................................

6.) When someone is being bullied do other prisoners try to help?

YES  NO  (please circle)

If YES, how; If NO, why not?
................................................
................................................

7.) Do you think members of staff try to stop bullying occurring?

YES  NO  (please circle)

If YES, how; if NO, why not?
................................................
................................................
................................................

8.) Have you seen anybody being bullied during the past week?

YES  NO  (please circle)
If YES, how many prisoners have you seen?

1  2–4  5–8  9–12  over 12
(please circle)

9.) Have you *heard* about anybody being bullied during the past week?

YES  NO  (please circle)

If YES, how many prisoners have you heard about?

1  2–4  5–8  9–12  over 12
(please circle)

10.) Have you bullied anyone during the past week?

YES  NO  (please circle)

If YES, on how many occasions?

1  2–4  5–8  9–12  over 12
(please circle)

Why did you bully them?
................................................
................................................
................................................

11.) Did you know the prisoner before you bullied them?

YES    NO   (please circle)

12.) Have you been bullied during the past week?

YES    NO   (please circle)

If YES, how many times have you been bullied?

1   2–4   5–8   9–12   over 12
(please circle)

Why do you think you have been bullied?
...................................................................
...................................................................
...................................................................

13.) If you have been bullied, did you know this person?

YES    NO   (please circle)

14.) Are there any specific names given to different types of bullying which takes place here?

YES    NO   (please circle)

If YES, what are they?
...................................................................
...................................................................

15.) When prisoners are bullied, how many other prisoners are usually involved?

1   2   3   4   5   over 5
(please circle)

16.) If you knew someone who was being bullied who would you advise they speak to? (Please tick the appropriate answer – you can tick more than one)

another inmate          ...............
a prison officer         ...............
their probation officer  ...............
the chaplain .............

their family   ...............
a prison psychologist   ...............
other (please specify)

17.) What do you think can be done to prevent bullying occurring?
...................................................................
...................................................................

18.) Is there anything you would like to add about bullying that you don't think this questionnaire has covered?
...................................................................
...................................................................

Thank you for your co-operation.

although prisoners were sitting away from each other and supervised, they still attempted to look at the responses of the other prisoners. They did this by either asking them directly what they had written, trying to encourage an open discussion about what to write, or by offering others help to complete their questionnaire.

Connell and Farrington (1996) also reported that many of the prisoners did not fully understand the questions or were poor readers and did not want to ask questions in front of the other residents. They argued that bullies in particular may be those who have difficulties with reading and writing. Thus, the use of self-completion questionnaires to measure bullying may underestimate the true prevalence rate, with an increased possibility of bullies being non-respondents (Connell and Farrington 1996). Dyson and colleagues (1997) identified a number of other problems associated with self-reports, namely honesty of prisoners, difficulties in guaranteeing anonymity, compliance of prisoners, low response rates and memory recall errors. It should be noted, however, that problems such as these are not limited to self-reports.

### Self-report: behavioural checklists

Although behavioural checklists are essentially a type of self-report questionnaire, they are a recent development and represent a unique method of measuring bullying and as such are discussed here separately. Behavioural checklists represent the only method that avoids both providing a definition of bullying to prisoners and also using the term itself (Ireland *et al*. 1999). Although problems with defining bullying have already been described at some length, it must be noted that there are also problems associated with using the term bullying either with or without an accompanying definition. The term bullying is an emotive one that holds negative connotations for both victims and perpetrators. Primarily, bullying is considered an activity restricted to schoolchildren, with prisoners, particularly adults and older adolescents, reluctant to admit to it for fear of being labelled childish (Ireland 2000a). They may also simply not view it as a behaviour that applies to them and therefore not admit to it when asked directly. Conversely, bullying in a prison environment carries with it a certain degree of status, with Connell and Farrington (1996) stating that bullying others in prison can provide you with 'jail respect'. Prisoners may be willing to admit to bullying others for this reason, regardless of whether or not they have engaged in such behaviour, which could lead to an overestimation of bullying. This may be particularly true for younger prisoners who tend to use the prison culture as a source of status (McCorkle

1992). Admitting to being a victim of bullying, however, is stigmatising in a prison with victims often construed as weak, and referred to with derogatory terms such as 'muppets', 'fraggles' or 'whingers' (Beck 1992). Furthermore, Connell and Farrington (1996) report that victimisation has to be severe before prisoners construe it as bullying, and argue that what incarcerated youths consider to be bullying may not be the same as the definitions generated by schoolchildren.

Such arguments led to the development of behavioural checklists such as the Direct and Indirect Prisoner behaviour Checklist (the DIPC, Ireland 1998b, 1999a). The DIPC incorporated a modified version of a behavioural checklist originally devised by Beck and Smith (1997) and included an Indirect Victimisation Index (IVI) created by Ireland (1997). The original Beck and Smith checklist was modified by Ireland (1997) following a review of prison-based research that described additional forms of bullying behaviour (McGurk and McDougall 1986; Brookes 1993). It addressed direct forms of bullying behaviour (notably physical, theft-related, psychological or verbal and sex-related bullying) and indirect forms of bullying. The definition of indirect aggression used by the DIPC is a broad one and is intended to encompass all forms of subtle aggression. The items in the DIPC were based on descriptions of indirect bullying found in schools (Ahmad and Smith 1994) and prisons (Ireland and Archer 1996). The DIPC has been used with male, female, adult, young (Ireland 1999a) and juvenile offenders (Ireland 2002e). It is a method of gathering information on bullying behaviour as opposed to a test or measure that yields a composite score. Its aim is simply to assess the presence or absence of a number of discrete behaviours. The DIPC consists of ninety-nine items describing both experienced events and actions. Sixty-five items represent those indicative of being bullied or bullying others, ten represent possible reactions to bullying, five items are indicative of negative behaviours towards staff or prison rules, four of involvement in the distribution and use of drugs, and five of proactive or positive behaviours towards others. The remaining items are fillers and relate to less specific behaviours. Prisoners complete the checklist on their own and are asked to identify which behaviours had occurred to them in the *previous week* or which behaviours they had engaged in by indicating 'yes' or 'no' to each item. Examples of items from the DIPC are presented in Table 2.3.

An additional question was also added to the DIPC by Ireland (2001c): participants were asked if the week that they had described represented a 'typical' one for them. It was hoped that this may provide some measure of what proportion of the sample may be experiencing such behaviours

*Table 2.3* Examples of items used in the Direct and Indirect Prisoner behaviour Checklist

| | |
|---|---|
| *Physical victim*<br>I was hit or kicked by another prisoner | *Physical bully*<br>I have hit or kicked another prisoner |
| *Theft-related 'victim'*<br>I had some tobacco stolen | *Theft-related 'bully'*<br>I have taxed another prisoner |
| *Sexual 'victim'*<br>I have been sexually harassed | *Sexual 'bully'*<br>I have sexually harassed someone |
| *Psychological/verbal 'victim'*<br>I was called names about my race or colour | *Psychological/verbal 'bully'*<br>I have called someone names about their race or colour |
| *Indirect 'victim'*<br>I have had rumours spread about me | *Indirect 'bully'*<br>I have spread rumours about someone |
| *Reactions to victimisation*<br>I have told an officer that I am being bullied | *Involvement with drugs*<br>I have smoked cannabis |
| *Proactive/positive behaviour*<br>I have helped a new prisoner on the wing | *Negative behaviour towards staff/prison rules*<br>I have been abusive to a member of staff |

Source: Ireland (1998b), a copy of the DIPC is available from the author.

on a weekly basis. It was not intended to be a measure that distinguished clearly between those reporting repeated acts of aggression and those that did not.

Importantly, the DIPC has attempted to overcome issues of definition by describing the discrete behaviours that constitute bullying and clearly defining the boundaries through indirect means, for example limiting it to a discussion of behaviours that have occurred in the previous week. It also leaves the definition of bullying to the researcher and not the respondent. Such checklists measure behaviours *indicative* of bullying others or of being bullied as opposed to bullying *per se*, as measured by the stricter school-based definitions, and as a result researchers prefer to use the term 'bullying behaviour' when describing the results. This is consistent with a growing trend in the school-based literature to measure a child's 'tendency to bully' or 'tendency to be bullied' using a similar behavioural method that does not use the labels bully or victim (e.g. Rigby and Slee 1993).

Checklists such as the DIPC, however, are subject to the same criticisms that are applied to all self-report methods. They also only address a small proportion of possible bullying behaviours and are subject to the researcher's definition of bullying. Research using the DIPC has found that the majority of prisoners reported that the week they described was a typical one for them, suggesting that the aggressive behaviours they reported for the week in question could also be applied to previous weeks. This could suggest that they were describing a behaviour that occurred on a regular (weekly) basis, thus allowing researchers to assess how much of prison-based bullying is repeated. Only a small percentage of participants reported the week to be atypical, which may suggest that they were reporting one-off incidents of abuse (Ireland 2001c). As argued previously, however, in a prison environment one-off incidents of aggression can be viewed as bullying since incidents tend to be severe and/or hold the potential of long-term consequences for the victim. The DIPC does not, however, measure how severe the victim or bully perceives the behaviour(s) to be or the consequences of the aggression for the victims, and there is no measurement of how fearful the victim was. The easy answer to these concerns would be to attempt to measure these variables in the DIPC. There are difficulties, however, with asking participants to rate severity or fear as these responses are open to individual perceptions. It would also be difficult to assess long-term consequences of the behaviours without following the participants over a set period of time. It is recognised that asking participants to indicate whether or not the week was a typical one for them is open to memory bias and is insensitive to gradations in behaviour, and there is no way of ascertaining if their response is based on the aggression items or on the other items listed in the DIPC (e.g. the filler items).

Thus, like other measures, the DIPC has flaws. It is a measure, however, that is currently in development and remains the only one to date that is specific to a prison environment and which clearly measures both direct and indirect behaviours. It is also the only method that avoids problems in defining bullying and using the term bullying. The definition of bullying behaviour is left to the researcher. At the very least, what the DIPC does not do is underestimate the problem of bullying. If anything, such methods over-include some aggressive interactions (Beck and Ireland 1997). The important point here is that the inclusion of certain types of aggression is left up to the researcher *after* data collection and not the respondent – if the researcher does not consider some of the interactions to be bullying, they can simply be excluded.

Nevertheless, there is evidence that the DIPC is reliable and produces consistent proof of bullying behaviour across different samples and time periods. There is also evidence that when the DIPC is compared with more traditional questionnaires that use the term bullying, the two methods converge for prisoners who did *not* bully or were *not* bullied themselves. For those prisoners who did engage in behaviours indicative of bullying others (as measured by the DIPC), only a small proportion admitted to being a bully when asked directly (Ireland 2002e). The lack of convergence between the measures, however, may be a result of the DIPC measuring both direct and indirect aggression, and prisoners tending not to recognise indirect aggression as bullying.

There is also emerging evidence that findings for prisoners classified as bullies, bully/victims or victims using the DIPC are similar to those reported among schoolchildren using more traditional and stricter methods of identifying these groups. Ireland (2002c), for example, found that bully/victims, as defined using the DIPC, were significantly more assertive on some components of assertiveness, with a non-significant trend for bullies. This was consistent with Stephenson and Smith's (1989) description of both bullies and bully/victims as assertive. Although Stephenson and Smith used a different method to define their groups from that employed in prison studies, the fact that the findings are comparable suggests that the DIPC is successful in identifying true bullies and bully/victims.

## Peer reports

Few studies have utilised peer reports to collect data. Peer reports primarily refer to using other members of the peer group (i.e. prisoners) to nominate individuals whom they consider to be bullies. This method is popular among school-based researchers but has been used to a limited extent with a prison population. Connell and Farrington (1996, 1997) represent the first researchers to specifically address the use of peer reports as a method of collecting data, with Connell and Farrington (1997) reporting that staff were more accurate than peers in identifying bullies, but that staff and peers were equally accurate in identifying victims. Interestingly, of the research that has used methods other than self-reports to measure bullying, the majority has included staff nominations of bullies and victims (e.g. Beck and Smith 1997). Although not strictly a form of peer report, it could be argued that staff reports are similar to peer reports in that you are requesting information from individuals who share the same environment. Staff reports have also been criticised, however, with Beck and Smith (1997) reporting that staff reports of prisoners who have been bullies did not relate to any self-report bullying items reported by prisoners. Similarly, those prisoners identified by staff as victims were also not likely to be the same prisoners who identified themselves as victims. Beck and Ireland (1997) made the point that staff may not be wrong in their judgements, but they may simply be attending to different behavioural cues that they then use to identify prisoners as bullies or victims.

Peer reports are potentially useful in terms of representing a method of collecting data on bullying that does not rely on the self-report of prisoners regarding their status as a bully or a victim. Their suitability for use in a prison environment has been questioned on the grounds that prisoner peer groups are not stable, with prisoners regularly being moved to new locations (Beck and Ireland 1997). Similarly, the number of prisoners held within one unit can be large, with some prisons holding over 100 prisoners on each living unit. The chance of prisoners knowing everyone on their unit well enough to say whether or not they are bullies or victims is therefore brought into question. This, coupled with the transient nature of the population, prevents the creation of a stable peer group that is necessary if peer methods of identification are to be effective. Importantly, Connell and Farrington's (1997) study was an exception to this in that the offenders were based in very small units (housing a maximum of twenty-three prisoners). Indeed, Connell and Farrington (1996) reported that although peer nominations of both bullies and victims were 'very accurate' in their research, this could have been a result of the small size of the facility under study.

## Official records

Official records have been used to a lesser extent than the other methods and have included an analysis of prison discipline or misconduct books (Dyson *et al.* 1997; Loucks 1998) and bullying incident reports (O'Brien 1996; Ireland 2002d). The use of such records appears related to an assumption made by some researchers that they represent an objective method of measuring bullying (Dyson *et al.* 1997). A distinction should be drawn at this point, however, between those records specifically designed to measure bullying and those that are not, for example prison discipline or misconduct books are designed to record a range of delin-quent behaviour including both specified and unspecified incidents of bullying and victimisation, whereas bullying incident reports (BIRs) are designed specifically to record incidents of bullying (Ireland 2002d). Bullying incident reports are raised if a prisoner is identified as a bully or a victim, or if they are suspected of bullying others or of being bullied themselves. Bullying incident reports are not used in all prisons and there is no standardised format for them. If used correctly, however, they can prove to be useful methods of recording incidents of bullying. Table 2.4 presents an example of a BIR format that is used at a male young offenders establishment.

Official records have been criticised by some researchers who suggest that they are inadequate for measuring the prevalence of bullying, that they severely underestimate the extent of bullying (Loucks 1998), and that the data are unreliable and produce only tenuous conclusions that should be treated with caution (Dyson *et al.* 1997). There are also difficulties in comparing the findings from different studies that have used such records, with considerable variance in the type of records used. It is important, however, to distinguish again between records that are designed to record general delinquent behaviour (such as prison discipline books) which are *then* used to estimate levels of bullying, and records (such as BIRs) that are specifically designed to record bullying. This latter form of official record may be of some use in describing bullying, particularly with regard to which individuals are involved in bullying and what their specific role was in an incident. They may also have some use in identifying the motivations behind bullying and the locations where it is most likely to occur. Bullying incident reports are intrinsically flawed, however, as a result of their use of the term bullying which in itself may lead to an underestimation of the problem (Ireland 2002d).

One of the main criticisms of official records is that they are dependent on staff recording information consistently and accurately. Therefore such records may be more a measure of 'staff willingness to report' than of bullying. Bullying is also a difficult behaviour to define, and the varying perceptions of what bullying includes are not limited to prisoners but apply to staff as well; it depends on the *perceptions* of the staff member recording the information and what may be construed as bullying to one member of staff may not to another. Such records are also not useful as a measure of indirect or covert forms of bullying, with such forms of bullying often being missed by staff because of their subtle nature and thus not recorded. As discussed previously, this is a particular problem in that indirect forms of bullying behaviour have been found to be more prevalent among prisoners than direct forms. Official records should not, therefore, be viewed as an accurate method of measuring the extent or the nature of bullying since they highlight only the 'tip of the bullying iceberg' (Dyson *et al.* 1997). They are useful, however, in providing good descriptions of direct bullying. As such, their usefulness may lie instead as a tool to inform the development of other methods of measuring bullying, such as behavioural checklists: methods that rely on providing

*Table 2.4* Example of a Bullying Incident Report (BIR)

| BULLYING INCIDENT REPORT (BIR) | Date received:   /   / |
| --- | --- |

Bully/bullies (name, number and wing location)   _____

Victim/s (name, number and wing location)   _____

Reporting member of staff _____(name) _____ (grade)

**LOCATION OF INCIDENT**

GENERAL[a]: BI  B2  DI  D2  WI  W2  CI  C2  Ed  VTC  Gym
Other:_____

SPECIFIC: (e.g. cell/classroom)_____

DATE of incident   /   /    Description of incident: _____
_____
_____
_____

*Motive for bullying (please circle)    Offence    Racial    Regional    Revenge    Debt*
*Drugs    Victim seen as weak    Protection offered    To make fun*
*Other: _____*

Support given to victim/s: _____
_____ When: _____

**BULLY STAGE RAISED[b]:        I        2        3        4**

Bully interviewed YES/NO By who: _____
Details of interview: I.) bully/bullies response   _____
_____
_____

2.) outcome _____
_____
_____

Source: HMYOI/RC Lancaster Farms, Lancaster, UK, LAI 3QZ. Form originally devised by J. L. Ireland, reproduced with permission of Governor David Thomas.
Note
a    refers to the living units and general locations within the prison.
b    relates to the number of occasions that a BIR has been recorded and proven for the individual bully concerned (see chapter 8)

descriptions of the discrete behaviours that make up bullying. If official records are used then they should represent only one of a range of methods (Dyson *et al.* 1997).

## Focus groups

Focus groups are not a popular method of collecting data and to date have been used only twice (Osiowy 1997; Ireland and Hill 2001). School-based researchers have begun to use such groups more widely to obtain information on bullying, recognising the importance of including the peer group as much as possible if anti-bullying strategies are to be effective.

Focus groups refer to small numbers of prisoners or staff selected to take part in an informal discussion concerning bullying. The groups are facilitated by other members of staff or researchers. Osiowy (1997) held focus groups with prison staff from two establishments, with the aim of having an open discussion about the effectiveness of anti-bullying strategies. I had a similar aim with the focus groups that I held (Ireland and Hill 2001), but held groups solely with prisoners. In this latter study three focus groups were held, each consisting of three prisoners. The first group included prisoners identified as victims of bullying and the second included those identified as bullies. The final group included those not identified as either bullies or victims. All groups were identified through the BIR system in place at the prison. In my own experience of running such groups, I found them to be very valuable in that they provided a rich source of information, particularly about how the anti-bullying strategy was working and how it could be improved. Focus groups also allow prisoners (and staff) to input directly into the development of anti-bullying strategies by allowing them to voice an opinion about its effectiveness. Focus groups would not, however, be an appropriate method of measuring the nature or extent of bullying, since you could only assess the perceptions of the group and could not ask direct questions about individual personal experiences in such settings.

## Problems in measuring bullying in a prison environment

Aside from the problems that are associated with each individual method of data collection, there are a number of issues, not specific to the methods used, that relate to how data on bullying are (or are not) collected and the conclusions that we can draw from the findings. The variety of methods that researchers have used to collect data, for example, makes direct comparisons between studies difficult if not impossible. There are also difficulties in making comparisons between studies that have presented prisoners with a definition of bullying and/or used the term bullying, with those that have not: avoiding use of the term has been shown to produce higher estimates of bullying behaviour (Beck and Ireland 1997). Of those studies that have presented prisoners with a definition of bullying, some have used global definitions taken from school-based research, some have tried to make the definition more specific to a prison environment, some have concentrated on definitions of direct bullying, and others have included specific definitions of both direct and indirect bullying. The lack of a standardised definition is a specific area of concern (Ireland 2002f).

In a number of studies the distinction made between direct and indirect bullying has not always been clear. Livingston and colleagues (1994) and Mosson (1994), for example, both report a type of bullying referred to as 'non-physical intimidation'. This intimidation clearly has indirect properties as well as direct, including instances of gossiping and ostracising. The studies, however, make no explicit reference to the indirect nature of bullying.

The sample sizes used in studies have been highly variable, including vast (e.g. Power *et al.* 1997), moderate (e.g. Ireland and Archer 1996) and very small sizes (e.g. Connell and Farrington 1996). The recall period between studies has also varied greatly. Some studies have restricted the recall period to one week (Ireland 1999a), others have used a longer recall period but have attempted to measure real frequency within it, for example by asking prisoners about their experiences of being bullied during their current sentence and how frequently this occurred, whether it was most days or every day (Power *et al.* 1997), or once or twice, about once a week or several times a week (Connell and Farrington 1996). Other studies have used a wide recall period with no real reference to frequency within this, either asking for the most recent incident, or asking for experiences during their stay, past or present, at a particular institution (Loucks 1998). There are obvious problems in requesting individuals to report on incidents that have occurred over a long time period. Research that has asked prisoners if they have engaged in bullying or been bullied during their time in prison *without* specifying a discrete time period should be interpreted with caution, and the accuracy of the responses should be questioned (Ireland 2002f).

There is also a lack of longitudinal research addressing how bullying changes and develops over time. This is important because 'Ideally bullying research will have a longitudinal component such that changes in policy can be assessed in terms of impact' (Beck and Ireland 1997: 71).

Only one study has attempted to measure bullying over time, using behavioural checklists that were repeatedly given to prisoners to complete on a weekly basis. Only limited results for this study (Beck and Smith 1999: cf. Ireland *et al.* 1999) are available, since it was not formally published. The findings suggest, however, that certain types of bullying increase over time whereas others do not. These findings hold a number of implications for interventions into bullying and highlight the need for more longitudinal research.

Researchers have also tended to concentrate on identifying bullies and victims, the prevalence of these groups, and the characteristics that they possess. Few studies have specifically attempted to identify the other groups involved, namely those who are both bullies and victims (bully/victims) and those that are not involved in either being bullied or bullying others (i.e. the not-involved group). Also to date there are no methods that have been developed for use within a prison environment that address the specific roles that prisoners adopt during incidents of bullying. By these methods I am referring to the Participant Role Scale approach (Salmivalli *et al.* 1996) that is becoming increasingly popular with school-based researchers. This method is based on self or peer reports and is presented in either a questionnaire or interview format (Salmivalli *et al.* 1996; Sutton *et al.* 1999a). A series of behavioural descriptions relating to six roles are presented to participants, and they are asked to rate how often the behaviour was displayed. A brief description of the six roles, based on Sutton *et al.* (1999a), is as follows

- *bully*   active, initiative taking, leaderlike behaviour
- *assistant*   active, but more follower than leaderlike
- *reinforcer*   inciting the bully, providing an audience, etc.
- *defender*   sticking up for or consoling the victim
- *outsider*   doing nothing in bullying situations, staying away
- *victim*   gets bullied.

Prison research has suggested the presence of some of these roles among prisoners (e.g. Ireland 2002d), but no empirical work using a 'participant role' approach has been used. Such an approach to researching bullying would be useful in providing a more detailed analysis of the roles involved, the prevalence of these roles and characteristics associated with each. It would be interesting to see how such methods could be adopted for use with prisoners. Categorising individuals into groups (e.g. as bullies or victims) is too arbitrary whereas 'Assessing the specific roles that they adopt during a bullying interaction would allow for a further understanding of the problem and the development of intervention strategies that are tailored to the individual' (Ireland 2002d: in press).

Finally, there is also a lack of research comparing the validity and reliability of the different methods used. To date only Connell and Farrington (1996, 1997) have attempted to address this empirically. However, the small sample size and the uniqueness of the prison facilities that they assessed make their findings difficult to generalise. Addressing issues of reliability and validity is important although this is not likely to be an easy task since bullying is a covert behaviour and victims are unlikely to report abuse for fear of retaliation from the aggressor.

Although it is unlikely that a perfect method of measuring bullying will emerge, there are a number of guidelines that researchers could refer to when researching bullying behaviour among prisoners. These guidelines are presented in the following section.

## What guidelines should researchers follow?

1   Researchers should avoid providing a definition of bullying to prisoners. They should also avoid use of the term bullying. The definition of bullying can be decided upon by the researcher after the data have been collected. As stated by Beck and Ireland 'the definition of bullying need not be decided in advance of data collection, but can be used as a guide to the behaviours of interest and then described later' (1997: 72). To date, the only method that is suitable for doing this is the behavioural checklist.

2   Researchers should aim to measure the discrete behaviours that constitute bullying. This should include examination of both direct and indirect forms of bullying.

3   If a self-report method is to be used, it should be administered on an individual rather than a group basis. If the method is questionnaire based, before administering the questionnaire, researchers should aim to identify any prisoner who may have difficulties in completing it and arrange for help to be offered to them.

4   Allowing prisoners to complete the questionnaires on their own, in their cells, is a useful method, particularly if the questionnaire can be administered and collected at a time when movement around the wing is not allowed for prisoners, i.e. during lock-up periods where cell doors are not allowed to be opened. Instructions regarding the questionnaire can be relayed to the prisoner by the researcher through the cell hatch or window, and the questionnaire passed to them under the cell door. This allows prisoners to complete the questionnaire

with no risk of interference from other prisoners. For prisons that have dormitories or shared cells in which this method would not be appropriate, prisoners should be allowed to complete questionnaires on their own in an allocated room.

5   The anonymity of all participants should be ensured. Researchers should avoid offering complete confidentiality. The mere inclusion of a prisoner's responses in a report, even if they are not identified, violates this assurance. Confidentiality should not be confused with anonymity.

6   Providing unmarked envelopes for prisoners to place completed questionnaires in helps to assure them that their responses will remain secure and anonymous.

7   It is good practice to ensure that questionnaires (and other forms of self-report) are administered by non-discipline staff. The involvement of officers in the administration of questionnaires may affect the responses of prisoners. This may be particularly true for victims and bullies who do not want to be identified by officers, and may not therefore be convinced that their responses will not be read by them. The ideal method of administration is by a researcher who works completely independently of the prison under study.

8   Prisoners should be asked to describe their experiences over a restricted recall period, ideally asking them what has occurred over the past week or perhaps even the past month. Researchers should aim to ascertain the frequency of the aggressive act(s) as they occurred during this period. Using longer recall periods or questions that do not specify a recall period (such as 'have you been bullied during your time in prison?') should be avoided.

9   Researchers should attempt to measure prisoners' *perceptions* of the aggressive act, for example if the prisoner is identified as a bully what was their intention or motivation for the act? What did they believe the consequences of their actions to be? If the prisoner is identified as a victim what did they perceive the intention of the bully to be? How fearful were they that they may be aggressed towards again? How did the behaviour affect them?

10   In view of concerns expressed by researchers regarding the literacy problems evident in prison samples, all questionnaires should be simply worded and easy to complete. Behavioural measures such as the DIPC are useful in this respect since they limit the amount of writing required: prisoners are asked to tick boxes and not to write answers. Although this does not solve problems of literacy, it is certainly more productive than questionnaires that, for example, ask

prisoners to 'Describe the type of bullying that takes place in as much detail as possible?' Methods should also be piloted to try and ascertain any items that may be problematic. Concerns regarding literacy are difficult to overcome. Another possibility would be developing auditory forms of questionnaires, i.e. recording the questionnaires onto an audiotape. Depending on the size of the study and the number of prisoners with literacy problems, such methods could prove to be expensive, particularly if the equipment to use the tapes also has to be provided. However, researchers could limit the use of such tapes to those prisoners with the most severe literacy problems.

11  Any method that is adopted must be tailored to the population that it is meant to serve. If a behavioural checklist is to be created or updated, for example, then it needs to be specific to the population under study. Individual interviews and official records are useful tools to use to gain a greater understanding of the discrete bullying behaviours that take place. These can then be used to inform the development of behavioural checklists.

12  Researchers should consider using more than one method to collect data on bullying. This may lead to more valid conclusions and allow for the different methods to be compared directly. The problems of each individual method, however, and the validity and reliability of the findings from each, must be noted in any discussion of the results.

## Summary

This chapter attempted to highlight some of the problems in applying school-based definitions of bullying to a prison setting, and argued for a broader more prison-specific and behavioural definition, one that takes into account a range of both direct and indirect aggressive behaviours. Researchers have used a range of methods to investigate bullying, each of which has its own problems. This, coupled with the varying definitions of bullying and differences between studies in terms of recall periods and sample sizes used, makes it difficult to compare findings across studies. What it does suggest, however, is that researchers attempting to investigate a behaviour as sensitive as bullying need to be aware of, and actively account for, these issues if they are to obtain a useful assessment. The way in which bullying is defined and measured has clear implications for estimates of both the extent and nature of bullying. Using the term bullying, for example, is likely to severely underestimate the extent of the problem whereas avoidance of the term is likely to overestimate it. Combining a method that avoids the term bullying (e.g. the DIPC) with one that does not will produce very different estimates of the extent of bullying. The different methods employed will also influence the types of bullying behaviour that are reported, with some methods more sensitive to indirect forms of bullying than others. I will discuss the nature and extent of bullying among prisoners in more detail in the following chapter and in doing so will reflect on some of the issues discussed here.

# Chapter 3

# The extent and nature of bullying

## The extent of bullying

Trying to estimate the true extent of bullying among prisoners is difficult. Estimates have varied across studies and appear largely dependent on how bullying has been measured, the definition that has been used and the type of sample addressed. There are three types of estimate that are generally referred to

- those based on asking prisoners directly if they have been bullied or have bullied others
- those based on the perceptions of prisoners (i.e. how much bullying they thought was taking placing or how much bullying they have seen or heard)
- those based on behaviours indicative of being bullied or of bullying others.

Based on the studies presented in Chapter 1 that have asked prisoners directly if they had bullied others or been bullied, the proportion of prisoners reporting to being a bully ranged from 0 to 67 per cent and the proportion reporting to being a victim from 5 to 57 per cent. Based on perceptions of prisoners, the proportion reporting to having seen an incident of bullying ranged from 15 to 76 per cent, and the proportion reporting to having heard about an incident from 13 to 86 per cent. Finally, estimates based on behavioural checklists measuring behaviours indicative of bullying others have produced ranges from 40 to 70 per cent, and for behaviours indicative of being bullied from 41 to 75 per cent.

As can be seen from these figures, there are differences between the different types of estimates. For example, estimates of bullying based on the perceptions of prisoners tend to be slightly higher than other types of estimate. Estimates based on perceptions, however, are not likely to be valid since they are not a measure of the frequency of incidents that have occurred. Instead they could easily relate to a small number of incidents widely known about. Also, the range of estimates based on behaviours indicative of being bullied or of bullying others appear to be much smaller than those based on perceptions or asking prisoners directly if they have bullied others or been bullied themselves.

These differences make it difficult to estimate with any certainty what the true extent of bullying is. This has led some researchers to argue that estimates of the extent of bullying should be based on ranges as opposed to static figures. For example, in a recent paper I asked prisoners directly if they had been bullied or had bullied others, producing figures of 5 and 6 per cent respectively. I also used a behavioural checklist to measure the extent to which they had experienced or engaged in any behaviours indicative of being bullied or of bullying others, producing figures of 45 and 53 per cent respectively (Ireland 2002e). I concluded from this that reports of being a bully or a victim fell somewhere between actual (i.e. direct) reports of bullying and those indicative of bullying, with estimates of being a victim falling somewhere between 5 and 45 per cent.

Regardless of the problems in trying to measure the true extent of bullying in prisons, two conclusions can be drawn from the estimates presented. First, that bullying does occur in prisons, and second, that it occurs among all categories of prisoners, i.e. adults, young offenders, men and women. Researchers should perhaps accept that measuring the extent of bullying accurately is not possible and instead focus on addressing the types of behaviour that occur.

## The nature of bullying

Bullying can include direct aggression where the perpetrator interacts directly and overtly with the victim. Direct aggression includes physical, psychological, verbal, theft-related and sex-related aggression. Bullying can also include more subtle types of aggression where the aggressor and/or the aggressive intent remains unclear, particularly to those observing or hearing about the incident. This is referred to primarily as indirect aggression and includes gossiping, ostracising and spreading rumours about someone. The types of bullying reported among prisoners range from what appear to be relatively minor incidents to the more serious incidents of abuse. In a prison environment, however, it is important that all types of abuse are viewed as serious with the potential for causing physical or psychological damage to the victim. Attempting to describe different types of bullying in terms of a hierarchy ranging from serious to minor behaviours is unlikely to be useful, and may focus research away from important types of abuse simply because they are perceived to be less serious. It should be acknowledged that the consequences for all types of bullying are potentially damaging for the victim. Recent research from school-based researchers, for example, suggests that non-physical forms of bullying, such as indirect aggression, may have a more damaging effect on victims than physical aggression (Boulton and Hawker 1997). Indeed, in a prison it may be more difficult for the victim to cope with bullying where escape from the environment is not possible, and the support that they receive from significant others outside the prison is limited. As a result the effects of all types of bullying on victims can be magnified.

The types of bullying behaviours that can occur between prisoners are summarised in the following sections. Examples of direct bullying are described first, separated into physical, psychological or verbal, theft-related and sex-related bullying. This is followed by a description of indirect bullying. The descriptions presented are based both on perceptions of bullying and actual accounts from bullies and victims.

## Direct bullying: physical

This can be separated into two main categories

- actual physical aggression
- indirect physical aggression.

*Actual physical aggression* This takes many forms including victims being slapped, hit, kicked, bitten, shoved in the ribs, being knocked unconscious, being pushed, having their food spat into, being thrown off landings, having their head banged against walls, having pieces of glass placed in their soap, having excrement thrown over them and having items such as hot water thrown at them (Livingston *et al.* 1994; McGurk and McDougall 1986; Ireland and Archer 1996; Beck 1995; Brookes *et al.* 1994; Loucks 1998; O'Brien 1996; Ireland 2002d). With regard to this latter form of aggression, a popular method of assault in a prison involves placing sugar into the hot water and then throwing this at the victim. The sugar sticks to the skin of the victim and can cause severe scarring. McGurk and McDougall (1986) also reported victims being forced to engage in an enforced type of breathing and shaking of the head that resulted in a loss of consciousness (termed a 'buzz'), being forced to drink urine, and having paper placed between their toes and then set on fire. Swift (1995) described a number of specific incidents of physical aggression that included

*   a prisoner having his chair removed while watching TV, when he sat back down a mop was then held over his head and set alight
*   a prisoner being stabbed in the back of the neck with a plastic fork who retaliated by hitting the aggressor with a food tray
*   a prisoner reporting to giving another prisoner a 'hiding' in the showers because he had failed to honour a debt
*   a prisoner reporting having batteries thrown at him, and also batteries and hot tea thrown through his window at night.

The use of weapons has also been reported, although researchers claim that their use is infrequent. Types of weapons include batteries or snooker balls placed in socks, bed legs, chairs, parts of a table, glass, razors, plastic utensils or food trays (Brookes *et al.* 1994; Ireland 1995; Swift 1995). A number of terms are also widely used to describe physical acts of bullying including 'beatings', 'slashings', 'giving someone a good hiding', 'giving someone a good kicking', 'razored' and 'rippings'.

*Indirect physical aggression*   This refers to the deliberate damage inflicted on the property of victims. Brookes (1993), for example, reports incidents where cold water was poured over, and/or excrement was placed in, bedding, and Loucks (1998) reports an incident where a victim's cell was set on fire. Other forms of aggression that fit this category include prisoners urinating or squirting water into adjoining cells (Swift 1995). Such behaviour has the aim of both humiliating the occupant and also damaging their property. Swift (1995) also reported an incident where prisoners had entered the cell of a victim and spat on their bed because they thought that the victim was a sex offender.

### Direct bullying: psychological and verbal

Psychological and verbal bullying are described together since researchers addressing this area don't usually distinguish between them: threats, for example, are often conveyed verbally yet can be considered as intimidation, and intimidation is often referred to as psychological aggression. There is also a lack of clarity regarding what constitutes psychological bullying and in my opinion it is a term used more to reflect the consequences of aggression, particularly of indirect aggression, than to describe an actual act of aggression. Since the aim of this section is to focus on describing the types of abusive behaviour that occur between prisoners as opposed to discussing the validity of each type, it will concentrate on providing a description of the psychological and verbal aggression reported among prisoners.

The types of psychological and verbal bullying reported include insulting someone, mental cruelty, calling someone names such as 'nonce' (sex offender), 'cell thief' or 'grass' (e.g. Brookes 1993; Swift 1995). Also described is racial humiliation or abuse, taunts about the physical appearance of the victim and/or about their home area, deliberately frightening the victim and encouraging prisoners to hang themselves. Pressuring victims to smuggle goods such as drugs and money into the prison or to smuggle contraband goods to and from areas within the prison is also reported (e.g. Home Office Prison Service 1999; Livingston *et al.* 1994; Brookes *et al.* 1994; Brookes 1993; Swift 1995). General intimidation is also described, either written intimidation or other intimidation such as staring at victims (O'Brien 1996; Brookes 1993).

Threats are frequently reported and can be delivered either in writing or verbally; they include threats of physical harm to victims and/or to their families or partners (Brookes *et al.* 1994; Swift 1995). In a recent paper I reported an example of a written threat, where a victim was sent a picture by a bully in the adjoining cell which depicted the victim's face with slash marks ripped into it with the words 'this is you' written underneath (Ireland 2002d). McGurk and McDougall (1986) also described incidents where victims would have petrol poured over their feet by a bully who would then threaten to set them on fire.

Demanding protection money to protect the victim from other prisoners has also been reported as well as demanding goods or services from the victim, for example pressuring victims into cleaning another prisoner's cell or clothes, or making tea and coffee for the bully at their request (Brookes 1993; Brookes *et al.* 1994).

## Direct bullying: theft-related

The most well-known forms of theft-related bullying are taxing and baroning. Taxing relates to goods being taken from prisoners under the pretence of taking for tax, whereas baroning refers to goods being given to prisoners by the baron with payment demanded at an extortionate rate of interest. Aside from these behaviours, researchers have also referred to property being stolen from victims. Brookes (1993), for example, reported victims finding that their clothes and trainers had disappeared whilst they were in the gymnasium, and Brookes and colleagues (1994) referred to instances where items had been taken from victims under the pretence of borrowing, with the bully having no intention of ever returning them. The types of goods taken from victims can include clothing, food, batteries, tobacco or medication (Brookes *et al.* 1994; Loucks 1998; Ireland 2002d).

In a prison where the amount of material goods that prisoners are allowed to have is limited by the prison authorities (including the amount that they can purchase), it is perhaps not surprising that such forms of bullying exist. Material goods, especially tobacco, become a valuable form of currency and are seen as one influence that is instrumental in causing and maintaining bullying in prisons.

## Direct bullying: sex-related

Few studies addressing bullying among prisoners have found evidence for the existence of sex-related bullying. This contrasts with research conducted into general prisoner violence where researchers such as Donaldson (1984) have asserted that eighteen adult men are raped every minute. Research into bullying, however, has tended not to focus on sexual aggression, instead viewing it as one of a range of abusive behaviours. Furthermore, the definitions of bullying applied by prison researchers have tended not to refer specifically to sex-related aggression, referring more generally to physical aggression. There is evidence, however, from some studies that sexual bullying does take place in prisons (e.g. McGurk and McDougall 1986; Brookes 1993; Ireland 1999a). One of the most descriptive accounts of such bullying was provided by McGurk and McDougall (1986) who reported instances where young offenders were held or tied to a bed and had their testicles covered in boot black and polished, or had their pubic hair shaved, offenders being forced to masturbate or perform oral sex on another prisoner and/or being stripped naked and then beaten with slippers.

Although evidence of sexual abuse has been provided, researchers tend not to indicate how prevalent such abuse is. Of the few papers that have attempted to estimate the prevalence of such abuse, the estimates tend to be small. For example, I found in one study that only 2 per cent of victims reported being sexually abused or harassed in the previous week (Ireland 1999a). Similarly, although the accounts of abuse offered by McGurk and McDougall (1986) are clearly sex related, it is possible that not all prisoners consider them as such, perhaps viewing them more as initiation ceremonies or horseplay. Connected to this, some types of sexual activity that occur between prisoners may not initially be viewed as abusive and will therefore remain unreported. This was noted by Ireland (1998) who reported an account from an adult male prisoner who stated that he had to 'sell himself' (i.e. prostitute himself) in order to pay his debts. Although the prisoner in this instance may have consented to the sexual act, it should be considered that indirect coercion had been used, i.e. the threat of what would happen if he was not able to repay his debts. Evidence from Brookes (1993) and Ireland and Archer (1996) suggests that a failure to repay debts is one of the main triggers for bullying. Thus such behaviours should be viewed as abusive – the victim has limited control over events and indirect coercion, regardless of how subtle, has been used.

Furthermore, any research into the area of sexual bullying should be interpreted with caution since it is expected that the underreporting of such abuse will be high. In a prison where prisoners are unable to escape from the abuse and where subcultural rules discourage 'grassing', it could be expected that victims would be reluctant to disclose abuse of any kind to a researcher, particularly sexual abuse. This may be particularly true for men who have been found to report less sex-related bullying than women (Ireland 1999a). It is perhaps more accurate to say that sex-related bullying does occur between prisoners but that the exact frequency and nature of this abuse are difficult to determine using current methods of measurement.

## Indirect bullying

Indirect bullying in prisons includes a range of subtle behaviours such as the spreading of malicious or false rumours, gossiping, ostracising, ignoring other prisoners (Beck 1995; Ireland and Archer 1996; Loucks 1998), crowding round or deliberately 'hogging' the prison phone, playing practical jokes on someone (Home Office Prison Service 1999), making fun of another prisoner (Brookes et al. 1994) or deliberately giving victims smaller portions of food at meal times (Brookes et al. 1994). Indirect behaviours can be very distressing to victims and this distress can be enhanced in a prison. Indeed, in 1996, I conducted an interview with an adult woman who was serving a life sentence for murder. She told me that all of the other prisoners on her house-block had decided not to talk to her and they had being doing this for a week. She told me that her only spoken contact that week had been with a few officers and myself and that she was finding this situation extremely distressing. Such a response is understandable in a prison where social contact is important; when this is removed from a prisoner the effects can be severe. Indirect bullying therefore becomes very effective in such environments, particularly since a number of the abusive behaviours are concerned with isolating the victim by distancing them from their peer group as much as possible.

Some types of indirect bullying are also particularly subtle. I am aware of one form in particular, which could be classed as indirect, that relates to the misuse of 'bullying information boxes'. Such boxes have been placed on the wings of some prisons with the purpose of allowing prisoners to place the names of suspected bullies into them without fear of being seen as a 'grass'. In this way, prisoners would be able to report bullies and yet remain anonymous. Staff would regularly survey the contents of these boxes and act on any information given. The use of such boxes, however, has been reviewed in some establishments where it was suspected that prisoners were using them to bully others, namely by placing the name of a victim into the box and then accusing them of being a bully when this was not the case. Similarly, when conducting research using anonymous surveys, I can also recall incidents where participants would deliberately list the names of victims as bullies on the questionnaires 'for a laugh'.

A number of the indirect behaviours presented in this section have been described by prisoners as 'just a laugh', 'a good crack' or 'entertainment'. This is perhaps particularly true of behaviours such as practical jokes. It must be remembered, however, that these 'jokes' are occurring in what can be described as a hostile environment where there are no significant attachment relationships between prisoners, and where prisoners are vying for a significant role in the prison pecking order. Practical jokes in a prison tend to be serious and focused on humiliating or embarrassing the recipient, while at the same time increasing the status of the perpetrator. How the victim responds to such jokes will determine how others will behave towards them in the future and in particular whether or not they will be seen as a future target. Popular jokes among young offenders include the delivery of parcels of excrement (termed 'shit parcels') to victims and the replacement of tobacco with excrement in roll-ups that are then given to the unsuspecting victim. Such behaviours are arguably serious, and use of the term practical joke to describe them serves only to minimise the impact of the behaviour on the victim and excuses what is essentially an act of abuse. If victims appear upset about the abuse then they will simply be told that they should be able to take a joke.

This section has only really touched on the range of behaviours that could be classed as indirect bullying. By its very nature this type of aggression is difficult to measure since it is not always obvious to those involved. The list of behaviours that could be classed as indirect aggression is increasing all the time, and as I described in Chapter 2, it is a form of aggression only recently recognised by researchers. As research into indirect aggression increases so too should our insight into the many different types of discrete behaviours that it can include.

It is obvious from the brief review outlined in the preceding five sections on direct and indirect bullying that the nature of bullying among prisoners can take a variety of forms. The present review is limited by the fact that there are, undoubtedly, numerous other types of bullying that occur between prisoners that are not yet identified in the research. The sheer range of behaviours reported here, however, reinforces the assertion that I made in Chapter 1, namely that a definition of bullying that encompasses all of the different types of bullying is virtually impossible to create.

It is also important to try and gauge the prevalence of each different type of aggression. Before moving on to discuss this, however, it is perhaps more appropriate at this point to describe briefly some of the terms that prisoners have used to describe specific types of bullying.

## Terms given to specific types of bullying

In addition to the behaviours of taxing and baroning previously described, a number of other terms have been used by prisoners to describe specific forms of bullying. The majority of terms are used by young offenders, with the most descriptive examples provided by McGurk and McDougall (1986) as follows

- *moon job*   a prisoner's bed is stood on end while the prisoner is asleep ensuring that he/she slides out of the bed
- *crocodile*   a prisoner is bitten by other prisoners
- *octopus*   a bucket of human waste is emptied over a prisoner
- *buzz*   the carotid artery in the neck is physically blocked by a stranglehold from another prisoner until the victim becomes unconscious
- *kangaroo court*   although this is not expanded on by McGurk and McDougall (1986), the general understanding of this in prisons relates to the creation of a mock 'court' set up by prisoners where the victim is judged and a sentence passed
- *tetley*   where a prisoner, naked except for a pair of underpants on their head and with a broomstick in their hand, sings a song (usually the 'Tetley tea bag' song from a TV advert) and dances round the dormitory; sometimes the prisoner is tied to a bed and a broomstick is pushed into their rectum
- *kestrel*   a cup of water is placed on the pillow of a sleeping prisoner and a boot is thrown at them, their startled response spills the water on their pillow and face
- *eagle*   a fire bucket full of water is placed on the bedside locker of

a sleeping prisoner and a boot is thrown at it, knocking the bucket
over onto the victim

- *whodunit*    a blanket is thrown over the head of a prisoner and the
  other prisoners hit the victim with sticks or kick them
- *dormitory death runs*    an initiation ceremony for new dormitory
  members where the new prisoner runs the gauntlet of prisoners who
  hit them with pillowcases, some of which contain boots
- *mock hangings*    prisoners are 'hung' from windows or threatened
  with being pushed off the top of a bed that is stood on end, a noose
  is placed round their neck which is then attached to the top of the bed
- *rape*    an incidence where a naked prisoner is beaten with slippers

The use of specific terms is not restricted to young offenders and
is also reported by adult prisoners. These include 'bed legged' where a
prisoner is hit with a bed leg (Brookes *et al.* 1994), 'broom legging',
where a prisoner is hit across the calves with a broom handle or similar
instrument (Ireland 1995) and 'blagging', referring to a gang beating
(Ireland and Archer 1996). Also reported are 'nonce kicking' and 'beast
bashing' both of which refer to the physical beatings given to sex
offenders (Ireland and Archer 1996), and 'joey bashing' referring to
beatings given to prisoners who act as the personal servants of bullies
(Ireland and Archer 1996). Brookes and colleagues (1994) also referred
to the act of being 'banjoed' although no explanation of this was offered
by prisoners, 'contracts on head' referring to having someone in mind
who is next to be bullied, and finally 'wind ups' where practical jokes are
used to make fun of a prisoner.

The use of terms to describe specific forms of abuse suggests that some
types of bullying are well established and possibly even tolerated to a
certain degree by the prisoner subculture. The use of terms to describe such
acts can also serve to minimise what is essentially an act of aggression.

### Prevalence of bullying types

There are difficulties in addressing the prevalence of each type of bullying,
particularly in view of the varying definitions of bullying applied in the
research (see Chapter 2). This applies especially to those studies that have
not included a specific definition of indirect bullying. Of the research that
has included indirect bullying the majority reports that it occurs at least
to the same extent as, if not more than, direct bullying.

Regarding the prevalence of each type of indirect bullying, gossiping,
deliberately ignoring someone or playing practical jokes on someone

appear to be most frequently reported. Assessing the prevalence of each type of indirect bullying is difficult with some researchers either not recognising certain behaviours as indirect bullying or confusing both direct and indirect behaviours and reporting them as one type (e.g. Livingston *et al.* 1994; Mosson 1994).

Regarding the prevalence of each type of direct bullying, psychological or verbal bullying tends to be reported most frequently, particularly being threatened, called names or harassed verbally. This is followed by physical and theft-related aggression, which in some studies are reported to an equal extent. As mentioned previously, sex-related aggression tends to be reported least frequently with researchers finding either little (Ireland 1999a) or no evidence of this (Connell and Farrington 1996).

The reported prevalence of each type of bullying is largely consistent regardless of the method that was used to collect data (i.e. whether researchers asked victims or bullies directly what behaviours they have engaged in or experienced, if rates were based on prisoners' perceptions of the types of bullying that took place, or if official records were used as a source of information). There are, however, subtle differences between them. When prisoners are asked for their perceptions of the most likely types of bullying, taxing and physical bullying tend to be reported more frequently than psychological or verbal bullying (Ireland and Archer 1996; Power *et al.* 1997). When official records are used, indirect bullying tends to be reported less frequently. For example, in one study I found that only 2 out of 102 incidents of actual or suspected bullying recorded on BIRs made reference to indirect aggression, compared to 72 describing psychological or verbal bullying, 32 physical and 23 theft-related bullying (Ireland 2002d). I concluded from this that official records were not a useful method of collecting data on indirect bullying and may under-estimate this particular type of aggression. Such records are dependent on the perceptions of those reporting the incident and, because of its subtle nature, indirect bullying may not be viewed as such by those observing or hearing of the incident. Although not yet assessed, it is also possible that the indirect bullying picked up by official records is limited to the most salient and well-known forms (i.e. gossiping, spreading rumours and ostracising), with the more subtle indirect behaviours being missed.

It is also worth noting that when victims and/or bullies describe the types of abusive behaviours that they have engaged in or experienced, it is not uncommon for them to report more than one type of aggression. For example, in one study I found that the majority of prisoners who reported aggressive behaviours indicated using or experiencing a combination of both direct and indirect aggression (Ireland 2002e). Research, however, has tended to focus on identifying those who have been bullied and not on addressing the many different types of aggression that victims may have been subjected to. In particular, research has not distinguished between those who have been bullied using one type of aggression and those who have been the victims of numerous types of aggression. This is surprising in view of evidence which shows that a small proportion of prisoners are, in fact, victims of many different types of aggression. Beck and Smith (1997), for example, found that of the 75 per cent of prisoners in their study who reported at least one behaviour indicative of being bullied, only 25 per cent reported one item indicative of being a victim with the rest reporting more than one item. Indeed, 1 per cent of prisoners in this study reported that seventeen victim items had occurred to them in the previous week with 1 per cent reporting eighteen items. Similarly, in a further study, I found that out of 52 per cent of prisoners reporting at least one behaviour indicative of being bullied in the previous week, 26 per cent reported between four and eight victim items, 4 per cent between nine and thirteen items, 4 per cent between fourteen and eighteen items and just under 1 per cent between nineteen and twenty-three items. A similar relationship has also been found for those reporting behaviours indicative of bullying others, suggesting that there are a small proportion of bullies who aggress towards others in many different ways over a short period of time (Ireland 1997).[2]

From the studies presented here, it is not possible to ascertain the extent to which the victims (or bullies) who reported more than one type of aggression were reporting separate incidences of bullying or a single incidence of bullying where more than one type of aggression was used. Regardless of this, it could be argued that prisoners reporting to being victimised in many different ways over a one-week period are victims of particularly severe bullying as opposed to those reporting that a single or a couple of types of aggression have been used against them. This does not take into account, however, the nature of bullying and that a single incident of bullying can be severe. What these studies do suggest, however, is that there is a clear distinction between victims reporting one or a couple of abuse items and those reporting many. We would expect, for example, that the victims reported by Beck and Smith (1997) who reported up to eighteen victim items would differ in some way from those reporting a single item. Addressing this issue is perhaps an avenue that future research should address.

These sections have addressed the overall extent of bullying, the general prevalence of each type of bullying and how this is influenced by the source of information used, for example prisoner perceptions or official records. It must be noted that there are also differences regarding the prevalence of the different types of bullying across samples in terms of sex, age (i.e. juveniles, young offenders and adults), and the type of prison where the study took place. These differences are described in more detail in the following sections.

## Sex differences in bullying

The majority of prison-based research has focused on men, with the first study addressing women published in 1996 and the first review of research among women in 2000. The paucity of research conducted among women prisoners is consistent with the pattern of research found in bullying among schoolchildren where boys were initially the focus of research. Indeed, Olweus (1978) in one of his first studies into bullying concluded that it was a behaviour that occurred so infrequently among adolescent girls that he limited his research to boys.

Where previously researchers have concluded that men were more aggressive than women and therefore focused research on them, more recently it has been recognised that women are also aggressive and therefore deserve further study. This is partly because of a recent trend in aggression research which recognises that sex differences in aggression are a function both of the type of aggression being examined and the context in which it occurs. Björkqvist and colleagues (1994b) argue that previous research has underestimated the level of aggressiveness displayed by girls as a result of operationalising a 'male' definition of aggression which has failed to assess forms of aggression relevant to the peer groups of girls, namely indirect aggression. It can be said, however, that the relationship between sex and aggression is a complex one, and subject to debate (Geen 1998). Björkqvist (1994) argued that if aggression is limited to physical forms then in western societies it is true that men are generally more aggressive than women, but that this is not a universal truth and does not hold for all cultures and contexts. Indeed, Björkqvist and colleagues stated that

> the claim that human males are more aggressive than females appears, however, to be false, and a consequence of narrow definitions and operationalisations of aggression in previous research, with a predominant emphasis on physical aggression. Recent reviews find fewer sex differences with respect to aggression, and these are more of a qualitative than quantitative nature.
>
> (Björkqvist *et al.* 1994b: 28)

This appears to hold for bullying as well as general aggression, with ample evidence from studies involving schoolchildren (Smith and Sharp 1994) and prisoners (Ireland and Archer 1996) that women do engage in bullying. Indeed, research focusing solely on samples of women prisoners has reported estimates of bullying comparable to those of men (Loucks 1998; Grant 1999; Mosson 1998). Of those studies directly comparing men and women prisoners, adult women have been found to perceive a higher extent of bullying in comparison to men, and also to be more likely to admit to being a victim than men when asked directly (Ireland and Archer 1996). Studies addressing behaviours indicative of bullying have found that men were significantly more likely than women to admit behaviours indicative of bullying others, and that more women than men were classified as pure victims (Ireland 1999a).

Overall, these findings could suggest that when it comes to admitting to the perpetration of bullying, men rank above women as the more aggressive sex. Women, on the other hand, are more likely to report being victimised. This could reflect true sex differences in the extent of bullying reported but it could equally reflect differences in reporting styles: women prisoners have been found to be more supportive of victims and disapproving of bullies than men (Ireland 1999b). Admitting to being a victim in a female prison may not carry the same stigma that it does in a male prison where admittance to victimisation is seen as a sign of weakness (which is construed as a feminine trait), and where prisoners are more supportive of bullies. Thus men may be more likely to admit to being a bully as this is reinforced to a greater extent in a male prison.

Although there are difficulties in comparing studies because of the different methods each has used to assess the extent of bullying and the differing definitions of bullying that they have applied, two conclusions can still be drawn, namely that both men and women do engage in and report bullying behaviour, and that women tend to perceive more bullying than men.

The question, therefore, has become, not 'do men and women both engage in bullying behaviour?', but rather 'how do the bullying strategies of men and women differ?' It is this question of 'how do men and women differ in the way that they bully?' that the present section will focus on, and in doing so will concentrate on those studies that have compared men and women.

Hypotheses about sex differences with regard to the types of bullying that prisoners would report were based initially on research among schoolchildren that reported 'male' and 'female' forms of bullying. These hypotheses related to research suggesting that men would report more direct forms of bullying than women, and women would report more indirect forms of bullying than men, but that neither form would be exclusive to each sex (Ahmad and Smith 1994). They were also based on evidence from research into general aggression among children that reported boys to favour direct and overt methods of aggression while girls focused on more subtle forms of aggression (Crick and Grotpeter 1995). Sex differences regarding the subtypes of aggression have also been predicted among prisoners, namely that men would be more likely to engage in physical bullying whereas sex differences in verbal bullying would be less clear. This, again, was based on general aggression research. In reviewing the literature, for example, Bushman and Anderson (1998) concluded that males were more physically aggressive than females but that sex differences regarding verbal aggression were minimal. The sex differences in physical aggression have been explained as a result of differences in physical strength between men and women: women are physically weaker than men and it is therefore likely that they have developed means other than physical aggression in order to obtain a goal (Björkqvist 1994). Both verbal and indirect aggression, however, are effective methods that are not dependent on the physical ability of the perpetrator. Thus it is no surprise that these forms of aggression have been found to occur to a greater extent among women than physical forms.

There is also evidence for sex differences within indirect aggression. In a study conducted by Björkqvist et al. (1994b) among non-incarcerated adults, two subtypes of indirect aggression were assessed, social manipulation and rational-appearing aggression (see Chapter 2 where these types are discussed in more detail). Björkqvist et al. (1994b) reported that adult women engaged in social manipulation to a greater extent than adult men, whereas men engaged in rational-appearing aggression to a greater extent than women. Although both forms of aggression are broadly considered to be indirect, rational-appearing aggression is argued to contain both direct and indirect strategies. Evidence for both types of aggression has been found among prisoners (Ireland 1999a), although they have not always been recognised as such. Subtle and indirect forms of bullying are a favoured type of aggression in a prison environment, and thus any consideration of sex differences in bullying needs to take into account indirect strategies as well.

Regarding bullying among prisoners, a review of the research suggests that men and women report similar types of bullying in a prison environment. Both sexes report psychological and verbal, theft-related, sexual, physical and indirect forms of bullying. Sex differences can be found in the *frequency* with which each form of bullying occurs. The first study that directly compared men and women was that of Ireland and Archer (1996). This study focused on perceptions of bullying and asked prisoners to describe the types of bullying that took place in as much detail as they could. Seven categories were reported and, presented in rank order, they were physical bullying, taking things, verbal bullying, threats, intimidation, gossiping or spreading rumours and ostracising the victim. Men were more likely than women to report physical assault, whereas women were more likely than men to report verbal bullying, gossiping or spreading rumours and ostracising. When the types of bullying were condensed into direct and indirect aggression, women were more likely to report indirect bullying than men (26 per cent versus 5 per cent respectively), who were more likely to report direct bullying (95 per cent of men versus 74 per cent of women). This provided evidence that there were indeed male and female forms of bullying, although neither form was exclusive to each sex. These findings corresponded with research into general aggression and bullying among children on which the hypotheses were originally based.

This study was, however, based on perceptions of bullying and these findings have not been replicated in later studies based on actual accounts of bullying, or more specifically with regard to behaviours indicative of bullying. For example, in a later study (Ireland 1999a), I found that women were more likely to report being victims of theft-related and sex-related bullying than men, and that more men than women reported being the perpetrators of psychological and verbal bullying. With regard to indirect and direct bullying, men were more likely than women to be the perpetrators of both these types of bullying. These findings are inconsistent with those of Ireland and Archer (1996). There was also no significant sex difference with regard to behaviours indicative of being the victim of direct or indirect aggression. An interpretation of these findings, however, needs to be made with caution. First, the later study (Ireland 1999a) was not, as mentioned previously, concerned with perceptions of bullying and it employed a different method to collect data than Ireland and Archer (1996). It also assessed a combined sample of adults and young offenders. Second, the prisoners studied in Ireland (1999a) reported indirect aggression to a greater overall extent than direct aggression. The findings regarding indirect aggression may therefore be a result of the overall preference of all prisoners in Ireland (1999a) to utilise indirect aggression and the fact that men did bully more than women. This study also focused on nine discrete types of indirect aggression whereas Ireland and Archer (1996) provided a definition of bullying to prisoners that included only three salient types of indirect bullying (i.e. gossiping, spreading rumours and ostracising). This could partly explain the differences between these studies. There is, however, another possible explanation. When the results of Ireland (1999a) are examined in more detail they suggest that men were more likely than women to report those forms of indirect aggression that could be described as rational-appearing aggression, which is consistent with Björkqvist and colleagues (1994b). More men than women, for example, reported the indirect item[3] 'I have had a practical joke played on me'. Such a form of abuse would seem to represent the most direct form of indirect abuse possible. Arguably practical jokes fall into the definition of rational-appearing aggression since they represent a form of aggression easily rationalised as 'only a joke'. They also represent a way in which the aggressor involves others in 'putting down' the victim. The victimised individual may be aware of who committed the act but not able to label it as overt aggressive intent. Similarly, the men in this study consistently reported more of those forms of indirect abuse that could be described as the most direct forms. A higher proportion of men than women, for example, also reported the items 'I have picked on another prisoner with my friends' and 'I have encouraged others to turn against another prisoner'. These items represent more direct forms of indirect aggression since the perpetrator is overtly encouraging the involvement of others in victimisation, and hence they are not as discreet as gossiping or spreading rumours about an individual. Thus, although men utilised more indirect aggression than women, they appeared to show a tendency to favour the more 'direct' forms.

Further evidence regarding the relationship between reporting behaviours indicative of bullying others and those indicative of being bullied would seem to add weight to this argument: a number of significant relationships were found between reporting being bullied and reporting bullying others. Men who reported bullying others indirectly also reported being victimised themselves both indirectly and directly. This was not found for women, where there were no significant correlations between bullying others indirectly and any form of victimisation (Ireland 1999a).[4] Research suggests that overt aggression carries a threat of overt retaliation (Björkqvist 1994), whereas indirect aggression minimises this risk. These correlational findings suggest that this may be true for women prisoners but not for men. Indirect bullying for women carried no risk of victimisation, whereas men who bullied others indirectly appeared at risk of both indirect and direct victimisation. It could be speculated that although men utilised indirect aggression more than women, women may be better at using it than men and at keeping it hidden. Alternatively, the indirect bullying behaviour of men may not be as surreptitious as that of women, simply because men prefer to utilise the less covert forms (i.e. the more rational-appearing forms). This interpretation of the findings, however, is purely speculative since the analysis used was correlational and therefore not necessarily indicative of a causal relationship between bullying and victimisation (Ireland 1999a).

In a later study conducted with adult offenders (Ireland 2000b), I reported similar findings to Ireland (1999a), in that there was no significant sex difference with regard to behaviours indicative of being the victim of direct or indirect aggression. Men in this study were again more likely than women to report the indirect behaviour of playing a practical joke on someone, or of being the recipient of a practical joke. There were also a number of differences between these two studies: women in the later study reported more physical and more psychological and verbal victimisation than men. There were also no sex differences this time with regard to the perpetration of direct or indirect bullying. The women in this study also consistently reported more of those types of indirect aggression that could be described as social manipulation in comparison to men, for example 'I have been gossiped about', 'I have had rumours spread about me' and 'someone has deliberately lied about me'. This latter finding is consistent with Björkqvist et al. (1994b). The differences between these studies could be explained in part by the different samples used. In Ireland (1999a) I reported on a sample that included both adults and young offenders, whereas in Ireland (2000b) I reported solely on adult offenders. As discussed in the following section, there is evidence to suggest that age is an important influence in deciding what type of aggressive strategy will be employed.

The present section has illustrated the difficulties in attempting to draw firm conclusions about sex differences in bullying. It is also worth noting that the original hypothesis that women would report more indirect aggression than men was based on studies of children, all of which involved peer reports, with most reporting higher values for girls than boys. Studies of non-incarcerated adults, however, have produced conflicting findings. Archer (2000a) criticised the claim that studies have shown that women are more indirectly aggressive than men, arguing that the characterisation of women as being more likely than men to show indirect aggression is incorrect according to current evidence. Such evidence shows that sex differences found regarding adults have been mixed in terms of the occurrence, direction and magnitude of aggression (Archer et al. 1997; Björkqvist et al. 1994b; Campbell et al. 1997; Green *et al.* 1996; Richardson and Green 1999). The results described in the present section provide further evidence for this, by highlighting that there is no clear sex difference in adults' usage of indirect bullying.

Although the research presented in this section regarding prison-based bullying is limited and conflicting, four tentative conclusions can be drawn from it

- it appears that women prisoners bully to at least the same extent as men
- both men and women engage in all of the different subtypes of direct aggression
- there is no clear and reliable sex difference in the frequency of direct and indirect aggression
- women appear to utilise different styles of bullying behaviour in comparison to men, although there are also a number of similarities between them.

What is clear, however, is that no definite conclusions can be made about sex differences until more research directly comparing men and women is conducted. There is a clear need, based on the evidence presented here, for research to specifically address the discrete behaviours that make up the different types of bullying, particularly indirect bullying. It is important that when assessing sex differences in bullying the research does not concentrate only on the most salient forms of indirect aggression. Only by examining the many different, discrete, types of bullying behaviours will researchers be able to explore exactly where sex differences in indirect aggression lie. In particular, this research should clearly distinguish between adults and young offenders. To date the only research to include a sample of both male and female young offenders is Ireland (1999a). Female young offenders are a particularly difficult group to study, with relatively few in the prison system in comparison to male young offenders. In addition, male young offenders are housed separately from adults in the United Kingdom whereas the same cannot be said for female young offenders who are housed with adults. Until female young offenders are housed separately from adults, a clear assessment of sex differences will be difficult to achieve. Age, as discussed in the following section, is a confounding variable in any analysis of sex differences and aggression, with aggression used to a greater extent by younger age groups.

## Age differences in bullying

Age differences relate here to differences between juvenile, young and adult offenders. Differences have been found both in the extent of bullying reported and also in the type of aggressive strategies used.

There is evidence that bullying is more prevalent among young offenders than adults, and this holds for reporting behaviours indicative of being a bully and behaviours indicative of being a victim. In a review of the literature, Ireland and colleagues (1999) reported estimates of the proportion of prisoners reporting to being a bully ranging from 20 to 70 per cent for young offenders and 0 to 62 per cent for adult offenders. Estimates of the proportion of prisoners reporting to being a victim ranged from 30 to 75 per cent for young offenders and 8 to 57 per cent for adults. Only one study (Ireland 1999a) has directly compared adults with young offenders and it reported that young offenders were more likely to report behaviours indicative of bullying others than adults. No differences were reported for behaviours indicative of being bullied. In a later study (Ireland 2002e) in which juvenile (aged 14 to 17 years) and young offenders (aged 18 to 21 years) were compared, bullying behaviour was more prevalent among juvenile than young offenders, although this only held for (direct) behaviours indicative of being bullied and not for bullying others.

There is also evidence for differences between offenders regarding perceptions of bullying, for example the average proportion of young offenders reporting to having seen a prisoner being bullied in the previous week is 56 per cent (based on combining the findings of McGurk and McDougall 1986; Swift 1995; Power et al. 1997), whereas for adults this is 40 per cent (based on Brookes 1993; Brookes et al. 1994; Livingston et al. 1994; Ireland and Archer 1996). Regarding juvenile and young offenders, in Ireland (2002e) I asked each how much bullying they thought was taking place in the prison and found that juveniles perceived a greater extent of bullying in comparison to young offenders.

The type of aggressive strategy employed is largely dependent on developmental change, with direct aggression (the most observable type) arguably decreasing over an individual's lifespan, while indirect and subtle aggressive strategies tend to increase. Björkqvist and colleagues (1992b) proposed a theory of aggression that is very applicable to a discussion of bullying behaviours among prisoners, a theory that conceptualises the level of aggression as falling along a continuum of development. They describe how physical, direct verbal and indirect aggression correspond to three developmental phases. Young children will resort to physical aggression to obtain a social goal simply because they do not yet have the verbal or social skills to utilise any other type of aggression. Boys, as mentioned in the previous section, appear to be particularly skilled at this form of aggression. Once verbal skills begin to develop, the need to use physical aggression is reduced. Verbal aggression is an effective method of aggression and one that is more socially acceptable than physical aggression. Hence, verbal aggression begins to replace physical aggression. This is not to say that physical aggression is no longer used, it is simply used less and is dependent on the culture and context under study. Once social intelligence develops the use of indirect aggression increases. Indirect aggression is a sophisticated form of aggression and as such requires a degree of social skill on the part of the perpetrator. However, although an individual may develop the skills to perpetrate indirect aggression, this is not to say that they no longer utilise other forms. Björkqvist and colleagues (1992b) state that indirect aggression is expected to coexist with direct verbal aggression during later adolescence and adulthood. The use of verbal or indirect aggression is also dependent on the context in which the aggression is taking place: direct verbal aggression may be more appropriate in a situation where anger is being expressed, whereas indirect aggression may be more appropriate when the perpetrator does not wish to be identified (Björkqvist et al. 1992b).

There is some evidence that this theory can be applied to prisoners although the evidence has not always supported a simple application. In Ireland (1999a), I found that the majority of bullying behaviours reported by young offenders included psychological and verbal abuse followed by physical abuse, and that in both categories young offenders reported significantly higher levels than adults. This is consistent with Björkqvist and colleagues' (1992b) theory in that it appears that the social skills of adults have evolved more than those of young offenders, with adults using direct forms of aggression less. It would be expected then, on the basis of this theory, that adults would utilise more indirect aggression than young offenders as this represents the most sophisticated form of aggression. There was no significant difference found between young and adult offenders, however, within this category of bullying although there was a trend with regard to reports of being bullied, with adults reporting more indirect victimisation than young offenders. An examination of the descriptive data across the categories of direct and indirect bullying did, however, show that young offenders utilised indirect bullying to a lesser extent in comparison to direct bullying (51 per cent versus 62 per cent respectively), with the opposite relationship found with adults, where indirect aggression was reported much more than direct aggression (44 per cent versus 26 per cent respectively).[5] Thus it would appear that young offenders utilise indirect aggression to complement their repertoire of aggression, whereas for adults indirect aggression represents the most dominant form.

In Ireland (2002e), where juveniles were compared to young offenders, I found that juveniles reported more physical, psychological and verbal and overall direct forms of victimisation (i.e. of being bullied) than young offenders. This again is consistent with Björkqvist and colleagues' (1992b) developmental theory. Both juveniles and young offenders, however, reported similar levels of indirect bullying. Unlike Ireland (1999a), there was no preferred strategy for either group with both reporting to favour direct over indirect aggression as a method by which to bully others. This was therefore not consistent with the theory, which would have predicted that the older age group would have used indirect aggression to a greater extent. It could be, however, that the age difference between the two groups in this study was not great enough for a difference to be detected: if the comparison was between adolescents and older adults (as it was for Ireland 1999a), then some of the expected differences may have been found.

The lack of significant differences found in both studies with regard to indirect aggression could be explained by the preference of prisoners to utilise indirect aggression more than direct since it carries the least cost for them in a prison environment. This highlights the importance of taking into account the environment in which bullying is taking place before attempting to apply theories of aggression developed for non-incarcerated samples. The influence of the prison environment on the nature and extent of bullying will be described in the following section.

## Environmental differences in bullying

How the physical characteristics of prisons differ and the influence that this may have on determining the extent or nature of bullying is not an area that has received much attention from researchers. Indeed, there has been little acknowledgement of the differences in environmental characteristics between the prisons under study. No two prisons, however, could be described as identical. Physical differences between them include variations in how prisoners are housed (i.e. either in single or double cells, dormitories or a combination of both), and differences between prisons that follow a more traditional design (i.e. wings, landings and spurs) and those that do not (i.e. accommodating prisoners in houses or billets). This section will focus on the physical differences between prisons.

The failure of research to address the issue of physical environment is surprising when it is considered that bullying is influenced largely by the environment. For example, it is acknowledged that bullying occurs where supervision from staff is limited. Environments that allow for certain areas to be poorly supervised by staff (i.e. with blind-spots) undoubtedly increase the opportunities for bullying. Indeed, a common suggestion for interventions into bullying is to change the physical environment in some way. This was a method emphasised in the 1999 Prison Service anti-bullying strategy (Home Office Prison Service 1999). Suggestions for making changes to the environment have included converting dormitories into single cells and installing extra gates or barriers on prison wings in order to break them up into smaller, more manageable units (see Chapter 7 for more detail).

Research that has incorporated more than one prison in a study has alluded to the importance of the physical environment as a variable that possibly influences the type of bullying reported. For example, the finding that women prisoners in one of my studies (Ireland 1999a) reported more theft-related abuse than men, could be explained with reference to differences in the physical structure between the male and female prisons under study. The structure of the female prison in this study was such that up to four prisoners would share a dormitory where the opportunity to steal was greater than in the male establishments where most cells were occupied by only one prisoner. Indeed, the women prisoners in this study reported that many of the thefts were from their dormitories.[6]

The environmental characteristics of a prison are largely a product of the security classification of the establishment. Although it may be impossible to control for all of the physical differences between prisons, researchers can address part of this issue by taking into account the security classification of the prison under study. Higher security establishments, for example, have more security gates and observation points than the lower security establishments. The failure of researchers to address the importance of prison type could be explained by a tendency for studies to concentrate on only one prison per study as opposed to collecting and comparing data from a range of establishments. To date only one study (Ireland 2000b) has attempted to address the importance of the type of prison in which bullying is being measured. In this study I addressed the nature and extent of bullying behaviour in six different prisons and reported a number of significant differences between them. Differences were found in relation to overall, direct and indirect bullying behaviours, and within the subcategories of bullying. This study reported more prison-based differences than sex differences, suggesting that the prison where bullying behaviour takes place is an important influence. The prison, as a variable, did not affect the classification of men and women into the different bully categories (i.e. pure bullies, pure victims, bully/victims and not-involved), suggesting that its influence was restricted to the nature and extent of bullying behaviour.

The finding that there were differences across prison establishments suggests that the type of prison in which bullying is being measured is an important variable to take into consideration and appears to be more important than sex differences. This may be particularly applicable to those studies that have directly compared samples of men and women and reported differences between them. The majority of female establishments in these studies were markedly different from the male establishments. The female prisons typically followed a dormitory-like structure and were made up of separate houses, unlike the male prisons which all followed a 'cell and wing/landing' format. This raises the question of whether or not the apparent sex differences reported in these studies are truly sex differences or rather environmental differences. Similarly, although not yet assessed, it is also possible that some of the differences described in the previous section between young and adult offenders could be explained by differences in the physical environment of the prisons under study.

## Summary

This chapter has focused on the extent to which bullying occurs among prisoners and has highlighted problems in trying to ascertain the true extent of bullying. Different types of bullying have been presented and the importance of measuring both direct (namely physical, psychological and verbal, theft-related and sex-related) and indirect forms of bullying has been highlighted. Accounting for indirect bullying is particularly important: studies that have focused solely on direct bullying may have severely underestimated the extent to which bullying takes place by failing to acknowledge the importance of measuring indirect aggression, which may be a preferred strategy in prison. The important of taking into account sex differences was also highlighted, particularly with regard to the impact that such differences may have on the extent to which bullying is reported. Age differences were also highlighted, with younger age groups tending to perceive higher levels of bullying and also reporting to bully in different ways to older age groups. Evidence for an application of a developmental theory of aggression was found, although it was acknowledged that a simple application of this theory was not possible and that the environment in which the bullying takes place needs to be taken into account. Related to this is the general impact that the environment may have on bullying, an impact that may be greater than either sex or age differences, in explaining the extent and nature of bullying. Only one aspect of the environment was discussed here, namely the physical environment. There are other elements of the environment that are just as important such as the social environment. The role of both the physical and social environment in the promotion and reinforcement of bullying among prisoners will be described in detail in the following chapter where I ask the question 'Why does bullying occur among prisoners?'

# Chapter 4

# Why does bullying occur among prisoners?

The circumstances of imprisonment can be seen as ideal conditions for bullying to occur where 'the demanding aspects of the prison environment, allied with the past behaviour of their prisoners, provide a combination where frequent bullying should be expected' (Beck 1995: 55).

If a prison reports that they have no or very little bullying in comparison to other prisons, it is likely that they are not measuring the extent of the problem accurately. Bullying will continue to take place in prisons regardless of the interventions that are put in place. As I discuss in Chapters 7 and 8, interventions can certainly help to alleviate the extent of bullying but they cannot eradicate it. This goal is unobtainable. Bullying is very much a product of the interaction between the prison environment and those housed within it. The environment acts to influence and reinforce the behaviour of prisoners who are predisposed towards bullying others.

Thus, describing a prisoner as aggressive or exploitative is not enough to explain why they bully their peers. The role played by the environment, both physical and social, is of vital importance in explaining why bullying takes place. The importance of the prison environment is the main focus of the present chapter. The importance of individual characteristics and how these may influence bullying are also discussed, although I discuss these more fully in Chapter 5. This is not a reflection of the importance of individual characteristics in explaining bullying, but rather of the amount of research conducted on such characteristics that merits a separate discussion. I conclude the chapter by presenting a model illustrating how each element of the prison environment and the individual characteristics of prisoners can be linked together to explain why bullying occurs.

As I noted in Chapter 1, there have been a number of papers on general aggression among prisoners completed outside the United Kingdom, primarily in the United States. Unlike research into bullying, the focus of papers on general aggression has been very much on *why* it occurs (e.g. Cooley 1993) as opposed to outlining the nature and extent of the problem. Thus, the present chapter refers to these papers as well as to those concentrating solely on bullying. In trying to describe why bullying occurs in prisons the first question that should be asked is 'why do prisoners think that bullying occurs?'

## Why do prisoners think bullying occurs?

Studies that have asked prisoners directly why they think that prisoners are bullied report a range of different reasons. Ireland and Archer (1996) found that the majority of prisoners reported that being unable to look after yourself in a prison was one reason why a prisoner may get bullied. This was followed by being convicted for a particular offence (mainly sex offences), for the possessions that they may have, for refusing to comply with the demands of a bully, for failing to repay debts, for not conforming, because a bully wishes to assert power and because victims were seen as easy targets. In addition, Brookes and colleagues (1994) found that prisoners were likely to be bullied because of a personal grudge held by another prisoner or by someone outside the prison, because the bully was bored or frustrated, in order to force unpopular prisoners to leave the wing, for fun, for drugs, to make the victim do something for them or to make the bully feel superior. Connell and Farrington (1996) also reported reasons for bullying that included the victim being seen as 'mouthy' (and hence considered provocative), the victim acting tough when this status was seen as not deserved or not knowing how to 'handle themselves' in custody (that usually meant that the prisoner was immature or not familiar with the informal subculture rules).

The reasons provided by prisoners provide some insight into why bullying may take place and how the prison environment itself may influence bullying. The role played by the social environment appears to be particularly important. The social environment in a prison is governed largely by the prisoner subculture and the unwritten rules dictated by it. Those who fail to conform to these rules, either by failing to repay debts, by not fitting in, by informing on others, or having a general lack of awareness concerning these rules, risk becoming targets of bullying. Issues of power and vulnerability were also included, with bullying others viewed as a way in which bullies can assert power over others, and victims viewed as easy targets. Both the importance of the inmate subculture and the role of power and dominance in explaining bullying will be discussed in later sections. The mention of possessions as one reason for bullying is also important. As discussed in the following section, possessions of any kind are a valuable currency in a prison where the type and amount of possessions allowed are carefully controlled by prison authorities. The careful control over material possessions is one aspect of the physical environment that is influential in explaining bullying. Although it is acknowledged that the impact of both the physical and social environment on bullying are inextricably linked, the two aspects are dealt with here separately for ease of discussion and interpretation.

## The physical environment

Prisons are environments where access to material goods is limited, large numbers of people are confined together within a relatively small space, staff supervision of prisoners is predictable and limited because of the high prisoner to staff ratio, and the level of environmental stimulation is low. Each of these aspects of the environment can help to explain why bullying occurs and each will be discussed in turn.

### Material goods

Goods are a valuable form of currency in a prison where prisoners are allowed to purchase and keep only a limited amount of possessions. Since goods are limited, there is marked competition to acquire them and their value on the prisoner black market is increased. This encourages prisoners to engage in theft-related bullying. Such bullying is an ingrained part of the subculture as evidenced by widely used terms to describe, and to a certain extent rationalise, such behaviour. Taxing (taking goods from prisoners new to the wing under the pretence of taking for tax) and baroning (loaning goods to prisoners and then demanding an extortionate amount of interest), for example, are well-known forms of theft-related bullying. Tobacco is a particularly valuable form of currency and some 'barons', known as 'tobacco barons', only trade in this. Other valuable items include food, batteries, medication, telephone cards and toiletries (Brookes *et al.* 1994; Beck 1995; Loucks 1998; Ireland 2002d). Indeed, as stated by Beck, 'Resources that may be taken for granted as freely available outside prison, become highly valued "inside". Tobacco, sweets and telephone cards are expensive in relation to prisoners' pay, and as such are the focus of intense competition' (1995: 55).

Incentives for bullying others to obtain material goods are high since bullies are in a powerful position where they can then bargain or trade their goods at extortionately high prices. Bullies do not have to take items directly from prisoners, instead they can charge extortionate prices for items that they have legitimately bought themselves but do not need. Material deprivation is an important component of prison life and is seen as one of the 'pains of imprisonment'. Violence and exploitation give prisoners the solution to such deprivation, even if it is at the expense of other prisoners. The greater the material deprivation, the more profitable exploitation becomes for the aggressive prisoner (Feld 1981).

Interestingly, the views of prisoners regarding theft-related bullying vary depending on the specific type of behaviour – stealing from the cells of other prisoners is viewed particularly negatively with such prisoners labelled 'cell thieves' (Ireland 2000b), whereas extorting money from someone (i.e. baroning) is often not viewed as bullying.

The fact that prisoners are provided with limited material resources also promotes a 'capitalist economic structure', something that increases predatory behaviour (MacDonald 1988). Such structures can be found particularly in large groups where the genetic and attachment relationships between individuals are low encouraging the exploitation of resources (Gilbert 1994). This can easily be applied to a prison and could describe the motivation behind prison bullying. Societies that are based on capitalist economic structures purposefully create arenas for conflict and are 'concerned only with winners, with little interest in those who are disadvantaged' (Gilbert 1994: 371). Bullying is a possible means through which an individual can be regarded as a winner (Ireland 2000a). The prison environment provides a good example of the physical environment (i.e. lack of material goods) interacting with the social environment (i.e. low genetic and attachment relationships) to maximise the conditions that generate bullying.

## Population

The effects of population density have been studied in humans since the 1960s with an increased density in population reportedly leading to an increased level of aggression (e.g. Hutt and Vaizey 1966). The effects of population density have been studied more extensively among animals where it is noted that the negative effects of population density, namely aggression, become exaggerated in confined conditions, where animals are unable to 'emigrate' to less dense conditions (Archer 1970). Although focusing on animals, this notion of aggression becoming exacerbated in confined conditions, where escape is not possible, could easily be applied to a prison environment.

Researchers addressing the effect of prisoner population on behaviour have tended to focus on the size of the prison in terms of the number of prisoners that it holds, and on two types of population density, the spatial and the social density. Prisons represent environments where the spatial density between people is limited, that is where the physical living space between individuals is low, and also where the social density is high, that is where the number of people encountered over time is high (i.e. the transiency of the population). These conditions can lead to crowding, with a large number of individuals (social density) crowded into limited space (spatial density). Nacci and colleagues (1977) described how, in a prison, high population density sometimes increases arousal levels resulting in increases in levels of aggression and hostility (Ekland-Olson 1986).

A link has also been reported between density and the number and type of disciplinary infractions reported. Nacci and colleagues (1977), for example, reported that high density was associated with high rates of assaults and that the relationship between density and this type of behaviour was greater than with other non-violent offences such as escapes. The importance of addressing both aspects of density was highlighted by Megargee (1976, 1977) who found only a weak correlation between population size and disciplinary infraction but a strong negative correlation between infractions and available living space (living space was reduced temporarily when renovations took place within the prison). In a discussion of this research, Farrington and Nuttall showed that variations in personal living space were associated with changes in other factors. When the available living space was reduced, prisoners were located to other areas of the prison which involved 'territorial intrusions and disruptions of social ties . . . and might have been more important in producing disruptive behaviour than the space reduction or change in population density' (1980: 223). The effect of density on other factors was also pointed out by Nacci and colleagues (1977) who argued that an increase in population may have a disruptive effect since it involves disturbing a pre-established social order among prisoners and occurs more frequently in a prison setting. To relate this back briefly to studies conducted among animals, there is evidence that group stability leads to lower levels of aggression in animals whereas a repeated turnover of animals acts to disrupt the cohesion of the group and leads to increases in aggression (Archer 1970). Nacci and colleagues (1997) argued that in a prison setting, social density was more disruptive than space reduction since fluctuations in social density occur more frequently in prisons, with the transient nature of the prison population acting to undermine any interpersonal trust among prisoners (Ekland-Olson 1986).

Although no studies have assessed the relationship between density and bullying, it could be expected that an association between the two may be found, not only because of the apparent link between aggression and density but also since bullying is an integral part of the prison subculture that is closely linked to where a prisoner will appear in the social order. Any disruption to this order will make prisoners attempt to defend their position, often by bullying others. As we shall see later, dominance relations between prisoners are particularly important aspects of prison life.

In reviewing studies addressing the relationship between prison size and behaviour within and outside prisons, Farrington and Nuttall (1980) concluded that the limited amount of research conducted into this area makes it difficult to draw firm conclusions. Although they stated that there were some suggestions in the literature that overcrowding produced violent or disruptive behaviour inside prisons, the authors comment on the difficulties in separating the effect of size from other potentially important influences. Thus, although population density may prove important in explaining aggressive behaviours such as bullying, it should be considered one of a number of influences that may indirectly contribute to bullying, an influence whose role may be related more to the disruption of the social order within prisons.

Importantly, in prisons where a large number of individuals are housed together in a relatively restricted and confined space, aggression may relate more to prisoners being unable to avoid unwanted social interactions as a result of these restrictions on living space (Cooke 1991), and being forced to associate with individuals with whom they would not normally do so. It is also important to note the types of individuals that are housed together, particularly those with histories of delinquency, many of which may involve aggression. This links to two further variables that may help explain bullying in prison. First, the individual characteristics that prisoners bring with them to the prison environment that influence their behaviour, and second, the role played by supervision, i.e. as more and more individuals are housed together the less supervision each will receive. This is captured by Nacci and colleagues who comment on how 'Crowding certainly means that line staff have less control over inmates if only because there may be too many to supervise' (1977: 26).

## Staff supervision

Bullying is an anti-social behaviour that will occur away from the attention of staff. The cost of being caught bullying can be high, and the official prison response includes severe penalties for bullies such as adding extra days onto their sentence, transferring them to another prison, placing them in cellular confinement or restricting their access to property. The cost of bullying for the perpetrator decreases, however, if the chance of being caught also decreases. In a prison, where a large number of prisoners are housed with comparatively few staff, it is unrealistic to expect staff to monitor the behaviour of each and every prisoner 24 hours a day. Thus, bullying can be expected to flourish under such circumstances. The number of staff on duty also varies depending on the activities taking place: bullying may be less likely to occur during association periods (i.e. times when prisoners are allowed to socialise freely) where the staff-to-prisoner ratio is increased, than during night-time periods where a small number of staff may be on duty and all prisoners are locked behind their cell doors. Although the majority of prisoners have no physical contact with each other during the night (unless they share a cell), bullying can and does continue in the form of verbal aggression.

Another way of assessing the impact of supervision is to look at its predictability. In a prison, staff shifts follow a routine that is, to a certain extent, predictable. Toch (1978) identified custodial supervision patterns as one feature of the prison environment that helps to increase opportunities for violence among prisoners. Toch (1978) suggests that the inmate aggressor is in the same position as the residential burglar who knows homeowner vacation patterns and can plan the time and location of their offences around these. It would be expected that prison bullies are also able to predict times when there are clear opportunities to bully because of predictable supervision periods. Indeed, anti-bullying intervention strategies have recommended varying the times when prison officers patrol prisoner living areas in order to make the patrol periods less predictable and more successful in identifying bullying (Home Office Prison Service 1999).

## Lack of stimulation

Another aspect of the prison environment that may prove important for a further understanding of bullying is the lack of stimulation in the form of activities and social contact that the prison environment provides compared to the outside environment. Cooke (1991) comments on how the monotony, frustration and poverty of institutional life promotes violence. One way of breaking this monotony may be through acts of violence that might provide a momentary distraction. As mentioned previously, prisoners report that boredom and frustration can be a cause of bullying (Brookes *et al.* 1994), and researchers have suggested a number of anti-bullying intervention strategies designed to increase the stimulation available for prisoners (see Chapter 7). This has included increasing the number and quality of activities available during association periods (Brookes *et al.* 1994) and locating televisions in each dormitory to combat boredom (McGurk and McDougall 1986). Researchers addressing assaults among prisoners have also found an inverse link between constructive activities and violence. Wright (1991) reported that prisoners who assaulted others perceived their environments as having little activity and social stimulation, and Gaes and McGuire (1985) reported that the number of prisoner assaults with weapons decreased when the percentage of programme enrolments in prison industry increased, particularly among younger inmates.

It may not be the feelings of boredom and frustration induced by a dull environment, however, that are important in explaining bullying. Instead, bullies may feel that they have nothing to lose by behaving badly since they are obtaining nothing meaningful from the environment. By providing prisoners with a meaningful activity that they can invest in, the cost for them to bully is increased. Any evidence of bullying could result in a withdrawal of their privilege to engage in such activities and thus deter them from bullying as they now have something to lose.

## The social environment

Although it is obvious from the previous section that the physical environment is influential in explaining why bullying occurs, on its own it is not sufficient. The impact of the social environment on the behaviour of prisoners is equally important and is influenced to a certain extent by the physical environment. Perhaps one of the most important elements of the social environment is the tendency for aggression between prisoners to be perceived to be so prevalent that it has become normalised or rather seen as expected behaviour. This is consistent with Connell and Farrington (1996) who reported that aggression had to be particularly severe before offenders would consider it to be bullying. This suggests that prisoners have become desensitised to a certain extent to the aggression that they see around them. Similarly, Jackson (1970) argued that prisoners are brutalised by the environment that they are in, with violence becoming one way in which individuals can adapt to the prison environment. If an aggressive response is successful, as it may well be in prison, the information about this strategy will be retained by the individual, and as a result the strategy will be repeated in the future (Rubin and Krasnor 1986). It should be recognised that in a violent environment, such as a prison, an aggressive response to a social problem, particularly one involving conflict with other prisoners, threats to status or possessions, may be an adaptive response (Ireland 2001a). Those who are unwilling or unable to aggress towards their peers are, as we shall see later, likely to fall to the bottom of the prisoner hierarchy and as a result suffer the consequences of such a position including social stigma and increased victimisation by others.

There are a number of aspects of the social environment that are important to a further understanding of bullying. These include the organisational structure of prisons, the prisoner subculture, attitudes of the social group and the role played by power and dominance structures. Each of these elements will be discussed in turn.

### Organisational structure

Prisons are authoritarian environments based on clear and accepted hierarchical structures (from governor through to officer), in which the maintenance of discipline is an essential part of the regime. This can contribute to bullying (Ireland 2000a) and combine with other aspects of the environment to create a climate that promotes bullying. This is not unique to a prison setting, however, as researchers based in the workplace and in schools, such as Leymann (1990) and Askew (1989) respectively, also identify a strict hierarchical structure and an authoritarian or disciplinarian atmosphere as risk factors for bullying.

There are a number of aspects of the organisational structure that are particularly important in understanding bullying. First, reliance on rules and procedures in prisons ensures that all new prisoners will experience some difficulty in adjusting to the regime. Established prisoners therefore possess a degree of power over newcomers who appear vulnerable because of their lack of knowledge, thus increasing the possibility that they will be exploited. Second, the high levels of overt security and control present in prisons may also increase the probability of violence, with a relationship reported between increases in security and control levels and increases in the risk of violence (Cooke 1991). Third, managing prisoners using an overly rigid, inflexible and authoritarian style may indirectly provide them with a target to attack: prisoners may resort to violence (particularly in front of their peers) in order to save face and demonstrate that they can resist the regime (Cooke 1991). Although it is expected that this violence may be targeted more towards staff and prison property, some of it may be displaced and directed towards other members of the peer group. If prisoners are trying to save face and are not able to do this by attacking the target of their aggression (i.e. staff), then they may opt for the next-best target and direct violence towards another prisoner. As shown in the following section, aggressing towards other prisoners can be an effective method of obtaining status among the prisoner peer group.

Connected with this, the structure of the prison can impact on other elements of the social environment, namely the type of prisoner subculture that is present in an establishment. Feld (1981) argued that such structures are more influential in distinguishing between different subcultures than the pre-imprisonment characteristics that prisoners possess. Studying prisoner subcultures within a range of different prison units holding juvenile offenders, Feld (1981) reported that the more custodial and punitive settings had subcultures that were more violent, oppositional and hostile than those units that were more orientated towards treatment. All prisons however, regardless of the regime that they adopt, are essentially custodial settings and as such are designed to contain individuals regardless of whether or not they wish to be there. All have rules and regulations that are enforced by an authoritarian structure. Although there may be differences between prisons in terms of the type of regime that they adopt, the mere existence of a regime ensures that prisoner subcultures will contain elements of hostility and aggression. The more custodial the setting the more extreme these subcultural elements become. All prisoner subcultures, however, are expected to support aggression to a certain extent and this links with bullying behaviour: if the subculture did not support aggression then it would be unlikely that bullying would take place. Thus, the inmate subculture is a particularly important part of the social environment that is crucial in helping to explain why bullying is maintained and reinforced, and this will be discussed more fully in the following section.

### Prisoner subculture

Feld (1981) describes prisoner subcultures as 'informal social systems' with norms and values that reflect the main concerns of prisoners. All prisoners new to the environment are quickly socialised into this system and expected to adapt. The subculture also refers to an 'inmate code' which all prisoners are expected to adhere to. The elements of this code include not backing down from conflicts, not informing on others, an approval of physical violence to protect oneself or one's possessions, a need to be tough and to resist exploitation and a need to maintain one's position in the prison pecking order. It also includes non-fraternisation with security staff, loyalty to the prisoner group, no respect for official rules and a recognition that you should mind your own business (Tittle 1969). Explanations of bullying are strongly related to the inmate subculture (Connell and Farrington 1996) and a number of these elements were evidenced in prisoner responses to the question 'why are prisoners bullied?' that were described earlier. Once incarcerated, prisoners are expected to live by the 'inmate code' and adoption of this code and the rules and structures that go with it is often referred to as 'prisonisation' (Gaes and McGuire 1985).

One of the most important elements of the inmate code includes not fraternising with staff and not informing on your peers. The inmate subculture creates opposition between prisoners and staff, with staff seen as the 'enemy'. The extent to which staff are viewed negatively is also influenced by staff perception of prisoners: if staff view prisoners as 'dangerous, unreliable and abnormal' then prisoners tend to hold corresponding negative views of staff regarding them as 'untrustworthy, unhelpful or indifferent' (Feld 1981: 356). The responses of prisoners to questions concerning bullying are often influenced by the existence of the inmate code. Informing on other prisoners (also referred to as 'grassing', 'snitching' or 'ratting', Tittle 1969; Connell and Farrington 1996), especially to those in authority such as prison officers, is seen as a clear violation of the code and is often cited as justification for bullying by other prisoners. Many prisoners fail to report their victimisation for fear of this (O'Donnell and Edgar 1996a). This element of the inmate code serves to reinforce the actions of the bully and provides them with an incentive to continue. If the subcultural rules maintain that others, particularly staff, cannot be informed then bullying will continue since the cost to the bully in terms of being punished is greatly reduced. This can be related to Björkqvist and colleagues' (1994b) effect/danger ratio theory of aggression, described in Chapter 2, where the aggressor will balance the cost of the aggression to themselves with the effect of the aggression on the victim. Even in the event that staff are informed (often by victims who are new to the prison system and not fully aware of the inmate code) and the bully is identified and punished, the bully can then aggress towards the informer with the full blessing of the prisoner peer group. In some cases, the victim who reports to staff that they have been bullied will also be aggressed towards by other members of the peer group as well as the original bully since they will have been labelled a grass. In such a situation it is unlikely that the victim will report bullying again. Informing and bullying appear, therefore, to be closely linked, with bullying becoming a way in which prisoners can control violations of the inmate code. The extent to which the inmate code is enforced is dependent to some extent on the type of regime that the prison operates. Prisoner approval regarding informing to staff is much greater in treatment-oriented regimes than in custody-orientated regimes. In the former regime, Feld (1981) reported that there were fewer incentives to engage in bullying since there was a greater availability of privileges and amenities.

The existence of a prisoner subculture can be explained with reference to two models, the 'indigenous origins' model and the 'direct importation' model (Thomas 1977). The first is sometimes referred to as the deprivation model and relates to aspects of the physical environment already discussed, namely relating the values and norms of the subculture to the deprivations of imprisonment and the prisoner's problems in adjusting to these. Essentially, the formal organisation of the prison is seen to shape the informal prison social system (Feld 1981). There is evidence for this, not only from the previously discussed findings of Feld (1981), but also from the existence of clear dominance relations or pecking orders found among prisoners that reflect the legitimate hierarchical structures found among staff. These are discussed in more detail in the section on power and dominance structures (pp. 88–91). The second model attributes subculture to the roles and values held by prisoners before incarceration. Indeed, Connell and Farrington (1996) report that many offenders enter prisons with a well-developed set of attitudes and values that are consistent with the aggressive, exploitative nature of institutional life. Both these models have been used to explain the violence that occurs within prisons and to explain the extent to which the prison subculture is adopted.

The most important point from this section is that bullying is not a behaviour that occurs in isolation between a few individuals. If bullying was not supported in some way by the prisoner subculture, either directly or indirectly, then it might not take place. The attitudes held by prisoners towards bullies and their victims are thus closely linked to issues of subculture, and can prove instrumental in offering an explanation regarding the motivation behind this form of aggression. This will be expanded upon in the following section.

## Prisoner attitudes towards bullying

Although the focus here is on the prisoner peer group, it must be acknowledged that prison staff also form part of the wider peer group and their attitudes towards bullying will influence the extent to which bullying takes place and how it is responded to. McGurk and McDougall (1986) found that when the results of a bullying survey conducted among prisoners were reported to staff, their initial reaction was one of indifference, with the majority of staff indicating that they believed bullying was endemic within prisons. If an attitude of indifference is expressed by staff it will undoubtedly reinforce the bullying that takes place. Bullies will continue to aggress towards others if they are assured that staff have accepted it as a behaviour that 'just happens' and therefore not worthy of any action on their part. Indeed, Rigby and Slee (1993) argue that school bullying will flourish in climates of opinion where a sufficient proportion of children admire the behaviour of bullies and feel either indifferent towards victims or despise them.

In a prison there is evidence for ingrained positive attitudes towards bullying. As I described in Chapter 2, prisoners who bully others are often rewarded with respect and status from their peers and, in contrast to children who bully, they tend to be quite willing to admit to bullying others. However, victims do not receive the same status from peers, with derogatory terms frequently used to describe them and the effects of bullying on them minimised.

It should be expected that prisoners who bully others will adopt the attitudes deemed appropriate to that group, notably a less sympathetic attitude towards victims and a higher approval of bullying behaviour. This is consistent with Turner's (1987) self-categorisation theory that argues that when individuals categorise themselves as a member of a certain group, they identify with that group and take on its rules, standards and beliefs about appropriate conduct and attitudes. Turner argues that the drive behind these processes is a motivation to improve self-esteem, and this can be achieved through rating themselves and their group positively. After identifying with a group they show a tendency to regard their own group favourably, resulting in 'between-group contrast' and 'in-group favouritism'. Prisoners do tend to categorise themselves into groups (e.g. Beck 1992), resulting in 'in-groups' (i.e. bullies) and 'out-groups' (i.e. victims).

To date only two studies have directly addressed attitudes towards bullies and victims in a prison environment, Ireland (1999b) and Ireland and Ireland (2000). In both of these studies I focused on 'provictim attitudes', an attitude first described and measured by Rigby and Slee (1993). Rigby and Slee described such attitudes as 'a readiness to give support, at least verbal support, to children who are victimised by bullies' (1993: 120). Although I found no differences in Ireland and Ireland (2000), in Ireland (1999b) I reported that prisoners who engaged in behaviours indicative of bullying others were less provictim than other prisoners in that they reported more positive attitudes towards bullies and more negative attitudes towards victims. There was also a marked difference between these studies. The prisoners in Ireland and Ireland (2000) reported much lower provictim attitudes overall than those in Ireland (1999b). This difference can be explained by differences in the prison environments: in Ireland (1999b) I studied prisoners in medium to medium-high security prisons whereas in Ireland and Ireland (2000) I addressed prisoners in a maximum-security establishment. It could be argued that maximum-security establishments are more authoritarian settings where rules and regulations are stricter and the focus of work is not on treatment but more on managing the risk posed by prisoners. To link back to the work of Feld (1981), this could influence the prison subculture making it more hostile and aggressive and thus more supportive of bullying. The subcultures present in medium-security establishments may not be so extreme in their support of aggression since the focus of the work within them may be more towards rehabilitation. Similarly, in a prison where the threat of harm from others is greater (in comparison to outside), it is perhaps not surprising that prisoners become more motivated to hold positive attitudes towards bullies and negative attitudes towards victims. In such threatening environments, prisoners may be more likely to hold 'just-world beliefs' (Lerner 1980), i.e. believe that victims deserve to be bullied, and to blame victims as a result. The differences between the two studies could also be explained in this way: although all prison environments are likely to be threatening, maximum-security prisons may be more threatening than medium-security prisons, and as a result prisoners may be more likely to hold just-world beliefs.

The negative attitudes held by prisoners towards victims, and the approval given to bullies, are an important element that helps to maintain bullying. The social approval for bullying is an important incentive for the bully since those who engage in such behaviour are also likely to attain a degree of status among their peers. Obtaining status is a valued goal for prisoners, and while positive attitudes towards bullying continue to exist, bullying will remain one way in which bullies can attain this. The importance of status and how this links to power and dominance is discussed in the following section.

## Power and dominance structures

Once incarcerated, prisoners become part of a highly structured social group that negotiates for power and dominance, where 'domination over weakness is paramount in gaining acceptance, satisfaction, and status, and inmates are constantly manipulating each other by manoeuvring for power' (Connell and Farrington 1996: 85). Bullying becomes one way that prisoners can dominate and obtain power and status over others.

The creation of such a social group is facilitated by the legitimate hierarchical power structure found among prison staff that is then reflected in the prisoner subculture. The dominance relations found among prisoners are often referred to as 'rank systems', 'pecking orders' or as the 'prisoner caste system'. Bullying is often seen as a normal part of prison life that helps to maintain these relations between prisoners (Connell and Farrington 1996). The existence of dominance relations or hierarchies between prisoners is widely documented and can be found in all prison establishments. Feld (1981) described a distribution of prisoner roles where there were a few aggressive leaders at the top and a few chronic victims at the bottom, with the majority of prisoners occupying a more intermediate status. The roles adopted by prisoners were largely dependent on their physical or verbal prowess, although Feld (1981) reports that the importance of such prowess was emphasised more in custody-orientated establishments. Bartollas and colleagues (1974) described the presence of pecking orders that defined which prisoners became exploited. They termed this the 'exploitation matrix' and described how it could consist of three or four different levels with the 'heavies' or 'inmate leaders' at the top followed by their 'lieutenants'. The third level consisted of a larger group of more passive prisoners, with the fourth level including the 'scapegoats' or chronic victims. Those at the top of the matrix were able to demand and receive personal favours and material goods from those below.

The existence of such exploitation matrixes can easily be applied to bullying. Bullying matrixes may consist of three levels. Level one may include the pure bully, someone who solely bullies others and who corresponds to the 'heavies' or 'inmate leaders'. Level two may include prisoners who both bully others and are bullied themselves, i.e. 'bully/victims'. Such prisoners generally represent victims who react aggressively to their own victimisation. They also represent those who are exploited by the pure bully and are used as their 'henchmen' or 'assistants'. This latter group roughly corresponds to the 'lieutenants' described by Bartollas and colleagues (1974). In both instances bully/victims will exploit those lower down the hierarchy as a way of preventing future victimisation and as a way of attempting to achieve peer recognition and approval. Finally, level three may include prisoners who are solely victimised by their peers (pure victims) and who correspond to the scapegoats described by Bartollas and colleagues (1974). Each of these levels will be described in more detail below.

Pure bullies, through their proven ability to dominate others using force will appear at the top of these hierarchical structures which is a privileged position to attain. As described previously, bullies are given a high status in prison by both prisoners and staff. Status is a valuable commodity in a prison in that it enables prisoners who possess it to make demands of those who do not and to secure greater access to resources. Successfully bullying others is one way of guaranteeing status among peers and any demands that bullies make of those lower down the hierarchy will be met, since they have proven their ability to successfully dominate and exert power over their peers using force. Once they have achieved high status among their peers, bullies must then maintain their position in the hierarchy. Continuing to successfully bully others, particularly those who threaten their status by attempting to bully them, is one way in which their position can be maintained. Once a prisoner has achieved a position as a pure bully, however, it is likely that they will no longer be seen as targets by other aggressors since they have provided consistent evidence of an ability to dominate others and no evidence that they can be victimised. Thus, the victimisation of the bully becomes less likely and the incentives to continue to bully are increased. These incentives include an increase in status and power, a privileged position among peers, a reduced chance that they themselves will become victims and increased access to material goods. It is also likely that the more successful and dominant the bully is, the more power they can exert over others and the more likely it is that they themselves will not carry out the bullying, instead getting other prisoners or rather 'assistant bullies' to do it for them. Bullies who have established themselves as barons, for example, will often get other prisoners to collect debts from prisoners on their behalf. This reduces the cost of the bullying for the baron since the chances of being caught are low. Even if these 'debt collectors' are identified by staff, the prison rules of not informing on other prisoners ensure that the baron will remain unidentified. Similarly, the more successful the bully, the less likely it is they will have to resort to direct aggression to obtain something from their victims. Once they have acquired a reputation for effective use of force, this can be conveyed to victims much more subtly. Thus subtle forms of intimidation become just as effective for them as direct forms and, as I described in Chapter 2, indirect aggression carries the least cost for the bully and yet can still be an effective method of bullying. This may be particularly true for indirect aggression that is ultimately backed up with a credible threat of violence.

Conversely, being known as a victim in a prison is much more stigmatising and victims appear at the bottom of these hierarchies. They are seen as vulnerable, weak and as prime targets for bullying by the rest of the peer group. This is evidenced by the derogatory terms used to describe victims such as 'whingers', 'muppets', 'fraggles' (Beck 1992) or 'herbets'. Research conducted into general prison violence also reports the use of terms such as 'lambs' or 'punks' to describe victims to indicate their weakness and vulnerability, whereas the term 'wolves' is reserved for their aggressors (Feld 1981; Wright 1991). The stigma may not be as great, however, for victims who are not solely passive and who do report aggressing towards others (Ireland 1999a). Indeed, some victims may try to increase their status among their peers by aggressing towards others (with such victims labelled by researchers as bully/victims). The fact that they are showing aggression towards others, regardless of the target of their aggression, suggests that they are attempting to assert and maintain their dominance, and in this way prevent any future victimisation. Although the target of their aggression is not important, it could be expected that they will bully those below them in the hierarchy, namely pure victims. The incentive for the bully/victim to aggress lies in the possibility that pure bullies may be less likely to target a bully/victim than a pure victim, since bully/victims have proven to the peer group that they can aggress towards others. However, bully/victims can also include the assistant bullies described earlier. Assistant bullies are exploited solely by pure bullies in order to bully others on their behalf. The existence of assistant bullies in a prison has not been empirically tested, however, although evidence has been found for their existence in a school environment (e.g. Sutton et al. 1999a). Although it is argued here that they are a subsection of the bully/victim group this may not necessarily be the case. There may be a number of assistant bullies who are not exploited by pure bullies but instead receive incentives in the form of material goods to bully their peers. Essentially they may be 'paid' by the pure bullies to work for them, particularly since pure bullies are able to obtain more material goods than other prisoners and can therefore afford their services.

The existence of prisoner hierarchies can also be linked to the presence of capitalist economic structures described previously in the section on material goods (p. 76). Any society based on such principles values traits such as dominance and aggression, with a disapproval of feminine traits such as fear and vulnerability (Gilbert 1994). This could help explain why the most dominant and aggressive individuals can be found at the top of these hierarchies (bullies) and the most fearful and vulnerable at the bottom (victims) (Ireland 2000a).

A link can also be drawn between population density and the existence of these hierarchies, with Archer (1970) suggesting that in crowded and confined conditions dominance hierarchies may represent a way in which animals regulate their increased aggression. Although focusing on animals, this raises the notion that dominance hierarchies, as they exist in a prison setting, may actually serve to regulate the increased aggression that occurs.

Thus it would appear that notions of dominance and power are important for a further understanding of bullying among prisoners, and that they are inextricably linked with other aspects of the environment that appear to encourage and maintain levels of predatory behaviour and competition among prisoners. The presence of prisoner hierarchies reinforces the importance of status in a prison environment, with status limited to those who display bullying behaviours and stigmas reserved for the victims of bullying.

## Individual characteristics

Feld (1981) describes how the prevalence of violence among prisoners may reflect the characteristics of those incarcerated. Many prisoners are from social backgrounds or cultures where emphasis is placed on toughness and an ability to protect oneself.[7] The characteristics that prisoners bring with them to the prison environment help to determine their responses to a violent prison culture. Indeed, Beck (1995) describes how the past behaviour of prisoners is often consistent with bullying in that many have been convicted of violent or acquisitive offences, with a link reported between bullying and delinquency.

Determining the actual characteristics of prisoners predisposed towards bullying others and/or being victimised, however, is not an easy task. Researchers have suggested the importance of intrinsic characteristics such as bullies being predisposed to use aggression to solve conflict situations, having a tendency to hold positive beliefs about the use of aggression (Ireland 2001a; Ireland and Archer 2002), and the possibility that bullies possess psychopathic traits (Ireland 2000b) including a lack of empathy (Ireland 1999b). Descriptive characteristics of prisoners have also been assessed, such as the length of time that they have spent in prison throughout their lifetime, with bullies likely to have more experience of institutional life than victims (Ireland 1999a), and some suggestion that bullies are younger than victims and more likely to be convicted of a violent offence, although the evidence for this is conflicting (Ireland 1999a; Power *et al.* 1997; Ireland and Ireland 2000). Also important is the level of social and physical skills possessed by the prisoner, notably their ability to bully others physically, verbally or indirectly. Some prisoners may have an increased tendency or willingness to bully others and yet do not have the skills necessary to do so. The level of physical and social skills that a prisoner possesses will influence whether or not they are able to bully, and also the type of aggression that they use. As I highlighted in Chapter 3, an individual has to have well-developed social skills if they are to engage in indirect bullying, whereas a certain degree of physical prowess is needed for physical bullying.

These are only a few individual characteristics that may prove important in explaining bullying. I will focus on the characteristics of bullies and victims and the relative importance of each in the following chapter. The present section serves to illustrate, however, the importance of taking into account individual characteristics as well as environmental characteristics in any explanation of bullying behaviour. This would certainly reflect the importance of referring to both deprivation and importation models of prisonisation to explain bullying in prison.

## A model to explain bullying in prisons

The most useful model for describing bullying behaviour is one that takes into account environmental and individual characteristics, and views bullying as an interaction between them. Viewing bullying as a product of either an individual or the environment will not provide a complete picture of this complex behaviour. It is equally important to acknowledge the extent to which the environment reinforces bullying behaviour once it has occurred. A model outlining the influence of the physical and social environment and how this is mediated by individual characteristics and subsequently reinforced by the environment is presented in Figure 4.1.

It must be noted that Figure 4.1 presents a simplistic model of what contributes to bullying and how it is reinforced in a prison. The elements described in it are closely linked with each other and have been separated here simply for ease of interpretation and description. For example, the organisational features of the environment (such as hierarchical structures) influence the prisoner subculture and hence the prevalence of violence and the incentives for violence. It must also be acknowledged that prisoners may engage in bullying for reasons not displayed in this model, and as yet not assessed by research. Indeed, the motivations behind bullying and the extent to which they are determined by the individual characteristics of the bully, is an area that has largely been neglected by research. It could be expected that some of the motivations behind bullying will be different for different types of bullies. Although all bullying may be motivated by a desire to dominate peers and to acquire status for example, bully/victims may bully primarily as a way of reducing their chances of being victimised in the future, whereas pure bullies may bully in order to obtain material goods. Masden (1997) also describes how motivations to bully can include emotive reasons (e.g. aggression or anger, dislike for the victim), personality and socialisation (e.g. background or a vicious streak), and enjoyment (e.g. enjoyment from seeing the victim suffer and thinking of ways to cause this suffering). Although Masden's study was based on schoolchildren, and the existence of such motivations has not been assessed among a prisoner population, they could provide further insight into the incentives to bully in a prison. It could be, for example, that some bullies simply enjoy aggressing towards their peers and that this is the main incentive for them and one that is not illustrated in the current model.

The environmental characteristics displayed in the model are expected to be the same for all prisons, although the extent to which they are present will vary between them and the type of regime that they adopt. As mentioned earlier, the type of regime present will influence the extent to which the prisoner subculture is violent and hostile, thus influencing the extent of bullying that takes place. The type of regime will also influence other aspects of the environment, with prisoners in custody-orientated regimes reporting more material and stimulation deprivations than found in other types of regime (Feld 1981). The environmental characteristics themselves, particularly low genetic and attachment relationships, high population and spatial density, an authoritarian or hierarchical structure, control, discipline and limited staff supervision, can also be related to other environments in which bullying has been found to occur, such as schools and the workplace.

The environment on its own, however, is not enough to make someone bully. If this were the case then we would expect all prisoners to bully others. Individual characteristics are just as important in deciding whether or not someone will, or can, bully others. These characteristics include those that prisoners bring with them to the environment and also the skills that they possess which will enable them to bully. Similarly, although environmental and individual characteristics may increase the probability

**Environmental characteristics**

*Physical environment*

Restriction on material goods

Capitalist economic structure

High social density

Limited spatial density

Physical escape not possible

Staff supervision limited as staff-to-prisoner ratio is high

Supervision is predictable

Lack of stimulation

*Social environment*

Aggression normalised and possibly an adaptive response

Authoritarian hierarchical structure based on overt control and discipline

Reliance on rules

Presence of a prisoner subculture

Negative or indifferent attitudes towards victims

Importance of dominance relations between prisoners

Importance of status and maintaining status

Low genetic and attachment relationships

Leads to →

**Increased Tendency To Bully**

**Mediated by individual characteristics**

*Intrinsic* characteristics of the individual, e.g. psychopathic tendencies, impaired ability to empathise, tendency to aggress and to have positive beliefs about aggression

*Descriptive* characteristics, e.g. length of time spent in prison, previous convictions, etc.

*Level of physical or social skill* possessed by the individual, e.g. ability to bully others physically, verbally or indirectly, will help to determine if they can bully and the type of bullying strategy used

Leads to →

**Bullying**
(probable outcome, dependent on opportunity)

**Incentives to continue to bully**

Increased access to material goods

Victims are unlikely to inform, e.g. inmate rules against informing

Increase in status and power

Privileged place in prisoner hierarchy

Proven ability to dominate that reduces the chance of being victimised by others in the future

Social support for bullies

Increase in stimulation and reduction in boredom

Figure 4.1 Model predicting why bullying may occur in prison

that bullying will take place, it cannot take place unless there is an opportunity to do so. It would be expected, for example, that bullying would not take place if the danger of being identified and punished was assessed as too high.

It is also important to recognise that the role of being a bully or a victim is interchangeable and not static: a prisoner can change from being a pure bully to a pure victim or a bully/victim and vice versa. This is dependent on the extent to which they can defend themselves from their peer group and the extent to which they can *successfully* bully their peers. It is also influenced by the responses of others, including staff and prisoners – for example if a pure victim is told to fight back then this could determine their role changing to that of a bully/victim. Similarly, whether or not a prisoner continues to bully others is dependent on the incentives to do so. If there were no incentives it would be unlikely that bullying would take place.

## Summary

This chapter has illustrated the importance of taking into account a range of influences if an adequate explanation of bullying is to be provided. There are a number of environmental aspects, both physical and social, that appear important in explaining why bullying may occur and reinforce the notion that bullying should be seen almost as an expected behaviour in prisons. I have also highlighted similarities between prisons and other settings where bullying is known to take place (e.g. schools, the workplace), demonstrating how some explanations put forward to explain prison bullying could also apply to the bullying that occurs in other settings. Although the focus has been largely on the environmental characteristics of prisons, the chapter has also touched briefly upon how this is mediated by individual prisoner characteristics. Indeed the model that I presented conceptualises bullying as an interaction between the characteristics of the individual and the environment in which they find themselves, with the environment also serving to reinforce subsequent bullying. Individual prison characteristics are just as important as environmental characteristics and will be the focus of the following chapter.

# Chapter 5

# Characteristics of bullies and victims

As the previous chapter highlighted, there are many aspects of the prison environment that act to promote and reinforce bullying. These aspects, together with the individual characteristics that predispose a prisoner to become a bully or a victim, either promote or reduce the likelihood of bullying taking place.

Research has supported the notion that those involved in bullying, either as bullies or victims, possess certain characteristics that distinguish them from the rest of their peer group. Early research tended to focus on the perceptions that prisoners held regarding the types of prisoners that became victims and, to a lesser extent, those that became bullies. Since then, researchers have focused more on the actual characteristics that those involved present with, focusing on a small number of basic personal/descriptive characteristics such as age, offence, sentence length and so on. Much more recently, researchers have moved away from addressing perceptions and basic characteristics to addressing actual intrinsic characteristics. These include empathy, ability to solve conflict situations involving bullying, beliefs about aggression, self-esteem and assertiveness. Researchers have also suggested a connection between bullying and psychopathy although this has yet to be assessed empirically. Finally, and perhaps most recently, researchers have begun to address the actual behavioural characteristics of the different groups involved with a view to determining if membership of any of the groups can be predicted by the behaviours that a prisoner displays within the prison environment.

Thus, in this chapter I aim to summarise the perceived and actual (basic personal/descriptive, intrinsic and behavioural) characteristics of the different groups involved in bullying. I will conclude with a summary of those characteristics that are most useful to include in typologies of the different groups. However, the first and most important question to ask before attempting to produce typologies is 'what are the different groups involved in bullying?'

## The groups involved in bullying

Prison-based researchers have tended to concentrate on two distinct groups – bullies and victims. Indeed, as I describe in Chapter 8, anti-bullying strategies tend to be based on the principle that only these two groups are involved. This is too simplistic a view, however, in light of the complexities of bullying behaviour. More recently, prison researchers have identified at least four distinct groups of prisoners relevant to a discussion of bullying

- *pure bullies*   those who solely report bullying others
- *pure victims*   those who solely report being a victim of bullying
- *bully/victims*   those who report both bullying others and being victimised themselves
- *a not-involved group*   those who report no bullying or victimisation (Ireland 1999a).

The prevalence of prisoners belonging to each group tends to be fairly consistent across studies, with bully/victims and those not-involved tending to be the most frequently reported groups, followed by pure victims and pure bullies. For example, in a recent study of 406 adult prisoners, I reported that 35 per cent were classified as bully/victims, 28 per cent as not-involved, 23 per cent as pure victims and 14 per cent as pure bullies (Ireland 2001c). I reported similar findings in a later study consisting of 502 prisoners (Ireland 2002b).

This four-group classification system is generally favoured by researchers using behavioural checklists as a method of collecting data, although it has been used by researchers employing more traditional methods of measuring bullying in which the term bully is used (e.g. Power *et al.* 1997). Behavioural checklists (see Chapter 2) avoid the use of the term bullying and involve the researcher assigning prisoners to one of these four groups after data collection. Since such methods do not require prisoners to label themselves as bullies, victims, etc., it would not necessarily be expected that they would perceive themselves to be members of these groups. This can limit the extent to which the findings can be compared to other studies using more traditional methods of measuring bullying in which prisoners are asked questions such as 'have you bullied?' and thus required to label their own behaviour.

There are three points regarding the use of a four-group classification system that are worthy of comment. First, such systems recognise the overlap between bullies and victims, which is an important development since bully/victims appear to be the most prevalent group in some studies. Second, they take into account those prisoners not-involved in bullying, another important development which recognises that bullying does not occur in isolation from the rest of the peer group. Indeed, as I highlighted in the previous chapter, if bullying behaviour was not supported to some extent by the wider peer group then it might not take place. Third, it should be recognised that membership to each of these four groups is not set in stone – over time prisoners can move from one group to another. Prisoners who bully and prisoners who are victimised should also not be seen as polar opposites: bullying others and being bullied varies along a continuum of behaviour, and individuals can be placed at any point along this continuum (Ireland 1999e).

Although prison-based researchers are now recognising that identifying a prisoner solely as either a victim or a bully is too simplistic, more work in this area is still required. I touched upon this briefly in Chapter 2 when referring to a method of measuring bullying that is popular with school-based researchers, namely the Participant Role Scale approach (Salmivalli *et al.* 1996). This method is useful since it concentrates on the roles that individuals adopt during bullying interactions. Identifying someone as a bully, for example, may not be sufficient. The specific role that they adopt also needs to be addressed, for example are they a leader bully or an assistant bully? I also touched upon this briefly in the previous chapter where it was argued that leader bullies tend to occupy the top of prisoner pecking orders, whereas assistant bullies do not and often work for leader bullies. Although such participant role methods have not yet been employed in prison studies there is evidence that prisoners may well adopt different roles during incidents of bullying. In a study addressing official records of both actual and suspected incidents of bullying, I reported a number of entries indicating occasions where one bully adopted a lead role with another there to back them up by reinforcing threats that had been made or by joining in with the name calling (Ireland 2002d).

Similarly, although not addressing participant roles *per se*, Marshall (1993) described a system of allocating prisoners to different parts of a prison based on an assessment of which 'prisoner typology' they belonged to. Each of these typologies was felt to be specific to the prison under study and included the following

- *gangsters*   self-confident, involved with other people but highly aggressive, their aggression mainly taking the form of attempts to bully, coerce or threaten other prisoners into doing what they want
- *mini-gangsters*   the same as gangsters but less aggressive
- *pure vulnerables*   not aggressive, but scared of other prisoners, they tend to be tense, withdrawn and submissive
- *vulnerable aggressives*   anxious, less involved with other prisoners but more fearful of them, highly aggressive but with their aggression usually taking the form of impetuous emotional outbursts perhaps because of poor temper control
- *mini-vulnerable aggressives*   the same as vulnerable aggressives but less aggressive
- *moderates/assets*   not aggressive, they involve themselves with other prisoners and staff and are not afraid of other prisoners.

The above classification system could quite easily be related to bullying. Indeed, it was used as one method of reducing the extent of bullying reported at the establishment under study. Gangsters and mini-gangsters clearly appear to be descriptions of bullies, perhaps leader bullies and assistant bullies respectively. Pure vulnerables can be likened to pure victims, vulnerable aggressives and mini-vulnerable aggressives perhaps to bully/victims, and finally, moderate/assets to those not-involved in bullying. Although the reliability of this system has not been assessed, it highlights the importance of addressing different typologies and reinforces how identifying a prisoner as either a bully or a victim is too simplistic.

In view of the absence of research addressing the many different types and roles of prisoners involved in bullying, I will concentrate, in the present chapter, on presenting typologies of bullies and victims and where possible of bully/victims. The first set of characteristics that will be addressed are those which victims and bullies are *perceived* to possess.

## Perceived characteristics of bullies and victims

The majority of studies addressing perceived characteristics have focused on victims, with few addressing bullies. Regarding victims, both prisoners and staff perceive them to possess a number of characteristics. These characteristics can be summarised into five main areas as follows.

1   *Characteristics indicative of vulnerability*   This includes physical vulnerability in the form of small physical stature, weakness, frailty

or a noticeable mental or physical defect (Brookes *et al.* 1994). It also includes characteristics indicative of potential vulnerability such as lacking confidence, a tendency to be under-assertive, shy, quiet, timid, of low intelligence or lacking in education, appearing inadequate and being easily influenced (Brookes *et al.* 1994), being different in some way from other prisoners, and finally, being gullible and thus easily exploited (Brookes 1993).

2   *Characteristics indicative of a prisoner being new to prison life* This may be because it is the prisoner's first sentence, they are a new reception into the prison, they are naïve about other prisoners and prison culture or they do not know their way around the prison (Brookes *et al.* 1994).

3   *Characteristics relating to the offence with which they are charged* Sex offenders and those who have committed offences such as assaults or burglary on elderly people are all considered to be potential targets (Brookes *et al.* 1994).

4   *Prisoners who remain isolated from the rest of their peers*   Prisoners who may have few friends or associates, having not been accepted into any of the previously formed prisoner groups (Brookes 1993; Brookes *et al.* 1994), because they are from a different home area from other prisoners (Power *et al.* 1997), because they appear introverted (Ireland and Archer 1996) or in some way are seen as unusual (Power *et al.* 1997).

5   *Other characteristics*   These include prisoners who are either young or elderly, those who have not repaid debts to other prisoners, drug users, those serving short sentences, those appearing childish or mouthy and those who scrounge off other prisoners (Brookes *et al.* 1994). A small number of prisoners also reported that bullies themselves became targets. This would appear to be surprising in view of the peer support that bullying receives. However, some prisoners who bully do not receive as much status as others, particularly bully/ victims, and it could be expected that they will be seen as targets. Pure bullies may also be targeted on occasion by prisoners attempting to secure a place at the top of the prisoner dominance hierarchy. Successfully bullying others, particularly a prisoner who is a pure bully, may be one way of guaranteeing this.

A number of further characteristics suggested by prisoners are also consistent with issues discussed in the previous chapter, for example that prisoners who violate the inmate code often become targets of bullying. This violation can include informing on other prisoners, being unable to defend or to stick up for themselves (Brookes 1993), or not conforming to the inmate subculture in some other way such as failing to hold contraband goods or to smuggle illicit items into the prison (Brookes *et al.* 1994).

Regarding bullies, only Power and colleagues (1997) and Loucks (1998) have asked prisoners what characteristics they perceive bullies to possess. Power and colleagues (1997) reported that knowing a lot of inmates, being aggressive, having a long criminal record and a large physical build were important contributing factors. Also included was the home area of the bully and the type of offence they were convicted for. In addition, Loucks (1998) reported that the more 'jailwise' and experienced prisoners were likely to become bullies.

Thus, there appear to be a number of characteristics that could predict whether or not someone is a bully or a victim. Very few of these perceptions have been directly assessed, however, and until this is completed they may inadvertently be helping to support myths regarding the characteristics that victims and bullies possess. The perceptions that both prisoners and staff have regarding which prisoners are likely to become victims and which are likely to become bullies are influential, regardless of their accuracy. If the peer group, for example, believes that a prisoner has the potential to bully others, either because of their physical stature or the experience that they have with prison life, then it is likely that they will allot reputations to these prisoners which in turn become self-fulfilling prophecies, ensuring that bullies become typecast in their respective roles. This was certainly something that I found in a study that I conducted in 1995, where prisoners who fitted the 'description' of a bully were thought to automatically take on that role because that was what was expected of them by the rest of the peer group (Ireland 1995). I remember one prisoner in particular who described to me how, because of his large physical build and general physical appearance, other bullies would often try and recruit him to bully for them, notably to collect debts for them or to physically assault other prisoners. He told me how he had never bullied others and had no intention of doing so, but that he struggled to get this message across to his peers who simply expected him to bully. The same prisoner had also been told by staff that he was not allowed to have another prisoner in his cell in case he was tempted to bully them. Although it is acknowledged that this prisoner may well have had the propensity to bully others, there was no direct evidence of this and the assumption of his status as a potential bully was made purely on his physical build and general appearance. The converse can also be true for prisoners who appear physically weak and vulnerable and are new to the establishment: staff will often watch such prisoners more closely and monitor their interactions with others, expecting them to become victims of bullying. The result of this, however, is that protection is often afforded to the wrong prisoners – what happens to the victim who is not considered physically weak and yet is being victimised? Similarly, many bullies are able to get away with their abusive behaviour because they do not fit the stereotype of a bully and it takes longer for their behaviour to be identified. Indeed, as will become apparent in the following sections, identifying the different groups involved in bullying through the observable behaviours and characteristics that they possess is not that straightforward and some characteristics are more useful than others. There is a definite need for more research addressing the actual characteristics that each group possesses as opposed to focusing solely on perceptions. Perceptions are of limited use, many have not been proven empirically and they can lead to stereotypes of bullies and victims that are simply not accurate.

## Actual characteristics of bullies and victims

The term actual is used here to refer to those characteristics that we know bullies and victims possess, as opposed to those that they are perceived to possess. Research has focused on three types of actual characteristics

*   personal/descriptive
*   intrinsic
*   behavioural.

Unlike research addressing perceptions, some limited research focusing on actual characteristics has also included the different groups involved in bullying, namely pure bullies, bully/victims and pure victims, as opposed to just focusing on bullies and victims. Thus the following sections will make reference to these different groups where possible. I will not address the not-involved group in this chapter. This is not to say that this group is not important to a discussion of bullying, simply that the present chapter will focus on those groups directly involved as either bullies and/or victims. The first set of actual characteristics that will be presented will be personal/descriptive characteristics.

### Personal/descriptive characteristics

Use of the term personal/descriptive characteristics refers here to basic characteristics used to describe prisoners such as their age, offence, sentence length, whether or not they are on remand, and also physical characteristics such as their height and build. Differences between bullies and/or victims in terms of some basic characteristics have been found, although the evidence is at times conflicting and not always supportive of perceived characteristics. A summary of the findings is presented here, beginning with victims.

## Victims

Some researchers have reported that the offence for which a prisoner has been convicted is related to their status as a victim. The exact relationship, however, is not clear. Loucks (1998), for example, reported that victims were more likely than non-victims to have been convicted for a violent offence, whereas Power and colleagues (1997) reported that victims were less likely to have been convicted for a violent offence in comparison to bullies, bully/victims and those not-involved. Some researchers have also reported no link between the type of offence and victim status (Ireland and Ireland 2000; Ireland 2002d).

As described previously, victims are often perceived to be prisoners with little prison experience and this has received some support. Both Falshaw (1993) and Beck (1995) reported that victims were more likely to be those with little prison experience, with a significant proportion of victims reporting that this was their first time in prison. The finding that it was their first time in prison, however, may relate more to other variables that could increase their chances of being bullied. Connell and Farrington (1996) suggest that young offenders begin their prison careers as victims and develop into bullies as their experience with prison life increases. Such experience allows their social network to expand, resulting in more friends (among prisoners) to gang up with. Indeed, research has reported that victims do have fewer friends in comparison with other prisoners (Duckworth 1998). I also found evidence among young offenders that bully/victims may well represent a victim group in transition to a bully group (Ireland 1999a). In this study, the more time that an offender had spent in prison throughout their lifetime, and hence the more prison experience that they reported, the more likely they were to belong to the bully/victim group. It could be suggested from this that as bully/victims accrue more experience with prison life (and increase their peer network) the more likely they are to become pure bullies as time progresses. Thus it appears that the amount of experience that a prisoner has with prison life is likely to influence other variables that will in turn impact on their assignment to a victim group. Incidentally, the length of sentence being served by a prisoner has been found to be important in only one study, where pure victims were predicted by a smaller sentence length (Ireland 1999a). This was only found for the adult sample with no such finding reported for young offenders. It was also not supported in two later studies (Ireland and Ireland 2000; Ireland 2002d).

Although the home area that the prisoner originates from is perceived to relate to victim status (with prisoners from a different home to that of other prisoners being more likely to be bullied, Power *et al.* 1997), this has not been assessed in any detail. Only two studies have commented on the impact of home area, one of which found no relationship between home area and status (Beck 1992) and one which reported that victims and bullies did come from different regions in the United Kingdom (Ireland 2002d).

Age has also been identified as an important variable by some researchers with victims tending to be slightly older than bullies (Grant 1999; Ireland 1999a). Findings regarding age are not consistent however, with both Beck (1995) and Ireland and Ireland (2000) reporting that it was not a predictor of victim status. Other variables that do not appear to relate to victim status (in any studies) include whether or not a prisoner is on remand (Ireland 2002d; Mosson 1998), their height or build (Connell and Farrington 1996; Falshaw 1993) and the number of previous convictions that they have on record (Falshaw 1993).

## Bully/victims

It is perhaps appropriate at this point to describe the actual characteristics of the bully/victim group. Although this group reports bullying others, they are conceptualised primarily as a victim group since their aggression arguably represents a defensive reaction (see Chapters 4 and 6). The results regarding this group are limited and have been assessed in only four studies to date (Bolt 1999; Ireland and Ireland 2000; Ireland 1999a; Ireland 2001c). Bolt (1999) found that bully/victims reported the longest current sentences and had spent the longest time in prison throughout their lifetime in comparison to the other groups. However, no statistical tests were employed on these findings. Of the remaining studies, significant predictors were found in only one study, Ireland (1999a). In this study I found that adult bully/victims were predicted by youth and were more likely to be violent offenders than non-violent offenders. Young offenders in this study, who were classified as bully/victims, also reported more overall imprisonment throughout their lifetime.

## Bullies

Research identifying the characteristics of bullies has been extremely limited. Variables such as age, time left to serve (Power *et al.* 1997) and offence do not appear to relate to being a bully (Ireland 1999a). As for victims, there has also been no relationship reported between an ability to bully others and either height or physical build (Falshaw 1993). Researchers have suggested a link, however, between whether or not the bully was on remand or sentenced: O'Brien (1996) reports that prisoners on remand were more than twice as likely to bully as convicted prisoners, suggesting that remand prisoners may feel that they have less to lose by being caught bullying whereas convicted prisoners may feel that they have a 'stake in the prison' and more to lose by bullying. Similarly, Falshaw (1993) reported that prisoners who stated that they could bully others were serving shorter sentences than those who said they could not. As with being on remand, it could be argued that the shorter the sentence length the less concerned the bully will be about the impact of their actions on themselves should they be caught bullying. Prisoners serving longer sentences, however, may be less inclined to bully others since they are aware of the long-term impact that their behaviour can have for them.

One influence that seems particularly important is the overall experience that bullies have with prison life. Bullies report spending a greater total amount of time in prisons than victims (Power *et al.* 1997; Beck 1995), to have more prison sentences and previous convictions (Ireland *et al.* 1998), and to be more likely than victims to have a previous history of custody (Connell and Farrington 1996). Falshaw (1993) also reported that the number of prisons that a prisoner had been in, before the current prison, correlated positively with their ability to bully others. Overall, this seems to indicate that the more experience a prisoner has with prison life the more likely they are to bully others. This is consistent with the points raised in the previous chapter, i.e. the longer a prisoner spends in prison the easier it becomes for them to bully others since they are able to familiarise themselves with the prison routines and the predictability of staff supervision: prison bullies may be able to predict times when there are clear opportunities to aggress because they have had time to observe the pattern of staff supervision. Similarly, the more familiar prisoners are with the informal inmate rules or inmate code the less likely they are to violate them and become a victim of bullying as a result. Those prisoners who are very familiar with these rules can sometimes use them to their advantage and exploit other prisoners who are less familiar with them. Established prisoners therefore possess a degree of power over newcomers.

Overall, by summarising the evidence relating to basic personal/ descriptive characteristics this section highlights their value in distinguishing between the different groups involved in bullying. The conflicting evidence surrounding many of these characteristics leads to the conclusion that only a small number may actually be important. Victims (not bully/ victims), for example, do appear to be relatively new to the prison system, although this may relate more to other variables such as the number of friends that they have managed to acquire over time which in turn influences whether or not they become a target for bullies. This lends some support to the perception that victims represent those who have violated the inmate code in some way, mainly through naïvety and a lack of prison experience, which in turn could isolate them even further from their peer group (as evidenced by their lack of friends). Bullies, on the other hand, appear more experienced with prison life than victims, lending support to the perception that bullies are those with a long criminal record (Power *et al.* 1997) and are the more 'jailwise' and experienced of prisoners (Loucks 1998).

It appears that neither bullies or victims can be identified by their height or physical build. This finding is inconsistent with the previously reported perceptions. This is interesting since such perceptions are widely reported by both staff and prisoners. The finding that they are not supported reinforces the importance of not focusing on perceived characteristics that have no basis in evidence and which, inadvertently, may perpetuate stereotypes of victims and bullies. Instead, research should concentrate on exploring actual characteristics associated with bullying, characteristics that may help researchers to understand why bullying occurs as well as providing insight into the types of prisoners predisposed to become bullies and/or victims. One such group of characteristics that may further such an understanding includes those that are intrinsic to the individual.

### Intrinsic characteristics

Prison researchers have only recently started to address the intrinsic characteristics that may be associated with bullying. Such characteristics are important since they help to explain why bullying may occur, as well as providing a further description of the different groups involved. The characteristics addressed to date include empathy, social-problem solving, assertiveness, self-esteem and provictim attitudes (I discussed this last area in the previous chapter and thus it will not be presented here). In the main, research has focused on distinguishing between pure bullies, bully/victims and pure victims, and thus the following sections will make reference to all these groups. Each characteristic and its relationship to each group will be presented in turn. In addition, researchers have also theorised a role played by psychopathy and, although this has yet to be assessed empirically, a brief discussion of the possible role played by this concept is presented since it represents a valuable avenue that future research could pursue.

## Empathy

Empathy is defined by Davis as 'a reaction to the observed experiences of another' (1983: 114). It is a multidimensional construct that includes either a cognitive or an emotional response to another's experience. To date only one study (Ireland 1999b) has specifically addressed the role of empathy in relation to bullying among a sample of male and female prisoners. Using the Interpersonal Reactivity Index (IRI: Davis 1983), I assessed how cognitive and emotional components of empathy related to the different groups involved in bullying. The IRI measured four separate constructs, two relating to cognitive empathy

- *perspective taking*   the tendency to adopt spontaneously the viewpoint of others
- *fantasy*   the tendency to become involved imaginatively in the feelings and actions of fictitious characters

and two relating to emotional empathy

- *empathic concern*   feelings of sympathy and concern for less fortunate others
- *personal distress*   feelings of personal anxiety in tense social situations.

All constructs have been identified as important and separate aspects of empathy (Davis 1980) and relate individually to emotionality, selflessness, prosocial motives and an increased concern for others (Davis 1983).

In Ireland (1999b) I predicted that prisoners reporting to engage in behaviours indicative of bullying others would report lower levels of empathy than those who did not. This was based on the assumption that an individual who bullies others would have to show deficits in some components of empathy in order to carry out their victimisation. This was supported, with pure bullies in particular showing deficits in a combination of cognitive (namely perspective taking) and emotional (namely empathetic concern) components of empathy in comparison to the other groups. Pure bullies and bully/victims reported similar levels of empathy although this latter group did not report significantly lower empathy scores in comparison to the other groups. Finally, pure victims were found to score significantly higher than those not involved in bullying on the component perspective taking.

Although potentially useful in adding to what we know so far about the typologies of prisoners involved in bullying, the absence of research in the area of empathy and bullying means that any conclusions drawn from this single study should be treated with caution. The findings presented here, however, suggest three things

- pure bullies differ from the rest of their peer group in terms of their capacity to empathise
- any deficit that they have is not made up of a specific component of empathy but of a combination of cognitive and emotional aspects
- both pure bullies and bully/victims are not entirely dissimilar to one another in terms of overall levels of empathy (Ireland 1999b).

## Social problem-solving

Social problem-solving skills have proven to be important in distinguishing prisoners who engage in bullying from the rest of their peer group. Dodge (1986) describes how an individual's behavioural responses to a social problem follow a series of information processing steps, which generally occur outside conscious awareness. The steps, in order, include encoding social cues in the environment, forming a mental representation and interpretation of these cues, searching for a possible behavioural response, deciding on a response and, finally, enacting the chosen response. Dodge (1986) argues that biases or deficits in any of these steps could lead to an aggressive response in certain individuals.

It has also been suggested that social cognition may play a role not only in whether or not bullying will take place but also in the type of bullying that a bully chooses to use (Sutton *et al.* 1999a). For example, indirect bullying, by its very nature, requires a certain degree of cognitive skill if it is to be carried out effectively (Ireland 2001a). Physical bullying may also require skills in social cognition to ensure that the victim's hurt is maximised and the risk to the bully, through detection and/or social retribution, is minimised (Sutton *et al.* 1999a). This may be particularly applicable to prison bullying where there is a need to hide acts of physical aggression since the punishments levied by prison authorities are severe (Ireland 2001a).

To date little research has addressed the relationship between social problem-solving and bullying among prisoners. In one study (Ireland 2001a) I focused on two specific skills that were identified by Richard and Dodge (1982) as being important for social problem-solving, namely the generation of solutions and the sequencing of generated solutions. In this study prisoners were categorised as pure bullies, pure victims, bully/victims or not-involved, based on a behavioural checklist, and required to complete a questionnaire that provided them with five hypothetical conflict situations involving bullying. Each scenario presented prisoners with a different type of bullying, for example theft-related, sex-related, physical, indirect or verbal bullying. An example of a scenario (verbal) that they were presented with is 'A prisoner has been calling you names in front of other prisoners. S/he has done this more than once in the past week.' Prisoners were asked to think of as many solutions to this problem as possible and from this to identify a 'best' and a 'second-best' solution. No differences were reported between the groups in terms of the number of solutions that they could produce. Differences were found, however, in the type of solutions reported with pure bullies appearing distinct from the other groups in favouring aggressive responses for all scenarios. This was found for both best and second-best solutions. I concluded from this that it was the type of strategy as opposed to the number of strategies produced that distinguished pure bullies from other groups, and that pure bullies lacked a range of non-aggressive solutions to conflict. Pure bullies appeared distinct from the bully/victim group who did not favour aggressive over non-aggressive solutions. I also suggested that the pure bullies' aggressive response to conflict may have proven to be an effective solution in the past, and that they may be accessing aggressive strategies sooner simply because of their previous success.

This study also highlighted the importance of taking into account the environment in which social problem-solving was taking place when interpreting findings. The findings regarding pure bullies, for example, could be interpreted in two different ways. If it is assumed that aggression is not an adaptive way of dealing with a social problem, then the present results suggest that pure bullies possess a faulty decision-making technique (Tversky and Kahnmann 1974), and that they have clear deficits in problem-solving skills. In a prison, however, where the range of solutions to a conflict situation is limited, aggression may not be an indication of a deficit but may, instead, represent an effective and adaptive way of dealing with bullying. Favouring an aggressive response may therefore be appropriate. Thus, the results could also be interpreted in relation to this – pure bullies may not be deficient in social problem-solving skills, they may instead be biased towards favouring aggressive solutions when compared to other prisoners. Indeed, I commented

> It is also worth noting that the model of social problem-solving proposed by Dodge (1986) is based on the assumption that overt aggression and intimidation are not adaptive ways of dealing with others. This may be an over-optimistic assessment for the prison environment, where the ability to coerce others through aggression is likely to confer benefits.
>
> (Ireland 2001a: 310)

With the same group of prisoners, I also addressed a further skill considered important for social problem-solving, namely the evaluation of (aggressive) solutions, as measured by the possible consequences that an aggressive response could entail (Ireland and Archer 2002). Following completion of each of the five hypothetical scenarios involving bullying, prisoners were asked what the consequences would be if they were to respond aggressively to the scenario (it is worth noting that prisoners were not asked to choose a consequence based on how they would *actually* respond to the situation, they were simply asked what would happen *if* they were to be aggressive). The specific consequences which prisoners could choose from were based on school and prison-based research that had suggested them as possible consequences of aggression. Two positive ('other prisoners would respect you' and 'you would feel better'), three negative ('the situation would get worse', 'you would feel worse' and 'you would get into trouble with the officers') and one neutral response ('the situation would not change') were included. Prisoners were only allowed to select one consequence, the one that they felt would be most likely to happen. The aim was to assess whether or not bullies and victims differed in their perceptions of the consequences associated with using aggression as a response to being bullied, and it was expected that bullies would hold favourable attitudes towards violence and the use of violence to solve problems.

Both pure bullies and bully/victims were found to report more positive than negative consequences of aggression when compared to the overall mean in response to some of the bullying scenarios (in response to theft-related bullying for pure bullies, indirect and physical bullying for bully/victims). This contrasted with the not-involved group who reported more negative than positive consequences compared to the overall mean for all scenarios. No differences were reported for pure victims (Ireland and Archer 2002). The finding that prisoners who engaged in bullying behaviour viewed the benefits of aggression differently from those who did not was explained with reference to the prisoner peer group, where peers can act to encourage the use of aggression as an appropriate and successful method of obtaining power over others (see Chapter 4). It is important again, however, to recognise the importance of interpreting these results with reference to the environment in which problem solving is taking place, specifically attending to the problems associated with interpreting the beliefs of bullies as 'deficient' in an environment where aggression may well be an adaptive response.

Both sets of results (Ireland 2001a; Ireland and Archer 2002) hold important implications for typologies of prisoners who bully and/or are victims. Although there appear to be no differences between the groups in terms of the number of solutions to conflict that they can generate, pure bullies do favour aggressive responses to conflict involving bullying, and they evaluate the consequences of aggressive responses more favourably in some situations. Bully/victims are less inclined to favour aggression as a solution but do evaluate the consequences of using aggression more favourably in specific conflict situations. Pure victims cannot be distinguished from other prisoners in terms of how they solve conflict situations or how they evaluate the consequences of aggression.

The research presented in this section, however, has addressed only the later stages of Dodge's (1986) model and there is a need for research to focus on the earlier steps as well (particularly those relating to hostile attribution biases). This would allow researchers to assess the extent to which such models can be applied to prison bullying. The initial results presented suggest that some elements of the model may apply to bullying although the interpretation of results needs to be done with an acknowledgement of the specific environment in which the model is being applied. It is also worth noting that both studies presented here classified prisoners using a behavioural checklist in which assignment to each of the different groups was made by the researcher after data collection. Thus, as I mentioned at the start of this chapter, since prisoners were not asked to identify themselves as either bullies or victims they may not necessarily be expected to perceive themselves as members of these groups. The results should be interpreted in accordance with this and caution is advised in attempting to compare these findings with research using more traditional methods of measuring bullying. This can be applied to the majority of research addressing intrinsic characteristics which has focused on behaviours indicative of being bullied and/or bullying others for reasons that are outlined in some detail in Chapter 2.

## Assertiveness

Baer (1976) describes assertiveness as a 'win–win' behaviour where an individual stands up for their rights without disregarding those of others. It contrasts with aggression where the intent is to violate the rights of others and to humiliate and dominate, and with passivity described as 'expressing feelings, thoughts and beliefs in such an apologetic, diffident, and self-effacing manner that others easily disregard them' (Ramanaiah and Deniston 1993: 336). It has been argued that assertiveness relates to bullying with many anti-bullying intervention programmes, both school- and prison-based, advocating assertiveness-skills training for victims (Ireland 2002c). This is based on the notion that victims lack skills in assertiveness (i.e. are passive), and that this has contributed to their victimisation: by providing them with assertiveness skills it is thought that they will be able to resist bullying attempts. Both bullies and bully/victims, on the other hand, are seen as assertive (Stephenson and Smith 1989), with some researchers suggesting that bullies are even over-assertive (Besag 1993).

The role of assertiveness can be discussed with reference to dominance and rank hierarchies among prisoners. As presented in the previous chapter, such hierarchies place prisoners who bully at the top (thus giving them a certain degree of status) and prisoners who are victimised at the bottom (thus stigmatising them). Gilbert and Allan (1994) suggest that comparing yourself unfavourably with others, particularly if you are assigned to a low status position, may contribute to assertiveness difficulties. Although focusing on animals, Gilbert and Allan (1994) further describe how subordinate animals tend to be non-assertive with more dominant animals, whereas dominant animals appear more confident in challenging subordinates. Applying this to a prison, we could expect that the victims of bullying would be relatively non-assertive towards bullies, whereas bullies would be more assertive as a result of their positioning in the hierarchy. Gilbert and Allan (1994) further state that however rank is derived, whether it be through aggression, fighting ability, attractiveness or prestige (as it often is among humans), inhibition of behaviour may relate to rank estimates. They suggest that this inhibition may arise from a fear of being labelled in a negative way. Individuals who compare themselves unfavourably to others, for example seeing themselves as weak or vulnerable, may be placing themselves at the bottom of these social hierarchies and as a result be prone to assertiveness difficulties. This could easily be applied to the victims of bullying in a prison, where the label of victim is seen as an unfavourable one. The bully, on the other hand, may view themselves as superior or equal to others during conflict or challenging situations and as a result be less socially inhibited and more assertive.

Empirical research addressing the role of assertiveness with relation to prison bullying is extremely limited and to date there have been only two studies (Falshaw 1993; Ireland 2002c). Falshaw (1993) presented prisoners with ten scenarios involving bullying and asked them to respond to each. The number of aggressive, passive and assertive responses that they provided was then totalled. It was reported that the more assertive an individual the less likely they were to report an ability to bully others. In contrast, the more passive an offender the more likely they were to report being bullied. In Ireland (2002c) I used a more standard method of measuring assertiveness than Falshaw, namely the Rathus Assertiveness Schedule (RAS: Rathus 1973), and assessed its relationship to being categorised as a pure bully, a bully/victim, a pure victim or not-involved. Assignment to each category was based on prisoner responses to a behavioural checklist. Assertiveness was found to consist of three components

- a tendency to be socially assertive and to show a lack of concern about displaying emotions to others
- a tendency to be argumentative and combative towards others
- a tendency to show a willingness to converse with others and to promote a personal opinion.

Significant correlations were found between total assertiveness and component scores, with the number of aggressive behaviours reported that were indicative of bullying others or of being bullied in the direction predicted, i.e. positively correlating with 'bullying others' items and negatively with 'being bullied' items. The magnitude of these correlations was extremely small (the largest being $r = 0.28$) and thus it could only be concluded that the relationship between assertiveness and the number of bully or victim items that a prisoner reports is poor. With regard to the assertiveness scores and membership of each of the different groups, lack of assertiveness was associated with being bullied, with pure victims scoring lower than the other bully categories on total assertiveness. Although this suggests that assertiveness-skills training for victims may be a valuable intervention, it is possible that the victim who is less assertive, particularly during conflict situations, may be acting in a fairly adaptive way. Such victims may have effectively judged the likelihood of being successful, and hence used non-assertive behaviours to avoid potential injury (Ireland 2002c). Interesting findings were also reported regarding bully/victims. Although this group did not show lower levels of overall assertiveness, they did report higher scores than the other groups on the argumentative and combative component of assertiveness (with a non-significant trend in the same direction found for pure bullies). On this basis it was argued that bully/victims may be somewhat over-assertive when it comes to this particular component. There was also a trend for both bully/victims and pure victims to score lower than other groups on the social assertiveness component and it was concluded from this that although bully/victims showed a tendency to be more argumentative and combative, they were more inhibited when it came to actually expressing emotions.

It is also worth noting at this point that although in Ireland (2002c) prisoners were allocated to each group based on their responses to a behavioural checklist, the finding that bully/victims were significantly more likely than the other groups to be more assertive on some components of assertiveness (and a non-significant trend for pure bullies to be more assertive on some components than the other groups), is consistent with Stephenson and Smith's (1989) description among schoolchildren of both bullies and bully/victims as assertive. Although Stephenson and Smith (1989) used a different method to define their groups from the one employed in Ireland (2002c), the fact that the findings are comparable suggests that the present behavioural method is successful in identifying true bullies and bully/victims.

Overall, this section provides some evidence for a relationship between bullying behaviour and assertiveness. Although assertiveness (and its components) may relate only poorly to the number of bully or victim items that a prisoner reports, there is evidence to suggest that pure victims are much less assertive in comparison to other groups whereas bully/victims are over-assertive when argumentative and combative components of assertiveness are considered. Since the findings reported by Falshaw (1993) regarding bullies were not replicated in my study (Ireland 2002c), predicting the role of assertiveness in prisoners who bully others is therefore difficult. There are also clear difficulties in comparing these two studies since they used different methods of measurement and Falshaw did not distinguish between pure bullies and bully/victims. This perhaps highlights the importance of conducting further research into this area using similar methods of classification that allow findings to be compared. Such research also needs to account for the problems in measuring assertiveness. There has been no universal agreement regarding the nature of assertiveness and what specific behaviours it includes: this has resulted in a number of the scales (including the RAS) tending to confuse assertiveness with aggressiveness and/or anxiety (Galassi and Galassi 1978). Thus, the reported findings regarding bullying among prisoners and assertiveness need to be interpreted with regard to this: the findings relating to the scores on individual components (i.e. those that I reported in Ireland 2002c) are perhaps the most useful since they distinguish between different behaviours associated with assertiveness. Future research should perhaps consider the importance of measuring individual components of assertiveness.

## Self-esteem

Self-esteem has been described as the affective and evaluative aspect of the 'self' (Blyth and Trager 1983; Hancock and Sharp 1985), an aspect that readily fluctuates, unlike the more stable self-concept (Calhoun and Morse 1977). The level of self-esteem that an individual reports is thought to relate closely to the influence of the peer group. Salmivalli, for example, comments on how 'for adolescents constructing their image of themselves, the feedback coming from their peers is of crucial importance and can certainly be thought to have a major impact on their self-view' (1998: 348). Harter (1993) argues that if others hold the self in high regard, self-esteem is high. In contrast, if others do not hold the self in high regard, self-esteem is low. A self-fulfilling prophecy may emerge from this where the negative views that others have of an individual become internalised and believed by that individual, which in turn leads to poor self-esteem. Harter (1993) argues that this process of comparing the self to others begins in middle childhood and increases with maturity. To relate this to bullying among prisoners, it could be argued that bullies represent those with high self-esteem since they have achieved a certain degree of status and respect among their peers. Victims should be expected to have low self-esteem since they fall at the bottom of the prisoner hierarchy and are stigmatised by the rest of the peer group.

The low levels of self-esteem expected to occur among victims can be explained with reference to Harter (1993) who describes how individuals with the lowest levels of self-esteem are those who report both incompetence in domains that are important to them and no supportive approval from others. In a prison, once an individual has been labelled as a victim and adopted the stigma associated with it, opportunities to obtain social support then become limited. Social support may then be offered on a conditional level (Harter 1993) and may be provided if the victim is able to display certain behaviours and attitudes deemed appropriate by the peer group. Bully/victims may represent those who are attempting to obtain support from others by displaying behaviours that are approved of by the rest of the peer group, for example by bullying others and not being submissive. If individuals are unable to display competence in domains deemed important to others, support cannot be obtained (Harter 1993). The issue of social support is important in a prison environment where such support, in the form of peer approval, becomes more critical with individuals distanced from peers important to them before their incarceration. Each period of incarceration creates a need for an individual to establish a new social network, and thus re-evaluate their self-esteem. Indeed, as I highlighted in the previous chapter, the peer group forms an integral part of the social environment that is closely related to bullying.

The actual relationship between bullying and self-esteem is far from clear. To date research has concentrated on bullying and self-esteem among children, with only three studies addressing self-esteem among prisoners. Regarding children, researchers have generally reported that low self-esteem is related to victim status (Rigby and Slee 1991, 1993; Slee and Rigby 1993) whereas the relationship between self-esteem and bully status is less clear: some have reported that low self-esteem is related to bullying (O'Moore and Hillery 1991) whereas others have reported no relationship (Rigby and Slee 1991; Slee and Rigby 1993).

Prison studies include one published paper addressing men and women adult offenders (Ireland 2002b), and two unpublished papers – one addressing male young offenders (Falshaw 1993) and one a mixed sample of young offenders and children under a care order (Duckworth 1998). The findings reported by Falshaw (1993) and Duckworth (1998) suggest that victim status is related to low self-esteem, for example Falshaw (1993) reported that the more an individual was victimised the lower their self-esteem, and Duckworth (1998) found that low self-esteem individuals were more likely than those with high self-esteem to report being bullied. The negative correlation reported by Falshaw (1993), however, could best be described as small ($r = -0.36$), and the fact that Duckworth (1998) addressed a combined sample of offenders and non-offenders questions the applicability of these results to a discussion regarding prison bullying. These findings were also not replicated in Ireland (2002b). In this study I assessed the level of social self-esteem reported by pure bullies, bully/ victims, pure victims and those not involved, and found no significant differences between them. There were some significant correlations reported between the level of self-esteem and the number of aggressive behaviours reported that were indicative of bullying others or of being bullied. These were found only for the male sample and were very small (with the largest r = 0.25), thus providing only weak evidence of a relationship between self-esteem and bullying behaviour. Indeed, the only significant finding was related to the offender's sex, with women reporting significantly lower levels of self-esteem than men.

In summary, the findings from these results suggest that the relationship between bullying and self-esteem is not conclusive, although there is some tentative evidence that victims may have low self-esteem. It is difficult to draw any firm conclusions, however, from the limited research conducted into this area particularly in view of the different methods employed by the studies. It is difficult to compare, for example, my study (Ireland 2002b) to the other studies since, unlike Falshaw (1993) and Duckworth (1998), I employed a behavioural checklist to assign prisoners to one of four groups. In addition, each of these studies measured self-esteem differently, for example Falshaw (1993) used a measure consisting of eight items and referred to it as a 'self-esteem questionnaire' with no further information provided, Duckworth (1998) used a single-item measure that asked participants to rate their self-esteem on a scale ranging from very low to very high, and in Ireland (2002b) I concentrated on one aspect of self-esteem (social self-esteem) using a standardised measure to assess it. One conclusion that can perhaps be drawn from this section is that the prison findings taken together with those based on children suggest that we should not be quick to draw conclusions about the relationship between bullying and self-esteem. At the very least all that can be acknowledged is that there *may* be a link between low self-esteem and victim status whereas a relationship between bullying others and self-esteem appears doubtful.

## Psychopathy

Although it is recognised that there is some disagreement between researchers regarding the exact definition of 'psychopathy' (e.g. Simonsen and Birket-Smith 1998), such arguments are outside the focus of the current section and readers are referred to other sources for a further discussion of these issues (e.g. Millon *et al.* 1998; Blackburn 2000). The aim of the current section is simply to provide a brief discussion of the possible relationship between psychopathy and bullying.

The most characteristic traits of psychopaths include their superficial charm, egocentricity, incapacity for love, inability to experience guilt, lack of remorse and shame, lack of insight and a failure to learn from experience (Simonsen and Birket-Smith 1998). Although no research has directly addressed the link between bullying and psychopathy there is reason to believe that they may be related. Sutton and colleagues, for example, have described some child bullies as 'cold, manipulative experts in social situations' (1999b: 2), suggesting that certain skills in bullying may be seen as 'low level manifestations of sociopathy' (1999b: 21), and that bullies may simply be thinking in instrumental terms without any expression of feeling or understanding of empathy. Indeed, Mealey (1995) describes the psychopath as a cold and detached individual who repeatedly harms and manipulates others. It is easy to see that such a description could also be applied to the prison bully. Evidence that the prison bully is cold and detached comes from the findings regarding emotional and cognitive empathy that I reported earlier (Ireland 1999b). Like Sutton and colleagues (1999b) I would also argue that the bully does not display high levels of psychopathy but, in accordance with Mealey's definition, they may show traits similar to the secondary psychopath. Such individuals fall at the low end of the psychopathy spectrum and their anti-social behaviour is more closely tied to social and environmental variables such as their competitive status within their referent group and changing environmental contingencies. They are also more responsive to changes in the environment (Mealey 1995). Such variables would seem to apply more readily to the bullying that occurs within prisons where the environment itself appears to foster such behaviour by allowing individuals the opportunity to increase their status by bullying others and by creating a competitive social structure.

Thus it could be argued that some bullying, particularly that carried out by pure bullies, may represent low-level manifestations of psychopathy. The bullying behaviour of bully/victims may not be so closely related to this concept since their behaviour is conceptualised more as a defensive response to their own victimisation. Indeed, it could be speculated that some bullying may be better described in relation to psychopathy as opposed to being described solely as a subsection of aggressive behaviour. Aggression may simply be one method that bullies use to successfully exploit their peers, whereas the intention to exploit may be related more closely to psychopathy. This latter point is based largely on conjecture and empirical research using a standard method of measuring psychopathy (such as Hare's 1991, Psychopathy Checklist Revised, PCL-R) is needed before any conclusions about the link between the two constructs can be drawn. However, at the very least the evidence presented here highlights the importance of researching this area further.

## Behavioural characteristics

The actual behaviours that prisoners display in the prison setting and how these relate to bullying has only recently received the attention of researchers. The importance of behaviours has been alluded to in the previous sections, i.e. the role played by assertive behaviours, and how bullies can be distinguished from the rest of their peer group by the behaviours that they report they would use during a conflict situation. Assessing the actual behaviours displayed by the different groups involved in bullying is an area that may prove useful in helping staff to identify prisoners who are bullies and/or victims and this is the focus of the current section.

Behavioural characteristics are defined here as prison-based behaviours (aside from bullying) that prisoners may display during incarceration. To date, researchers have addressed three main groups of behaviours, namely those indicative of

1   *negative behaviours towards staff or prison rules*   including reporting being shouted at by an officer, being sacked from a job or course, being placed on a governor's report or being abusive to an officer
2   *involvement in the use of and the distribution of drugs*   including reporting having bought, sold or used drugs
3   *proactive or positive behaviours towards others*   including breaking up a fight, making new friends or helping new prisoners on the wing.

These categories are based on the work of Beck and Smith (1997) among young offenders, and on my own studies addressing adult offenders (Ireland 2000b, 2001c). They were originally included in the Direct and Indirect Prisoner Behaviour Checklist as filler items (see Chapter 2 for a detailed description of this checklist). When they were analysed as distinct groups of behaviours in their own right, however, and related to the different groups involved in bullying, they proved to be useful in distinguishing between the groups. For example, in Ireland (2001c), I reported that bully/victims displayed the highest frequency of negative behaviour towards staff or prison rules and they also displayed the highest frequency of behaviours indicative of involvement in drugs. They were followed by pure victims who displayed the next highest frequency of these behaviours. For men, membership of the bully/victim group was predicted by more involvement in drug-related behaviour and increased proactive behaviour whereas membership of the pure victim group was predicted by decreased proactive behaviour. With regard to women, membership of the bully/victim group was predicted by increased negative behaviour.

I also reported similar findings in Ireland (2000b) in that bully/victims again displayed the highest frequency of negative and drug-related behaviours. The only difference here was with pure victims who did not display the next highest frequency of negative and drug-related behaviour. Instead, pure bullies displayed the next highest frequency of these behaviours followed by pure victims. With regard to behaviours predictive of group membership, I reported similar findings to Ireland (2001c) with regard to bully/victims in that men classified as such were predicted by more proactive behaviour, whereas women were predicted by more negative behaviour. Differences were reported, however, for the other groups in comparison to the previous study: men classified as bully/victims were predicted by more negative behaviour, men classified as pure victims were not predicted by any behaviours and women classified as pure victims were predicted by decreased negative behaviour.

The most interesting finding to emerge from these studies is perhaps that those prisoners most likely to come to the attention of staff (either through negative behaviour displayed towards them or suspicion of involvement in drug-related behaviour) were likely to belong to one of the victim groups, i.e. bully/victims. The behaviours reported for this group were also largely consistent between studies with the exception that male bully/victims in Ireland (2000b) were also predicted by increased negative behaviour. It could be speculated that such prisoners may be identified as troublemakers by staff and seen more as the instigators of behaviours that contravene prison rules than as victims of bullying in need of support. It is perhaps ironic that those prisoners potentially most visible to staff through the behaviours that they display are those most in need of such support. One could theorise a number of reasons as to why such prisoners may want to make themselves known to staff. They may, for example, wish to be removed from the wing or unit (and hence from the bully) since they know that this will be a potential consequence if they are abusive to staff. The reasons why prisoners may respond in this way will be discussed more fully in the following chapter when I consider reactions to being bullied.

These findings suggest that addressing the behaviours displayed by the different groups may prove useful in encouraging staff to focus on the behavioural symptoms of bullying as opposed to relying solely on stereotypes of which prisoners are likely to become victims and/or bullies. I would argue that it is also easier to identify the different groups by the (often observable) behaviours that they show rather than by focusing on the other more intrinsic characteristics that they possess. This is not to say that behavioural characteristics are the most important, simply that they may prove more useful in helping staff to identify the different groups. If staff can learn to identify the types of behaviours that pure victims and bully/victims are likely to show then this will make their identification easier and ensure that staff do not have to rely solely on victims reporting the abuse themselves. Both the studies presented here, for example, suggest that one of the best ways of identifying bully/victims (and to a lesser extent pure victims) may be to monitor the negative and drug-related behaviours that prisoners show since such behaviours appear to be good indicators of victimisation.

Undoubtedly more research is needed to address the specific types of behaviours that the different groups may display. Those described in the present section are based on a relatively small number of possible behaviours. Researchers should consider addressing a wider range of behaviours that can help predict group membership, and not base an analysis of these behaviours solely on prisoner self-report but also use other sources of information such as official records (e.g. wing files). However, this section has highlighted the potential importance of including actual behaviours in any typology of bullies, bully/victims or pure victims.

## What characteristics are important?

In view of the limited research available, it is difficult to assess with any certainty which characteristics are the most important in describing the different groups and which are not. In addition, a number of studies, particularly those addressing perceived and personal/descriptive characteristics, have separated their sample into only two groups – bullies and victims – with no recognition of bully/victims. It therefore becomes difficult to compare findings from these studies to those that have adopted a different classification system that recognises this third group. Comparison also becomes difficult because of the range of different methods used to measure bullying.

Attempting to describe the characteristics associated with status as a bully and/or victim is important since decisions about which group prisoners belong to can be based on poor evidence. In addition, anti-bullying intervention programmes, as I shall highlight in Chapters 7 and 8, are often based on perceptions of which types of prisoners bully and which are victimised. Addressing which characteristics should, and should not, be taken into account therefore becomes important.

One group of characteristics that should be interpreted with caution are those perceived to relate to bully or victim status. A number of these characteristics are either not supported by research addressing actual characteristics or the support is inconsistent. Physical stature, for example, does not relate to victim or bully status and there is conflicting evidence regarding the importance of home area and offence type. There is also conflicting evidence regarding the importance of age and the perception that victims are those serving short sentences. Some perceived characteristics have been supported by research. In particular, bullies (and bully/victims) tend to be those who report the most experience with prison life, whereas victims are those with limited prison experience. This appears to be the most important distinguishing variable between the groups. In addition, victims do report having fewer friends, to be less assertive than other prisoners and more involved in drug-related behaviour (although this latter characteristic is more pronounced for bully/victims), and bullies do report longer criminal records as evidenced by an increased number of previous convictions. There are many perceived characteristics, however, that have yet to be assessed. These include the perception that victims have poorer education or intelligence levels than other prisoners, that they have mental or physical deficits and are quiet. Until empirical evidence emerges supporting the importance of such perceptions, their use in describing the groups involved in bullying should be limited. At the very least any reference to the importance of these characteristics should highlight the fact that they are merely perceptions.

There are a number of intrinsic characteristics important in distinguishing between the different groups that add considerably to typologies of these groups. In summary, pure bullies show deficits in both cognitive and emotional components of empathy, they are inclined towards favouring aggression as an appropriate response to a conflict situation and are more likely to evaluate the consequences of using aggression as a favourable solution in some conflict situations. They cannot be clearly distinguished from other groups based on an assessment of their level of self-esteem or assertiveness. Pure victims display increased levels of empathy in comparison to those not-involved in bullying in terms of 'perspective taking' but cannot be distinguished from other groups with regard to social problem-solving skills. They are also less assertive than the other groups and do not consistently report lower levels of self-esteem. With regard to this latter point, however, it is acknowledged that there may be some tentative evidence that victims present with low self-esteem, but the poor quality of the studies showing this coupled with the fact they do not distinguish between pure victims and bully/victims questions the validity of their findings. With regard to bully/victims, this group did not show significant deficits in cognitive or emotional empathy and were not inclined towards favouring aggression as a response to conflict, although they did report positive consequences related to using aggression. Bully/victims also reported higher levels of assertiveness than the other groups but this was restricted to one specific component of assertiveness, namely argumentative/combativeness, and they could not be identified based on their reported level of self-esteem.

Bully/victims can also be reliably distinguished from the other groups in terms of the increased negative behaviour that they show towards staff and prison rules. Distinguishing between the different groups in terms of the actual behaviours that they display is proving to be an interesting development and one that is potentially more important than focusing solely on the other characteristics that they possess, such as personal/descriptive characteristics. In Ireland (2001c), for example, I reported that whereas behaviours consistently predicted membership to some of the groups, the personal/descriptive characteristics prisoners possessed were of poor statistical quality and not expected to generalise outside the specific sample under study. There was also evidence that the behavioural characteristics reported were reliable, with the findings from both Ireland (2001c) and Ireland (2000b) fairly consistent, particularly with regard to describing bully/victims and identifying that both this group and pure victims engaged in negative and drug-related behaviour. Indeed, in Ireland (2001c) I concluded that

> personal/descriptive characteristics such as length of sentence, offence type, institutional history, age and ethnic origin may not be wholly predictive of group membership. The prison-based behaviours displayed by these different groups may be more important in distinguishing them.
>
> (Ireland 2001c: 245)

Thus, it appears that pure bullies, pure victims and bully/victims do possess certain characteristics, some of which potentially could help to explain how they become assigned to each group. More research is needed however, particularly that which attempts to replicate the findings reported here so that some estimation of the reliability of the characteristics can be obtained. I have also highlighted the importance of two issues in this chapter. First, that of taking into account the environment in which bullying is taking place before trying to explain why prisoners may possess certain characteristics. This was certainly considered in the sections on social problem-solving and assertiveness where it was recognised that certain behaviours, although initially interpreted as maladaptive (i.e. using aggression to solve conflict situations and being under-assertive), may actually be adaptive in a prison environment. Second, also highlighted is the importance of distinguishing between the different groups involved in bullying, i.e. pure bullies, pure victims, etc.

There is a clear need for more research addressing the characteristics of the different groups involved in bullying. This applies in particular to behavioural and intrinsic characteristics, both of which have been under-researched yet potentially are very useful in helping researchers to understand why prisoners bully and/or become victims. One intrinsic characteristic in particular that could be addressed is that of psychopathy since it is speculated that this concept may relate closely to bullying.

## Summary

This chapter has attempted to describe bullies and/or victims in terms of the different characteristics that they may or may not possess. In doing so it focused on a range of perceived and actual characteristics that are potentially important in providing a further understanding of bullying behaviour, and attempted to evaluate the relative importance of each. There are a number of characteristics that appear particularly useful in distinguishing between bullies and/or victims. These include intrinsic characteristics such as self-esteem, assertiveness, social problem-solving and empathy, and behavioural characteristics such as negative behaviour towards staff or prison rules, proactive or positive behaviour and drug-related behaviour. Behaviours may be particularly useful characteristics to emphasise to staff since many of them are observable, making it relatively easy for staff to identify them.

What I hope is clear from this chapter is a need for more research addressing the characteristics of the different groups involved in bullying, research that focuses on actual as opposed to perceived characteristics. Research could also assess which characteristics predispose a prisoner to become a member of a bully and/or victim group and which are likely consequences of the behaviour that they engage in or experience. Are victims, for example, less assertive before they are victimised or is this a behaviour they adopt as a consequence of their victimisation? Obviously, in view of the lack of research available, such questions are outside the scope of the present chapter and indeed the present book. It is a question, however, that relates in part to the following chapter where I discuss in more detail how victims may respond to being bullied.

# Chapter 6

# Reactions to bullying

The impact on prisoners who have become targets for bullies should not be underestimated. This impact is undoubtedly accentuated by the fact that prisons are environments in which there may be no means of physical escape from the bully (or bullies), and where the existence of an inmate code prohibits prisoners from reporting to others. Victims do not, therefore, have the option of reporting the abuse to those in authority, or even to other prisoners, for fear of rejection or retribution for violating this code (Ireland 2000a).

Victims can respond to bullying in a number of ways with O'Donnell and Edgar (1996a) arguing that their responses can fall along a continuum ranging from passive acceptance to active resistance. Responses include those that happen at the time of the bullying and those that occur after the bullying has taken place. These latter responses can include 'preventative reactions' and represent the ways in which a victim responds in order to prevent future victimisation. They can also include other responses that may be less visible but may become more evident over time, such as emotional responses.

In the current chapter, I aim to provide some insight into the range of possible reactions that victims of bullying may show, as well as providing a rationale behind these reactions. Where possible, two distinct groups of victims will be referred to, pure victims and bully/victims, and the differences between them will be explored. It should be acknowledged that a number of the intrinsic and behavioural characteristics that I described in the previous chapter could also be construed as reactions to victimisation. I mentioned this briefly at the end of the chapter, as well as the problems in separating the characteristics that predispose a prisoner to become a victim from those that are consequences of their victimisation. In view of the lack of research into this area, these problems are considered to be outside the scope of the present chapter and represent a direction that future research could perhaps take. In the present chapter I aim simply to describe the possible reactions that victims may display.

As an area of research, victim reactions have not been systematically studied. Researchers outside the United Kingdom have focused to a greater extent on how victims may react to aggression, including the precautions that they may take to avoid future victimisation (McCorkle 1992). However, this research has been studied in the context of either general prison violence (McCorkle 1992), or it has focused on specific types of aggression such as sexual assault (Lockwood 1980), but not bullying. This research is useful, however, in helping to describe how the victims of bullying may react and thus I will make reference to it in the present chapter.

It is undoubtedly an omission on the part of prison researchers not to focus on the victims of bullying. Indeed, as I highlight in Chapter 8, the focus of intervention strategies has been very much on identifying and punishing the bully and less on supporting the victim and exploring the abuse with them. As the research area develops it is hoped that the focus will move on to the victims of bullying. Thus I will concentrate specifically on victims in the current chapter, referring both to anecdotal and empirical evidence in my discussion of the many ways in which they can respond to bullying. The reactions that have been highlighted in the research to date include various emotional responses, avoidance and/or social isolation, aggression and self-injurious behaviour. I will focus on these reactions in the present chapter and discuss each in turn. Although each will be discussed separately this does not mean that they are not related: undoubtedly victims can display more than one reaction and, as we shall see later with regard to self-injurious behaviour and aggression, each can serve a similar function.

## Emotional responses

Emotional responses can include a range of feelings such as fear, anger, paranoia, anxiety, depression, distress, hopelessness or vulnerability that can manifest themselves in a number of behaviours such as crying, physical illness, avoidance, social isolation, aggression and self-injury. Many of these behaviours will be described in later sections, serving to highlight how each can be interlinked. The fact that they are described here separately is deliberate and illustrates how not all instances of aggression, social isolation, avoidance and self-injury should be conceptualised as purely emotional responses.

The emotional responses of the victims of bullying in a prison environment have received very little attention from researchers. Thus, the present section aims to summarise briefly the research conducted to date that has included reference to an actual or possible response that could be conceptualised as emotional, and to make some suggestions for further research. In view of the lack of research it will be necessary at times to refer to literature that has focused on aggression among prisoners and used different concepts or terms such as violence and victimisation.

One of the most commonly reported responses to being aggressed towards is fear (Lockwood 1980). Fear can be conceptualised almost as an expected part of imprisonment; prisons can be violent and threatening environments and anyone entering such an environment, particularly if it is their first time, may be fearful of what they may be subjected to. One of these fears may represent the possibility of being bullied. Fear therefore, can occur before an incident of bullying takes place, representing a motivating drive in some prisoners and encouraging them to take certain precautions against the possibility of being bullied. This will be touched upon in later sections with reference to the work of Grant (1999) and McCorkle (1992), particularly that of Grant (1999) who reported how those prisoners who reported being most afraid of bullying were most likely to engage in precautionary behaviours. There may also be a link between fear and the type of precautionary behaviour that a prisoner displays, with some suggestion in the literature that the more fearful the prisoner the more likely they are to use avoidance behaviours as a precaution to victimisation (McCorkle 1992). Fear, however, can equally be viewed as a consequence of bullying. This is captured in a letter from a young offender that was presented to officers following numerous incidents of bullying. I presented this letter in full in Chapter 1 but it is useful to present an extract here to highlight the fear that bullying can induce in an individual.

> I have been getting bullied off lads on this unit for about 8 weeks . . . one of the lads is in court on the same day as me. He told me that he's going to batter me there and I think that he would . . . I'm really scared what might happen now when I go to court with him and what he might do. Even if he doesn't do it at court he might do it at reception. I don't want anything like that to happen.

Not surprisingly, prisoners who report being bullied also report higher levels of fear (about being bullied) than prisoners who have never been bullied (Grant 1999). The intensity of fear reported by those who have been bullied regularly versus those who have been bullied once or twice is also reported to be similar (Grant 1999). This suggests that the severity of bullying (in terms of the number of times that a prisoner has been bullied) may have little to do with the level of fear that victims experience. A single incident of bullying may cause as much fear as multiple incidents.

Prisoners who are visibly fearful of their peers may encourage further victimisation (Johnson 1987). Toch describes fear reactions in prisons as 'red flags in bullrings' (1992: 203) and a way of communicating to other, more dominant, prisoners their vulnerability and hence their victim potential. It is thus left to the victim to try and control those aspects of their behaviour that indicate their fear of others. This can include adopting certain roles or images that the victim feels will help them to avoid victimisation. This is captured in the following account from a male victim reported by Toch

> All my motions, you know, like walking, you know, talking, and any movement at all, I always try to make myself look like if anyone would fuck with me I would kill them.
>
> (Toch 1992: 203)

Indeed, fear is seen to be an important component in the definition of bullying that is applied to a prison environment (see Chapter 2), where it is the fear of repeated aggression that characterises bullying, not the actual incident (Randall 1997). In a prison this fear can include a fear of being labelled a victim unless the prisoner is able to defend themselves adequately. The fear in this situation is not just limited to the possibility of being aggressed towards again by the same perpetrator, but is also a fear of becoming a viable target for other aggressors in the future. This fear is likely to impact on other emotions such as anxiety, apprehension, feelings of paranoia or worthlessness that in turn may manifest behaviourally through self-injurious behaviour or social avoidance. Fear can become a powerful emotion that ultimately places restrictions on the level of interaction that victims engage in with their peers. Victims can begin to see potential aggression or aggressors in every part of their prison world (Lockwood 1980). Undoubtedly if victims and their bullies remain in close proximity to each other following an incident of aggression, feelings of fear can persist and may even be intensified. The actual effect that feelings of fear in response to bullying can have on the victims has not been systematically studied. In view of how crippling such an emotion can be, it is perhaps an area that future research should address.

Crying can be described as an obvious emotional response to being bullied. It is a reaction that is a clear sign of the distress of the victim and the emotions that they may be experiencing. This is captured by Falshaw who presented the following account from a male victim in a letter that he sent to his family.

> People have been punching me and throwing water at me because I won't lend them a tape, because I won't lend them anything as I may not see whatever I lend to them again . . . there is one lad by my cell who said he is going to cut my throat with a knife. I'm not bloody having that going on. I can't wait to get out, it's doing my head in now, I cannot stand any more of this and have been crying because of what is going on at the moment.
>
> (Falshaw 1993: 18)

In a study by Bolt (1999), 21 per cent of pure victims and 20 per cent of bully/victims reported that they had cried in the previous week. This was considered a reliable indicator of victimisation with only 12 per cent of prisoners not involved in bullying as either a bully and/or a victim reporting this behaviour. The similarity in frequency with which each victim group reported this response was also found in two studies that I completed (Ireland 1999c, 2001c). The proportion of victims reporting to have cried was, however, much higher in these studies, with 32 per cent of victims in the first study reporting to have cried and 43 per cent in the second. Women in both studies also reported this response to a much greater extent than men and this was consistent across victim groups. Whether this latter finding reflects an actual sex difference remains unclear. It could be speculated that it is more reflective of a difference in reporting styles, with men reluctant to report that they have cried since this is not compatible with a masculine stereotype. Similarly, the extent to which this crying occurred in public is also not clear since no studies have explored this response in any detail. It could be expected that it would occur away from other prisoners since to openly display such a reaction could be viewed as an indication of vulnerability and increase the likelihood that they would be bullied in the future.

Anger is another emotional response that has been found to occur among prisoners reporting to being victims. Biggam and Power (1998), for example, reported elevated levels of anger and hostility in prisoners admitting to staff that they were being bullied, and Duckworth (1998) reported that the majority of victims felt angry (50 per cent) and frustrated (40 per cent) following an incident of bullying. The proportion of victims reporting such a response is consistent with research addressing sexual aggression between prisoners that reports anger to be the most common emotion next to fear (Lockwood 1980). The following victim account provided by Lockwood illustrates the impact that anger can have.

> He said I was a pussy and he is going to break me. So I picked him up and I threw him against the wall. When he came off the wall I just beat the pulp out of him. I kind of just lost my head and I know that if I get in that state I am really going to break because, you know, after a while it builds up. You can't take it no longer.
>
> (Lockwood 1980: 45)

Anger may also play a role in the aggression displayed by bully/victims. This group, as will be discussed later, can be described as reactive aggressors. Such reactive aggression has also been referred to as angry aggression and is thought to be carried out primarily by individuals viewed as short-tempered and volatile, and who tend to overreact to minor provocations. The consequences of anger can be serious, regardless of whether or not they lead to an expression of aggression. If the anger leads to aggression, regardless of the target, the victim risks potential injury or retribution. If the anger is not expressed it can lead to internal or psychological discomfort (Lockwood 1980).

Research has also begun to address other reactions to bullying such as depression, anxiety, distress, hopelessness and feelings of vulnerability. Duckworth (1998) found that 27 per cent of victims felt anxious or depressed following an incident of bullying, with 23 per cent feeling insecure and vulnerable. Biggam and Power (1998) reported mild levels of depression, clinical levels of distress, elevated levels of hopelessness and tension anxiety in prisoners admitting to staff that they were being bullied. Livingston and Chapman (1997), focusing on the relationship between self-injury and bullying, reported that depression had a more important association with self-injurious behaviour than it did with bullying.

The only conclusion that can be drawn from these few studies is that more research is needed that addresses the emotional reactions of victims in a prison setting. In view of how such reactions may help to inform the motivation behind the other reactions that will be presented in this chapter (i.e. avoidance, aggression and self-injurious behaviour), such research should be seen as essential. The lack of research is perhaps a reflection of the tendency for researchers to focus more on the perpetrators of bullying and less on the victim's account of the effect that the aggression has had on them. There is a clear need to ask the victim directly about the impact of bullying. Indeed, many of the reactions that I present in this chapter are to some extent observable, thus avoiding the need to question the victim directly, but they present only a limited view of the true range of reactions that a victim can experience.

## Avoidance and social isolation

Being victimised can encourage victims to make changes to the way and extent to which they interact with others. Such changes equate with the 'passive reactions' element of the victimisation continuum described by O'Donnell and Edgar (1996a). They can include formal changes such as the victim requesting protective custody, to be locked in their cell or to be moved to another location within the prison. They can also include informal changes such as victims staying in their cell when they could be out, restricting the amount of time that they spend with other prisoners and avoiding certain areas of the prison. All represent ways in which the victim is attempting to avoid areas, or times, where the risk of being aggressed towards is high. This is captured in the following account from a male victim reported by Lockwood 'And I started not going to those places, the mess hall or the recreation room at night or the yard. And I kept to myself in my room' (1980: 74).

Isolating themselves from their peers can be the most common change that a victim can make to their lifestyle (Lockwood 1980). Such isolation is often termed 'secondary victimisation' because it indicates the disruption that the aggression has caused to the prisoner's life (Lockwood 1980). It also represents precautions against future victimisation, i.e. behaviours that prisoners will engage in if they are fearful that victimisation is likely to occur (McCorkle 1992). Although the studies of Lockwood (1980) and McCorkle (1992) did not address bullying among prisoners there is enough evidence to suggest that similar reactions should be expected to occur among the victims of bullying as well. The following accounts, taken from Bullying Incident Reports[8] completed by staff in a male young offenders' institution, highlight the tendency for victims to respond to bullying by avoiding interactions with others and/or certain areas of the prison.

> The prisoner requested to be taken off education as he is being given a 'hard time' by other prisoners on education. He refused to give details. Was returned to the unit on this occasion but remains on the education list.

> This prisoner refused to attend education claiming that he is being taxed for tobacco by two prisoners in education.

I spoke to this prisoner and asked him why he is refusing to attend work. He told me that other prisoners in the workshop have threatened to beat him up. He has also asked to be locked in his cell during association periods.

Grant (1999) reported that the most frequently reported precautionary behaviour used to avoid bullying was 'keeping more to oneself', followed by 'avoiding certain areas of the prison'. Behaviours such as 'spending more time in one's cell', 'avoiding association activities' and 'avoiding work/leisure or education' were reported to a lesser extent, with 'asking to be placed in protective custody' one of the least frequently reported. Both victims and bullies were found to report more of these precautionary behaviours than those not involved in bullying. This could be explained by the fact that Grant (1999) did not separate the sample into pure victims and bully/victims. It could be expected that both these victim groups would engage in precautionary behaviours such as these to a greater extent than those not involved in bullying. Indeed, Grant (1999) reported that almost half of those prisoners identified as bullies in this study also reported being victims at some point. Thus, there appear to be two conclusions that can be drawn from this study: first, that victims of bullying (and bullies) engage in precautionary behaviours to a greater extent than those not involved in bullying, and second, that informal avoidance (e.g. keeping more to oneself) is a preferred type of strategy in comparison to more formal methods of avoidance (e.g. requesting protective custody).

Support for the apparent preference of avoidance and social isolation as a response to bullying also comes from Bolt (1999) and two studies that I completed (Ireland 1999a, 2001c). In these studies behaviours indicative of avoidance, namely 'staying in my cell when I could be out' and 'I have tried to get moved', were some of the most frequent victim reaction items reported. Differences were found between victim groups, with bully/victims reporting 'staying in their cell' to a greater extent than pure victims (Ireland 2001c; Bolt 1999). Bolt (1999) also found that 'trying to get moved' was reported to a greater extent by pure victims than bully/victims. In Ireland (1999a), however, I did not find overall differences between victim groups but I did find differences across status and sex (this latter study included a combined sample of young and adult offenders, whereas Bolt (1999) and Ireland (2001c) addressed only adult offenders). With regard to status differences, adult bully/victims reported staying in their cell to a greater extent than young offenders, whereas the opposite was true for pure victims, with adults reporting this behaviour to a lesser extent than young offenders. With regard to sex differences, women classified as pure victims reported the behaviour 'I have tried to get moved' to a greater extent than men classified as pure victims. Thus, taken as a whole these results suggest that bully/victims will isolate themselves in their cells to a greater extent than pure victims, but that this only holds for adult offenders and the relationship may be reversed for young offenders. The sex of the victim may also influence the particular avoidance behaviour that they adopt.

By engaging in such behaviours the victim ultimately limits the opportunities that bullies will have to target them. They may be particularly useful for victims who feel unable to defend themselves from the bully or who feel that they have too much to lose by behaving aggressively. The physical cost to victims preferring such avoidance behaviours may be reduced although the social costs, in terms of the limits that it places on peer interactions and the consequent support that they can receive, are increased. Isolation may, however, have some positive consequences for the victim. Those who choose isolation not only adjust to it but may learn to appreciate the safety and privacy that it offers (Lockwood 1980). Deliberate isolation and avoidance can, however, carry a hidden cost. Prisoners who respond in this way may send a clear signal to others that they are vulnerable with few friends and therefore represent potential targets for bullying. Toch (1992) describes how victims who present with such a pattern of behaviour make it obvious to the aggressor that they are afraid, which in turn provokes the aggressor to aggress towards them. If a victim isolates themselves from their peers this will result in fewer opportunities for them to develop a social network that could act as a protective factor against being bullied. This may be particularly true for bully/victims for whom avoidance appears to be a preferred strategy. For the bully who targets such a victim, the cost for them in using aggression in terms of retribution from other prisoners (i.e. the victim's social network) remains low. This was captured by Lockwood who noted the following account from a male prisoner.

> If you are by yourself, those are the people that turn out to be real preys of those other people. Because the guy is a loner, they know he doesn't have anyone to run to his aid if anything starts.
>
> (Lockwood 1980: 77)

Victims who respond to bullying by isolating themselves may not come to the attention of staff. Instead, staff time may be taken up with those victims displaying more overt reactions such as aggression (as we shall see in the following section). The danger here is that the passive victim(s) may get overlooked. In addition, victims who formally request protection from officers can expect to be stigmatised to a greater extent than those who use other means of achieving protection that allow them to maintain some status among their peers, yet ultimately protect them from their bullies (i.e. victims who choose to be aggressive). Victims are thus in a very difficult position. They may want protection from staff but are unable to ask for it formally unless they are willing to break the inmate code and suffer the consequences. Thus the only options they have left include becoming difficult and disruptive in the hope that staff will then move them because of their bad behaviour, or dealing with the situation themselves by avoiding their peers and entering a state of self-imposed isolation.

## Aggressive responses

Aggression can be an encouraged method of responding to bullying in a prison. It can form a fundamental part of prison life where the subculture rules of 'not backing down from conflicts' and an 'approval of physical violence to protect oneself or one's possessions' are revered elements of the inmate code to which all prisoners are expected to adhere. It is likely that in a violent environment (such as a prison) aggressive responses may represent adaptive ways of responding to bullying. Although such a view is unfortunate, it reflects the realities of prison life. Indeed, prisoners may advise victims of the advantages of using violence when threatened by others, a sentiment captured by Toch who reports the following account from a male victim.

> Everyone has been talking to me and telling me that I should fight, and I've tried everything else, so now I might as well fight.
>
> (Toch 1992: 208)

In some instances officers and other prison staff may recommend to the victim that they should fight back. Again, this is illustrated in the following accounts from Toch, the first from a male prisoner describing how he had told an officer that he was being victimised, and the second from a male prisoner reporting what his counsellor had advised him to do.

> He said, 'well there is nothing we can do about it, and there is nothing that the brass can do about it, so hit him'. He came right out and told me, just like that.
>
> (Toch 1992: 208)

they told me that you can't run away from it. You have to knock them down, face up to them . . . I said that these guys were big, and I would have to jump three feet to reach them. And they said that I would have to bring them down to my size. And he told me to kick them in the nuts, and that would bring them down to my size.

(Toch 1992: 208–209)

Countering aggression with aggression is very much a prevailing norm in a prison environment (Toch 1992) and its use as a way of responding to victimisation is well documented. This is highlighted in the following account from a male young offender provided by O'Donnell and Edgar.

He demanded phonecards and threatened me. I ignored his threats for a few days but then I thought it had gone too far and I cracked him. When he went to hit me I hit him once. He was stunned – two black eyes and a broken nose. An officer saw his injuries – blood pumping out of his nose. I was brought back to my cell. One of the officers congratulated me and shook my hand. Another officer made me a cup of tea. The bully was not popular with officers on the wing.

(O'Donnell and Edgar 1996a: 69)

O'Donnell and Edgar (1996a) also reported instances where the aggressive reaction on the part of the victim was not carried out at the time of the bullying but was enacted at a later date. These were described as revenge attacks with such attacks aptly illustrated by the following victim statement. The victim in this account, a male young offender, had previously been assaulted with a knife by two bullies. After hiding his injury for 3 weeks he reported how

I decided to do them, and planned it for weeks. I got a flick knife on a visit. I always carried the knife on association in case I could do them. Five weeks after the attack, I was coming back from gym and they were coming back from the wing. I felt a surge of energy in my body. They turned around and said 'Look who it is'. We were in the corridor. There were three officers close by. I stabbed one in the ribs. I slashed the other from the ear, across the throat and down the chest.

(O'Donnell and Edgar 1996a: 70)

Even when asking prisoners directly how they would respond to a hypothetical incident of bullying, a sizeable proportion include aggression as one way of dealing effectively with it. In Ireland (2001a),[9] I presented prisoners with five conflict situations involving different types of bullying (physical, theft-related, verbal, sexual and indirect) and asked them to generate as many ways of dealing with the bullying as possible. Prisoners generated both aggressive and non-aggressive responses, with men more likely to report an aggressive response than women (see Chapter 5 where I discuss this study and its relationship to social problem-solving in more detail). Overall, an aggressive response was favoured by up to 40 per cent of prisoners. Whether or not aggression was reported as a response, however, was largely dependent on the type of bullying that prisoners were asked to respond to, with physical bullying producing the highest proportion of aggressive responses and indirect bullying the least. With regard to victim groups, pure victims were more likely to report a non-aggressive response (to some scenarios) in comparison to other prisoners. No such difference was reported for bully/victims, suggesting that they were no less likely than the other groups to report aggression.

One of the most important observations that can be made from this study is that victim responses appear dependent on two variables – the type of bullying that victims are subjected to and the type of victim that they are (pure victim versus bully/victim). Indeed, the victim accounts presented earlier all relate to direct aggression, namely sexual (Toch 1992), physical and theft-related (O'Donnell and Edgar 1996a). Similarly, not all victims will respond aggressively to bullying, with studies describing how pure victims tend to be more passive than bully/victims who tend to respond in a more active and aggressive way. In one study, for example, I found that a higher proportion of bully/victims than pure victims reported defending themselves against another prisoner (24 per cent versus 11 per cent), and only bully/victims reported hitting or kicking someone after being victimised. This appeared to be particularly true for young offenders, with a higher proportion of young offenders classed as bully/victims reporting such reactions in comparison to adults. There were no sex differences suggesting that the status of the prisoner (i.e. young offender versus adult) was more important in helping to determine how they reacted to bullying (Ireland 1999a).

It is also important to acknowledge that the target of the victim's aggression may not necessarily be the bully. The aggression can be directed towards another prisoner or, in some instances, a member of staff. The victim who successfully aggresses towards their bully will undoubtedly increase their status among their peers and substantially reduce the possibility that they will be victimised in the future. Victims who aggress towards other targets (not the bully), however, may also be able to increase their status and prevent future victimisation, albeit to a lesser extent. Although such victims may remain at risk of being bullied by the original bully, they are able to communicate to the rest of the peer group that they are not an easy target and therefore deter other potential bullies.

I would argue that this applies in particular to the bully/victim group. Bully/victims are conceptualised primarily as a victim group for whom bullying others has become a way in which they can avoid further victimisation and increase their status among their peers. They can be described primarily as reactive aggressors, with aggression for them representing a reaction to bullying, one that is motivated by fear and a desire to defend themselves from other prisoners. In some instances their aggression towards others may represent displaced aggression towards the bully. This contrasts with pure bullies who can be described as proactive aggressors, for whom aggression is planned, organised and used instrumentally to obtain a social or material goal. Dodge (1991), however, argues that the distinction between reactive and proactive aggression is only a relative one, and it is possible for reactive aggression to contain proactive elements and vice versa. This can be related to the reactions of bully/victims in the following way: although bully/victims may be displaying reactive aggression there may also be a proactive goal, namely a way of communicating to the rest of their peer group that they will not readily submit to being bullied and thus are not likely targets for future victimisation. By communicating to the rest of the peer group that they are able to aggress towards another prisoner, regardless of whether or not this prisoner has bullied them, bully/victims are able to maintain a certain degree of status that in turn may help to prevent future victimisation. Indeed, bully/victims may not construe themselves to be victims in the same way as pure victims in that they are not wholly passive and thus the stigma associated with being known as a bully/victim may not be as extreme as that associated with being known as a pure victim (Ireland 1999a).

It could also be argued that by aggressing towards other prisoners the bully/victim is attempting to ensure their removal from the wing or unit to a safe environment away from the bully and/or to increase the level of supervision that they receive from staff. Both of these consequences will help to reduce the opportunity that other prisoners have to bully them and, as we shall see in the following section, may be similar in function to self-injurious behaviour. The display of aggression towards staff by bully/victims was mentioned briefly in the previous chapter in a discussion of the actual behaviours that they show, namely negative behaviours towards staff, which includes being abusive towards them. Indeed, in one study I reported that the largest proportion of abusive behaviour towards staff was reported by bully/victims, with only a very small proportion of pure victims reporting the same (Ireland 2000b). Undoubtedly it is easier for a victim to aggress towards a member of staff than towards another prisoner, with the consequences of such aggression more predictable and carefully controlled in accordance with prison policies and procedures: aggression towards a member of staff can lead to extra days on a sentence, cellular confinement, a restriction on privileges, etc., whereas aggression towards another prisoner is less predictable – the prisoner may retaliate and the victim may risk serious injury.

Aggressing towards staff may also increase the victim's status among other prisoners, although it is unlikely that such aggression will be an effective way of preventing victimisation in the long term. Unless the prisoner is able to increase their status substantially among other prisoners and prove to them that they are adhering to the inmate code (which includes a need to be tough and to resist exploitation), their status as a victim is unlikely to change. It is worth acknowledging, however, that some victims may not be overly concerned with the prison code and the status that they have among their peers. Some may feel sufficiently ostracised from their peer group that they either do not care about how this group perceives them or they have simply given up on attempts to increase their status. The main intention of the victim in this case may simply be to limit the opportunities that the bully has to aggress towards them by actively encouraging their own removal from the wing or unit.

It is also important to recognise that a victim who responds aggressively may be perceived and treated differently from one who self-injures. While both behaviours may ultimately ensure the victim's removal to a safe environment, the victim who self-injures is likely to receive increased staff support whereas the same cannot be said for the aggressive victim. Both self-injury and aggression, however, represent possible reactions to bullying although the former is more likely to be conceptualised as a victim behaviour since it is consistent with the stereotype of how victims are perceived, i.e. weak, vulnerable and poor copers. This highlights the importance of recognising that victims can also use aggression as a way of communicating their victimisation to others, and in these instances they should be supported in the same way as victims displaying other types of behaviour such as self-injury.

As I mentioned previously, an aggressive response to bullying should almost be expected in a prison where aggression can represent an adaptive and effective response (see Chapter 5). The danger here is that victims who display such reactive aggression, particularly that directed away from the original bully towards other innocent prisoners or to staff, can quickly become labelled as troublemakers. Once labelled as such it then becomes increasingly difficult for them to receive the support that they need since it becomes harder for others to perceive them as victims. Their aggressive behaviour, however, may represent the only way in which they can communicate to others what is happening without violating the inmate code of not informing on others. By being aggressive the victim may be aiming to draw as much attention to themselves as possible in the hope that someone will recognise their distress, remove them from the vicinity of the bullies and/or increase the supervision that they receive from staff. As victims begin to learn how effective their aggression can be in achieving these goals, the more likely they are to continue using it. The obvious consequence of this includes an increase in the number of prisoners who are bullied, with the victims of these bully/victims also having to be supported. This highlights the importance of recognising such aggression as a response to bullying. If bully/victims in particular are supported early on, then there will be less need for them to bully others which should lead to a reduction in the overall number of victims.

An aggressive response will be dependent to some extent on the ability of the victim to carry out such behaviour effectively. If victims are not confident of successfully aggressing towards the bully, either by physical or verbal means, then they will be unlikely to respond in this way. Indeed, as I suggested in the previous chapter, victims who respond less assertively (i.e. more passively) during conflict situations may actually be acting in a fairly adaptive way since they may have effectively judged the likelihood of being successful, and hence used non-assertive behaviours to avoid potential injury. In these circumstances, victims may choose to aggress either towards prisoners whom they consider to be more vulnerable or weak than them, or even towards staff through the use of verbal aggression. In this way they are using aggression but are attempting to reduce the personal cost of their actions. On the other hand, victims who do not possess the skills needed to aggress towards others, who are not inclined towards the use of aggression to solve conflict, or who feel that they have too much to lose by being aggressive (e.g. parole), may simply choose to react in another, non-aggressive, way.

## Self-injurious behaviour

Self-injurious behaviour is defined by Livingston as 'any instance in which a prisoner deliberately harms him/herself regardless of the method(s) used or the expressed intent to die' (1997: 22). It is used broadly in this section to include both threats to self-injure and actual self-injury. The experiences that prisoners report during incarceration are viewed as particularly important in distinguishing between those who self-harm and those who do not. Liebling and Krarup (1994) argued that prisoners who self-harmed could be identified less by their background and criminal justice histories and more by the descriptions that they provided of their experiences in prison. Since bullying can represent an element of the 'prison experience' it seems reasonable to expect that there may be a link between this and self-injurious behaviour. Indeed, O'Donnell and Edgar (1996a) describe how it is generally accepted that self-harm is regularly preceded by victimisation and that this represents the most passive response that victims can engage in. It also represents an extreme reaction to bullying and one that has received only limited attention in the research. Of the research that has been completed, a link between this and bullying has been found with a higher incidence of self-injury found in prisoners who have been bullied in comparison to those who have not. Livingston (1994), for example, reported that young offenders who actually self-injured were twenty to twenty-five times more likely to report bullying-related difficulties in the prison setting than young offenders who did not self-injure. Liebling and Krarup (1994) compared a sample of prisoners who had self-harmed to those who had not, and reported that prisoners placed in the self-harm group were more likely to report suffering from bullying in prison. Duckworth (1998) found victims were more likely than non-victims to feel like self-harming and to have had thoughts of killing themselves, and finally, in one study that I conducted, victims (identified via Bullying Incident Reports, BIRs[10]) were more likely than bullies to have been seen as at risk of or to have actually displayed self-harm at some point during their prison sentence (Ireland 2002d). This is also illustrated in the following accounts of bullying that were recorded on BIRs by staff in a male young offenders' institution after prisoners had attempted to harm, or had actually harmed, themselves[11]

> The prisoner in question had borrowed tobacco and toiletries from two other prisoners. He was unable to repay them within the time that they had allowed. With the pressure from these two prisoners he attempted to take his own life by hanging.

> The prisoner was taken to the Health Care Centre during the night after making attempts to cut his wrists. The prisoner states that he is being bullied for tobacco. He has asked to be locked up during association and has also refused some meals.

When the prisoner returned from court, two orderlies told other prisoners the nature of his offence. This has led to several incidents of abuse by other prisoners and threats. The prisoner has self-harmed due to this.

Few studies, aside from those conducted by me (Ireland 1999a, 2001c), have addressed differences between pure victims and bully/victims. In the first study, self-injurious behaviour was found to be one of a range of possible reactions to bullying. This study addressed behaviours indicative of bullying others and/or of being bullied, in a sample of men and women (adult and young offenders), and reported that both pure victims and bully/victims were more likely to report to have threatened to harm themselves and to have cut themselves in the previous week than those prisoners who did not report any victim items. Both bully/victims and pure victims reported an equal extent of self-injurious behaviour.[12] The self-injurious behaviour reported by pure victims and bully/victims was confined to men, particularly the male young offender sample, for whom threatening to self-harm was favoured over cutting themselves. Women in this study did not report self-injury. Similar findings were reported in the second study. This addressed both men and women adult prisoners with the exception that only female pure victims (and not male) reported to have threatened to harm themselves and/or to cut themselves.

Not surprisingly, there is also some suggestion from the research that a link may exist between completed suicides and bullying. Marshall (1993), for example, described how bullying was implicated in the suicides of four young offenders during 1991 and 1992 in one institution alone. HM Inspectorate (1999) describes how bullying was referred to in suicide notes left by prisoners who had committed suicide. Loucks (1998) reports how being bullied in prison was viewed as one of the most likely reasons for suicide, and Swift (1995) reported occasions where prisoners had incited victims to commit suicide.

Thus, there does appear to be some evidence for a link between self-injurious behaviour and bullying and this has been found both for pure victims and bully/victims. The finding that both groups appear to be at equal risk of self-injury suggests that they should be treated similarly (i.e. as victim groups) and monitored accordingly (Ireland 1999c). In view of this, the most important question to ask then becomes 'why do victims behave in this way?'

This question can be considered with reference to the inmate code that I described in some detail in Chapter 4 and touched upon at the start of the present chapter. The existence of such a code ensures that any instances of bullying are not likely to be reported to staff for fear of violating this code. This places victims in a difficult position and limits the options that are available to them. It could be argued that they are left with four main options. They can

1   tolerate the abuse
2   reduce the opportunities that the perpetrator has to aggress towards them by isolating themselves
3   retaliate aggressively towards the bully, another prisoner or member of staff
4   engage in another behaviour that ensures that they will receive the attention of staff and, indirectly, their protection, albeit for a short period of time: self-injury can represent such a behaviour.

Livingston and Beck (1997) view self-injury as one way in which a prisoner can communicate their distress to staff without having to be specific about its cause. If there is sufficient concern about their risk of future self-injury, or if the incident is considered severe, then the prisoner may be moved to another location within the prison, either to the hospital on a temporary basis or to a vulnerable prisoner unit for a longer stay. This will ensure that the victim is protected, at least on a temporary basis, from those who are bullying them. This is supported by Power and Spencer (1987) who reported that 50 per cent of offenders who self-injured reported doing so to avoid friction with other prisoners: their self-injury ensured that they would be closely watched by staff thus reducing the chance that they would be victimised.

Self-injury can therefore serve an instrumental function[13] for *some* victims: it enables them to avoid further victimisation without informing on the prisoner who is bullying them (Livingston and Chapman 1997). This may be particularly true for prisoners who cope with difficult situations by attempting to escape or avoid them. This was highlighted by Livingston and Beck (1997) who argue that avoidance strategies are difficult to employ in a prison environment where legitimate ways of avoiding the bullying (i.e. by requesting a change of location) may be refused. Since the options available to avoid the situation are limited, self-injury becomes an effective method of coping. As noted by Livingston and Beck (1997), not only may self-injury ensure sanctuary for the victim but it may also serve an anxiety-reducing function. Similarly, in the same way that aggression can be an adaptive response to bullying, so can self-injury: the potential for physical injury may be greater for the victim if they are unable to avoid the bully. At least if they self-injure they have some control over the extent of this injury.

It could also be argued that bullying indirectly encourages self-injurious behaviour by reducing the extent to which the prisoner social network is available to victims. Victims tend to be stigmatised by the rest of the peer group and will appear at the bottom of the prisoner hierarchy. The victim label that they carry ensures that the social support they receive from other prisoners is limited. This loss of social support may increase their potential to self-injure (Livingston 1997) and force them to rely on staff for support and/or on external forms of support such as family or friends. Both these sources of support are limited and regulated to a certain extent by the prison authorities (e.g. they are allowed a certain number of visits from family and friends per month and limited phone calls). Self-injurious behaviour can thus become effective in two ways

- externally, by producing some (any) change in the prisoner's significant (external) others such as encouraging relatives to get in touch
- internally, with the self-injurer being taken to the hospital with a chance of staying there in what is essentially a comfortable environment and where staff may take more notice of them, for example enquiring as to why they self-injured (Livingston 1997).

Similarly, in a prison where the control that a prisoner is able to exercise over their environment is limited, being bullied may have an increased impact on them by reducing the level of control that they feel they have. If the victim feels that they are unable to control the bullying, or its consequences, self-injury may become one way in which they can exert control on other aspects of their environment. If a prisoner self-injures, a number of procedures are automatically put in place that include an interview by an officer, a visit by a doctor and possible removal to the prison hospital. Control therefore is achieved by virtue of the behaviour's impact on others.

Although a link between self-injurious behaviour and bullying can be suggested, the magnitude of this link is less clear and seems largely dependent on how bullying has been measured and the time period referred to by researchers. This is illustrated by two studies that I conducted that I have already described (Ireland 1999a, 2002d). In the first study, I found levels of self-harm among victims ranging from 4 to 9 per cent, which contrasted with the second study where 35 per cent of victims had been seen as at risk of self-harm or had actually displayed self-harm at some point in their sentence. The difference between these studies can be explained by the different methods that were employed to measure bullying and the different time periods observed. In Ireland (1999a) I measured behaviours indicative of bullying over a 1-week period whereas in Ireland (2002d) I measured self-injurious behaviour retrospectively over a prisoner's sentence using official records. This serves to highlight the importance of further research to clarify the relationship between self-injurious behaviour and bullying before any firm conclusions are drawn. Indeed, O'Donnell and Edgar (1996a) suggest that the strength of the relationship between self-harm and bullying may have been exaggerated. In many ways self-injurious behaviour may represent a perceived response to bullying. In the same way that the perceived characteristics of bullies and/or victims should be interpreted with caution until consistently proven by empirical research (see Chapter 5), so should the perceived link between bullying and self-injury. It is perhaps more appropriate to consider self-injurious behaviour as one of many possible responses to bullying.

It is also important to note that self-injurious behaviour can occur for a range of complex reasons, with the experiences reported by a prisoner during their incarceration, such as bullying, seen as only one of a number of risk factors that also include demographic, mental-health, personal and familial variables (Livingston 1997). Thus, linking self-injury directly to bullying may be too simplistic. Being bullied may sometimes contribute to the victim's behaviour but it may not be a direct cause. The characteristics that a victim possesses may help to determine their response to bullying. It is perhaps more appropriate to say that although bullying can be an important component in the aetiology of self-injurious behaviour (Livingston and Chapman 1997), such behaviour may represent an extreme reaction to being bullied.

Indeed, Liebling comments on how 'one of the limitations of . . . studies of prison suicide has been an assumption that it is a single problem with a single, identifiable profile and a single explanation' (1995: 182). Liebling (1995) describes how there are typologies of prisoners who go on to commit suicide. These include poor copers, prisoners serving long sentences and those who are mentally ill. It is perhaps poor copers for whom being bullied may be a contributing component since it is also this group whose history of previous self-injury is rated as high and whose motivation behind suicide includes isolation, fear and distress (Liebling 1995). All of these motivations have been described in the previous sections as possible reactions to being bullied. Thus the victim who isolates themselves from their peers and displays marked emotional reactions in response to being bullied may be at an increased risk of self-injurious behaviour and possibly suicide. This risk may be increased for those prisoners who also present with a history of self-injurious behaviour.

## Summary

In summary, victims can react to being bullied in a number of ways and it should be expected that they will display more than one response. As I have mentioned throughout this chapter, however, research into reactions to bullying is surprisingly scarce, thus limiting the conclusions that can be drawn. There is a clear need to address other possible reactions to bullying such as stress, physical illness and attitude changes (particularly those towards the use of violence) to name but a few. It would also be of interest to explore the short- and long-term effects of bullying on victims, the extent to which the coping style adopted by the victim mediates these effects, and differences between those who are described as severely bullied versus those who are bullied to a lesser extent.

Undoubtedly, it is only when the reactions of victims are fully understood, along with the context in which they occur, that intervention strategies can be tailored to their individual needs. This will certainly become evident in the following chapters, particularly Chapter 8 when I discuss intervention strategies for dealing with victims. Identifying the range of reactions that victims present with will help to inform staff when a prisoner is being victimised. I touched upon this in Chapter 5 where I argued that staff need to attend to the *symptoms* of bullying, particularly since it is recognised that victims are unlikely to tell staff of their situation. What I have highlighted in the present chapter is that victims should be expected to respond in a range of ways, including ways that may not at first appear to be linked to victimisation, such as displaying aggression towards others including members of staff. I have also highlighted the importance of taking into account the type of victim and the specific population from which they are drawn (men, women, adults or young offenders) when trying to describe how they might react. Such variables are important in the design and implementation of intervention strategies, as I will highlight in the ensuing chapters.

# Chapter 7

# Strategies: I preventing bullying

## Focus of research

As the previous chapters have highlighted, research has focused on the nature and extent of bullying and on the characteristics of those involved. By contrast, what can be done to address bullying is not an area that has been studied systematically and to date there has been no research evaluating the effectiveness of intervention strategies. Being able to offer some guidance on what should, and perhaps more importantly what should not, be used to both prevent bullying and to deal with it once it has occurred is undoubtedly important. This is captured by Beck who states

> Despite the fact that our knowledge about bullying is expanding rapidly, our strategies for combating it are varied and sometimes conflicting. This is a reflection of the recent increase in concern and motivation to improve the conditions and the influences of prison. The attribution of suicides and other self-harm to bullying has highlighted the seriousness of the effects of bullying and focused the attention of management on dealing with the problem.
>
> (Beck 1995: 68)

The UK Prison Service launched its first anti-bullying strategy in 1993 with the publication of a booklet entitled *Bullying in Prison: a Strategy to Beat It* (Home Office Prison Service 1993). It was not mandatory, however, for prisons to have an anti-bullying strategy until 1999 with the publication of a Prison Service Order (PSO) entitled *Anti-bullying Strategy* (Home Office Prison Service 1999). The order represented a comprehensive update of the 1993 strategy and included detailed methods of preventing bullying and a clearer supporting rationale for the interventions suggested. It also included an example of a survey that prisons could use to measure bullying and provided examples of good practice. The improvement in this strategy was probably because of a marked increase in prison-based research conducted between 1993 and 1999 that would have proved helpful in informing the policy. For the 1993 strategy the Prison Service would have had to rely primarily on school-based research (e.g. Olweus 1978, 1992; Askew 1989; Tattum 1989), which may have provided the impetus and ideas for the prison-based research but is of limited value when applied to a prison environment. The Prison Service, however, is now in a position to draw on a developing body of prison-based research specifically addressing bullying.

The UK Prison Service recognises that a number of issues are important for the introduction or review of anti-bullying strategies. These include

1   not focusing on the characteristics of bullies that may help identify them and concentrating instead on the specific types of bullying that are taking place
2   making the strategy meaningful to the local environment and recognising that different groups of prisoners will bully differently
3   recognising that bullying can be both open and hidden
4   recognising the need to avoid stereotyping bullies and victims
5   recognising that prisoners can be both bullies and victims (Home Office Prison Service 1999).

There also appear to be two broad aims of the 1999 strategy: to prevent bullying and to address it constructively when it occurs. To reflect this, in the present chapter I will focus on what are primarily considered *preventative* strategies, whereas in the following chapter I will address *reactive* strategies, namely what should happen once bullying has occurred. Although there is undoubtedly some overlap between preventative and reactive strategies, they are separated here simply for ease of interpretation. In developing a strategy, however, both need to be included. It is also worth noting that although the focus in the present chapter, and in Chapter 8, will be on prison-based bullying, the strategies described can potentially be applied to a range of secure settings including secure hospitals. They may need to be adapted to accommodate the specifics of these environments but in many cases can be adapted with relative ease.

In reviewing the literature on bullying it became apparent that a number of recommendations for improving anti-bullying strategies have been made. Since 1991 there have been a total of thirty-two papers (relating to twenty-five studies, five reviews, one paper addressing specific interventions for bullies and/or victims, and one discussion of an earlier paper) that have made some recommendations for dealing with bullying in a prison setting. Some of these papers dedicate a substantial amount of discussion to how anti-bullying strategies could be improved (e.g. Brookes *et al.* 1994; Ireland and Hill 2001). Developing anti-bullying strategies that have some impact on bullying can be a difficult task: bullying is not a behaviour that can be removed entirely from secure settings and eradicating it is an unobtainable goal that should not form the focus of any strategy. As I described in Chapter 4, bullying is a product both of the environment and the individuals housed within it, and it should be considered an expected element of incarceration. Instead the main focus of intervention strategies should be on reducing bullying. Importantly, it should be acknowledged at this point that strategies can only have an impact on bullying if they are well resourced. This would allow them to be implemented correctly and maintained and developed over time.

In reviewing the recommendations made by researchers and those included in the 1999 Prison Service anti-bullying strategy, a number of broad themes relating to prevention emerged. These were

1   making changes to the environment
2   educating staff and prisoners about bullying
3   improving communication
4   increasing prisoner involvement in the strategy
5   assessment and monitoring
6   other strategies.

Each of these themes will be described in turn. Some have already been implemented in some prisons. The implementation of a recommended strategy, however, is not necessarily an indication of its appropriateness. In some instances strategies have been implemented based on poor evidence and assumptions made by researchers. Thus in the present chapter I aim not only to describe the recommendations but also to evaluate them where possible. I will conclude with a summary of the elements that anti-bullying strategies should contain if they hope to have an impact on preventing bullying, with an aim of informing the development of consequent anti-bullying strategies.

## Themes of intervention

### Making changes to the environment

This theme refers to changes that could be made both to the physical and social environment. It includes making changes to the structure of the physical environment, changing the supervision of prisoner areas, increasing stimuli for prisoners, increasing vigilance, controlling and monitoring material goods and increasing the involvement of officers through raised levels of prisoner contact. Intervening at an environmental level is important, particularly since it is recognised that both the physical and social environment play an important role in encouraging and maintaining bullying (see Chapter 4). Although certain aspects of the environment are outside the control of prison authorities, some, as will be highlighted below, are not. Indeed, a number of strategies can be employed to reduce bullying or rather make it harder for bullies to engage in such behaviour by reducing the opportunities that they have to bully.

## Structural changes

Approximately one-fifth of papers reviewed suggested such changes. This included installing gates or barriers within prison wings in order to break them up into smaller more manageable units (Brookes *et al.* 1994), installing CCTV cameras on the wing and in locations where bullying is known to occur (Brookes *et al.* 1994; Loucks 1998; Brookes and Pratt 1996), and fitting locks to cell doors that would enable prisoners to lock their own cells on departure (Brookes *et al.* 1994), thus reducing incidences of theft-related bullying. For prisons that housed prisoners in dormitories as opposed to cells, McGurk and McDougall (1986) suggested placing light switches on the outside wall of each dormitory as opposed to within the dormitory. This would enable officers patrolling at night to view inside the dormitory quickly if they suspected that bullying may be taking place. O'Donnell and Edgar (1996b), however, suggested that dormitories should be abolished altogether and converted into double cells where possible. This latter point would be one way of reducing bullying, with dormitories considered a prime location for bullying. Converting dormitories into cells is an expensive option and prisons may choose instead to use less expensive strategies such as monitoring dormitories more closely and carefully selecting which prisoners are placed in dormitories together. Specifically selecting prisoners to be housed in dormitories is not an easy task: there has been some suggestion of accommodating friends together in the dormitories as one method. O'Donnell and Edgar (1996b) raise particular concerns about this, stating how it may allow for the development of a cohesive and potentially troublesome group that could lead to control problems on the wing.

Making changes to the structure of the physical environment is an intervention emphasised in the 1999 Prison Service strategy, with many of the strategies described above forming part of this strategy. This strategy also describes making changes aimed at reducing particular types of bullying, for example in order to reduce bullies intimidating victims by shouting out of the cell window at them, it is suggested that numbers be placed on the outside of each cell window so that the location, and thus identification, of the bully can be quickly ascertained by staff.

## Changes to the supervision of prisoner areas

Sixteen per cent of papers reviewed suggested making improvements to how prisoners were supervised. Suggestions included increasing officer patrols of prisoner areas and supervising prisoners more closely at vulnerable times such as recreational periods, movement to the dining hall and the prison shop (Brookes *et al.* 1994; Brookes and Pratt 1996). Brookes and colleagues (1994) also suggested employing more staff, particularly at the weekends or during periods where prisoners are allowed to associate with one another. Both O'Donnell and Edgar (1996b) and McGurk and McDougall (1986) suggested that dormitory accommodation should be supervised to a greater extent than cells, and that officers supervising dormitories at night should vary the timing of their visits. McGurk and McDougall (1986) also suggested that a governor should make one visit at night to each prisoner unit. The 1999 Prison Service strategy also referred to this area in some detail and mentioned all of the above suggestions.

Supervision is an important area to address and was highlighted as such in Chapter 4. Although it is accepted that staff cannot monitor all prisoners 24 hours a day it may be more important to vary the amount of supervision that they can provide, particularly by increasing it at times of high risk for bullying (e.g. during recreational periods). In addition, recommendations include making the supervision less predictable. This is a particularly useful suggestion: by making supervision less predictable (i.e. by varying the frequency and timing of staff patrols) it becomes less easy for bullies to predict when they will have an opportunity to bully others. Thus, strategies should consider not only ways of increasing supervision at times of high risk but also ways of making supervision less predictable. In addition, strategies could consider increasing the visibility of staff. This may be just as important as increasing the actual physical supervision and may help to improve levels of perceived supervision (Ireland 2002a).

## Increased vigilance

Approximately one-third of papers reviewed referred to increasing the general vigilance of staff. Brookes and Pratt (1996) suggested searching prisoners more on visits, on outside work parties and on return from temporary release, in order to prevent bullies from successfully pressurising victims to smuggle contraband items into the prison. Encouraging greater staff vigilance to prevent prisoners from borrowing from and lending to each other, which is against prison rules (O'Donnell and Edgar 1996b), and compulsory body checks on prisoners by staff every morning to detect physical injuries (McGurk and McDougall 1986) were also suggested.

O'Donnell and Edgar (1997) also argue that although officers may not be directly informed about bullying at the time that it occurs, they are likely to learn about some types of bullying such as cell thefts and even exclusion. Evidence for cell theft may become apparent after a cell search and for exclusion by observing how prisoners interact with one another during association. O'Donnell and Edgar (1997) suggest that officers should therefore make a record of all prisoners suspected to be victims of cell theft or exclusion to help them identify those who are likely to be vulnerable to other types of bullying as well such as physical or verbal assault. Indeed, as I highlighted in Chapter 3, it is not uncommon for victims to report more than one type of aggression (Ireland 2002e).

This notion of looking for evidence that a prisoner is being bullied is also consistent with the views that I expressed in Chapter 5. It is acknowledged that victims will find it difficult to report bullying and instead the onus is on staff to look for the 'symptoms' of bullying. These symptoms should include not only the more direct indicators of bullying, such as physical injuries or stolen possessions, but also more subtle indicators such as the behaviours displayed by suspected victims. These behaviours can include increased negative behaviour towards staff, involvement in drug-related activity, self-injurious behaviour, aggression, avoidance and/or social isolation (see Chapters 5 and 6). The more vigilant staff are in observing and recording such behaviours or responses the more likely it is that they will correctly identify prisoners who are being bullied. This highlights the importance of staff becoming more vigilant and learning to recognise how victims react to bullying. This may be particularly important in a male prison where victims may be more reluctant to admit to being victimised because it conflicts with the masculine image of toughness (Ireland 1999c).

## Increased stimuli for prisoners

Ten per cent of papers reviewed made reference to increasing the stimuli available for prisoners. This included increasing the number and quality of activities available during association periods (Brookes *et al.* 1994), locating televisions in each dormitory[14] (McGurk and McDougall 1986), increasing the number of privileges available (Power *et al.* 1997), making attendance at education compulsory, creating opportunities for more purposeful activities such as creating extra work parties and encouraging prisoners to take part in them (Brookes *et al.* 1994), and providing prisoners with more activities that they can do in their own time such as cell work and board games.

Lack of stimulation was identified as one aspect of the prison environment that may prove important to a further understanding of bullying (see Chapter 4). Thus, addressing this may go some way in helping to prevent bullying by alleviating the monotony, frustration and boredom of prison life that may act to promote violence (Cooke 1991; Brookes *et al.* 1994). As I noted in Chapter 4, however, it may not be the feelings of boredom and frustration induced by a low-stimulation environment that are important in explaining bullying. It may instead be that prisoners bully since they do not have anything to lose by not co-operating with the regime, as they are not taking part in any meaningful activities. By encouraging all prisoners to take part in and invest time in activities such as work or education the cost of bullying for them is increased. As I stated in Chapter 4 'Any evidence of bullying could result in a withdrawal of their privilege to engage in such activities and thus deter them from bullying as they now have something to lose.'

It should be recognised, however, that a lack of stimulation may not explain all incidents of bullying. This would be too simplistic a view and would fail to acknowledge the many different motivations behind bullying. In addition, it may well be that only bullies who possess psychopathic traits would be motivated to bully others in order to alleviate feelings of boredom. Indeed, a need for stimulation or proneness to boredom is one component of psychopathy (Hare 1998). Although research has yet to be completed addressing the role of psychopathy in bullying, I speculated in Chapter 5 that pure bullies may be the group most likely to possess such traits. In view of the small proportion of bullies who are classified as pure bullies, however, it could be speculated that a lack of stimulation may only help to explain a minority of bullying incidents.

## Controlling and monitoring material goods

I discussed the role of material goods in the promotion of bullying in Chapter 4. In short, access to material goods is limited in prisons making them a valuable form of currency. Goods such as tobacco, phonecards and toiletries are particularly sought-after items, as well as illicit items such as drugs and alcohol. Theft-related bullying is well established in prisons as evidenced by the specific terms that prisoners use to describe it, namely baroning (where material goods are provided to prisoners and repayment demanded with a high rate of interest by the baron), and taxing (taking goods off prisoners under the pretence of taking for tax). Failure to pay back a loan to a baron can lead to the victim being verbally threatened or physically assaulted, and the behaviour of taxing can include the use of verbal and/or physical bullying in order to secure goods. Thus, the monitoring and controlling of material goods becomes a high priority in prisons. Approximately one-fifth of papers reviewed suggested this as a useful intervention in bullying. Specific suggestions included marking phonecards with the owner's name and holding them in the wing office when not being used, marking valuable items with an ultraviolet pen that would assist in the identification and return of stolen property (O'Donnell and Edgar 1996b), a closer checking of prisoner property cards (Home Office Prison Service 1999), discouraging the use and trafficking of controlled drugs and thus making it harder for them to be brought into the prison (Brookes *et al.* 1994; Ireland and Archer 1996; Willmot 1997), and helping prisoners with drug problems in order to reduce the market for drugs (Brookes *et al.* 1994).

Other suggestions included advancing earnings to all new prisoners who have not yet had the chance to earn any money in the prison and keeping prison shop prices low (Brookes and Pratt 1996). This would discourage prisoners from getting themselves into debt. Similarly, the 1999 Prison Service strategy suggests providing new receptions who have no belongings with a 'reception bag' that will help get them through the first few days of incarceration without having to borrow from other prisoners (Home Office Prison Service 1999). O'Donnell and Edgar recommended changes to how canteen facilities are provided to prisoners (e.g. how they purchase goods from the prison shop), stating that this could be a high-risk time for bullying, where prisoners had to 'run the gauntlet of other prisoners who had the opportunity to judge whether items were worth taking or trading' (1996b: 4). O'Donnell and Edgar (1996b) felt that such difficulties could be avoided if prisoners were able to submit an order that could be delivered to them individually and in private. It has also been suggested that prisoners be allowed to spend more of their own money (Brookes *et al.* 1994) and that their wages should be increased (Ireland and Archer 1996; Power *et al.* 1997). Both these latter suggestions were made by prisoners themselves. It is unlikely, however, that they would be useful: by allowing prisoners to spend or earn more money you could encourage them to harbour more materials that they could then sell at a higher cost to other prisoners.

Although it is accepted that there will always be restrictions on material goods in secure environments that will help to maintain their value to prisoners and encourage bullying, strategies can still be introduced that will help to reduce bullying. The most important elements of such strategies relate to the close monitoring of the material goods that prisoners have, or conversely don't have, and the generation of ways in which prisoners can avoid getting themselves into debt in the first place. Once they have accrued a debt it becomes difficult to help victims, since failure to repay a debt is a violation of the inmate code and a rationale for their continued victimisation. Eradicating the need for some material goods is a particularly useful strategy that can be employed. One of the best examples of such a strategy relates to current developments in the UK Prison Service with regard to the management of prisoner phonecards: the Prison Service is at present developing a phone system for prisoners that will replace the need for such cards. All prisoners will be provided with a personal identification number which they can key into the phone to allow access. In some prisons (high-security establishments), prisoners will be asked to provide a list of phone numbers that they intend to use and these will be verified by the authorities and placed onto their individual account. Numbers not placed onto this account by the prisoner concerned cannot be accessed (Home Office Prison Service 2001). It is hoped that this will reduce the incidence of bullying relating to phonecard thefts.

### Involving officers through increased prisoner contact

This is included here since it focuses on one aspect of the social environment, namely the relationship between staff and prisoners. Bullying is not a behaviour that occurs in isolation from the peer group. The extent to which the peer group supports bullies and disapproves of victims can determine the prevalence of bullying as a whole. In order to tackle bullying effectively, all members of the peer group must become involved. The involvement of prison officers in anti-bullying strategies becomes essential since they too, by means of sharing the same environment as prisoners, become part of this wider peer group, and the attitudes and beliefs that they hold towards bullying may help to reinforce it as much as those of prisoners. Encouraging prosocial, co-operative relationships between prisoners is one way of tackling bullying. The effectiveness of such a method would be enhanced further if officers ensured that they were also involved in promoting such relationships. This is recognised by the 1999 Prison Service strategy which encourages staff to act as positive role models and states how both staff and prisoners must work together to reduce bullying. It also corresponds to the idea of a 'whole prison approach' that will be addressed later in the section on multidisciplinary approaches (pp. 170–171).

One-fifth of papers reviewed suggested ways in which staff and prisoners could work together to prevent bullying. Ireland (1998) recommended that prisoners and staff work together on induction programmes[15] to help promote co-operation and trust, and both Brookes and colleagues (1994) and Willmot (1997) recommended that staff be seen as available, approachable and sympathetic listeners. In prisons where personal or group officer schemes are not in place, consideration should be given to setting up such schemes where prisoners are allocated a nominated officer(s) should they have any concerns that they wish to discuss. Brookes and colleagues (1994) also argued that by improving the quality of staff–prisoner relationships, prisoners may begin to trust staff more and provide more information about bullying. Interestingly, this latter point was a suggestion made by both the staff and the prisoners in this study. One way of achieving this may be by increasing the presence of staff on the units to allow them to interact more with prisoners to discuss problems (McGurk and McDougall 1986; Loucks 1998). In addition. Loucks (1998) and O'Donnell and Edgar (1997) suggested that prisons encourage a sense of 'joint responsibility' between staff and prisoners regarding the prevention of bullying. This is an important point: if an anti-bullying strategy is simply imposed on prisoners by staff, prisoners will be less likely to buy into it. If, however, the strategy is seen as a collaboration between staff and prisoners, with each having a clear role in its creation and development, then its effectiveness could be enhanced. The importance of increasing prisoner involvement will be discussed in more detail in the section addressing involving prisoners in the strategy (pp. 163–166).

## Educating staff and prisoners about bullying

Education is an area often not emphasised enough in anti-bullying strategies. Indeed, it receives only a brief mention in the 1999 Prison Service strategy where it is recommended that staff receive awareness training on the nature and consequences of bullying and about the local strategy that is in place to tackle bullying (Home Office Prison Service 1999). Educating both staff and prisoners on all aspects of bullying behaviour should form a fundamental part of any strategy. It is crucial in terms of preventing bullying, helping staff and prisoners to recognise when bullying is taking place, developing and maintaining intervention programmes and ensuring consistency in staff approaches to bullying. Indeed, over half of all papers reviewed referred to educating staff and prisoners on a variety of issues relating to bullying.

The content, or rather the accuracy, of the education is also important and it should include both an overview of the literature on bullying, an avoidance of the stereotyping of bullies and victims, and training in how the anti-bullying strategy operates. It should also occur at regular intervals to ensure that staff and prisoners do not become complacent about bullying and to ensure that they are kept up-to-date with findings from the literature. I highlighted this in Chapter 1 where it was recognised that knowledge about bullying among prisoners is steadily increasing. Providing additional and/or regular booster training on what bullying is and how to deal with it, is one way of minimising the effects of complacency and ensuring that staff remain up-to-date with the most recent research evidence (Ireland and Hill 2001). Equal weight should also be given to the education of both staff and prisoners and this reflects earlier comments that I made about ensuring that strategies are seen as a collaboration between staff and prisoners. The elements of this education are summarised below.

### Staff education

Eighteen of the papers reviewed (Ireland 2000; Ireland and Ireland 2000; Ireland 1998; O'Donnell and Edgar 1996b, 1997; Ireland 1999b, 1999c, 2000c; Osiowy 1997; Bolt 1999; Brookes *et al*. 1994; Brookes and Pratt 1996; McGurk and McDougall 1986; Ireland and Hill 2001; Willmot 1997; Ireland and Archer 1996; Marshall 1993; Ireland *et al*. 1999) made some suggestions about what areas education should address. These included

- the importance of attitudes in bullying, namely that negative attitudes towards victims and positive attitudes towards bullies may help to maintain bullying behaviour
- the different types of bullying, particularly the distinction between direct and indirect bullying
- the prevalence of indirect bullying and its effects

- awareness of the different types of bullying preferred by different groups of prisoners (i.e. adults, young offenders, juveniles, men, women)
- awareness of the distinction between the different bully categories (i.e. pure bully, bully/victim, pure victim, not-involved)
- awareness that the victim's aggressor may not always be another prisoner but can be a member of staff: just over one-quarter of prisoners in the study conducted by Ireland (1998) raised the concern that they were being bullied by staff
- the use of terms to describe the vulnerable and victimised, for example terms such as 'fraggle', 'nonce' and 'muppet' are widely used by prisoners, and sometimes staff, to describe such prisoners. These terms are dehumanising, cause great distress, and trivialise the seriousness of the problem. O'Donnell and Edgar (1997) state how use of such labels is unacceptable, should always be challenged by staff, and never used by them
- how the victim can be supported
- how incidents of bullying should be recorded and what information is essential
- how incidents of bullying should be responded to
- all aspects of the anti-bullying strategy
- how to identify the symptoms or signs of bullying including the distress felt by victims
- how to identify the characteristics of bullies and/or victims
- the skills needed to interview prisoners suspected of bullying others.

*Prisoner education*

There were some similarities between the suggestions made for the education of prisoners and those made for staff. This included making clear reference to the importance of attitudes in bullying (Ireland and Ireland 2000; Ireland 1999b), highlighting the effects of bullying (Willmot 1997; Ireland and Archer 1996), the different types of bullying, particularly the distinction between direct and indirect bullying (Ireland and Ireland 2000), and reinforcing all aspects of the anti-bullying strategy and what it includes (Bolt 1999).

In addition, Willmot (1997) emphasised the importance of educating prisoners on the benefits of a bullying-free environment and on the responsibility that they all have for stopping and reporting bullying (even if they just witness it). Training on the specific skills needed to help prisoners avoid being bullied has been suggested, including advising them not to have valuable goods in their possession and to avoid getting into debt, or providing advice on how to budget their money and resources to avoid having to borrow from others (Brookes and Pratt 1996; Willmot 1997; Brookes *et al*. 1994; Ireland 2000c). Ireland (2000c) also suggested educating prisoners that baroning is a form of bullying, and that just because it is a widespread behaviour does not mean that it is acceptable. The consequences of failing to repay a debt in this instance could also be emphasised, namely that it can lead to further bullying. Other specific recommendations have included providing more information to prisoners on who can help should they become victims (Brookes *et al*. 1994) and encouraging prisoners to report victimisation and not to be supportive of bullies (Ireland *et al*. 1999; Bolt 1999).

The timing of the education is also important. Ideally it should be provided when prisoners are first received onto the unit or as part of the prisoner induction programme (O'Donnell and Edgar 1996b; Osiowy 1997; Ireland 1998). Brookes *et al*. (1994) recommended that on arrival into the establishment prisoners should be provided with compacts that they should sign which clearly state what the prison policy is with regard to bullying. This was viewed as one way of obtaining prisoner commitment to the strategy. Targeting prisoners while they are still fairly new to the environment also provides the prison with an opportunity to set ground rules by making its own definition of bullying. Prisoners are thus aware of what constitutes bullying from day one (Loucks 1998). The same should also apply to staff new to the prison. All should be aware from their first day what bullying is. As mentioned earlier, it is also important that any education provided to both prisoners and staff should be continually reinforced and additional training, or booster training, provided at regular intervals.

In summary, although this section has highlighted a number of areas that both staff and prisoner education should include, there are four areas that are perhaps most important.

1   Ensuring that staff and prisoners are aware that there is an anti-bullying strategy in place and how it operates. Ensuring that they are simply aware that a strategy is in place is not sufficient, all must have a good working knowledge of it.

2   Both prisoners and staff should be able to recognise all of the different types of bullying, in particular indirect bullying. Ireland (1999c) states how it is easy to dismiss activities such as social exclusion, gossiping and playing practical jokes as a widespread form of behaviour, and therefore normalising it. Many individuals,

however, remain unaware of the negative effects that this has on victims, and being educated in this way helps them to recognise it when it takes place and thus prevent it. Making indirect bullying easier to detect increases the likelihood that it will be responded to and punished appropriately, and thus decreases its use by bullies.

3    The distinction between the pure bully and bully/victim group needs to be reinforced, particularly to staff. The 1999 Prison Service strategy does state that a prisoner can be both a bully and a victim. This is not expanded on in any detail, however, and no specific recommendations are made for the different interventions that should be applied to these two groups. Research has consistently shown bully/victims to be one of the most prevalent groups among prisoners (Ireland 1999c). Intervention strategies should not, therefore, be based on the principle that there are just two groups – bullies and victims – with an emphasis on punishing the bully and supporting the victim. Strategies need to recognise bully/victims as a distinct group, and also to generate ways of dealing with their behaviour (Ireland 2000c). I will discuss this in more detail in Chapter 8.

4    The importance of tackling bullying in a prison environment from both a staff and a 'prison' perspective. This should also include discussion of the impact of bullying on victims and recognition of the range of reactions that they may show.

In addition, there are three rules that education or training programmes should observe.

1    That the content of the education is as accurate as possible and grounded in literature. It should not be based solely on anecdotal evidence and the perceptions of staff and prisoners, for example education should not focus on describing the characteristics of the different groups involved in bullying according to the perceptions that prisoners and staff have of them, without assessing the accuracy of these perceptions. As I highlighted in Chapter 5, a number of the perceived characteristics associated with bullies and victims have not actually been supported by empirical research and reinforcing these characteristics as facts may be potentially damaging and lead to the stereotyping of both bullies and victims.

2    That the content of the education is regularly updated and improved as knowledge about bullying increases.

3    That both staff and prisoners receive education on bullying at regular intervals to avoid complacency and encourage consistency in responses to bullying from staff.

## Improving communication

Although this theme is closely related to that of education it refers in this instance to a general level of communication about the strategy across the regime as a whole that is not restricted to a period of training or education. It refers to improving communication in three ways

1    communicating the anti-bullying policies and strategies effectively
2    discussing bullying within the prison
3    involving prisoners' families and visitors as much as possible.

Each of these areas will be discussed in turn.

### Effective communication of policies and strategies

Having an anti-bullying strategy and/or policy in place should represent the starting point of dealing with bullying and the importance of such strategies is emphasised in the 1999 Prison Service strategy (Home Office Prison Service 1999). Once in place it is essential that these strategies are then communicated effectively both to staff and prisoners. One-third of all papers reviewed recognised this as an important element in reducing bullying. Communicating the consequences of being suspected of bullying others to all prisoners (Brookes et al. 1994; Ireland and Hill 2001), the effects of bullying on victims and the benefits of a bullying-free environment (Brookes et al. 1994) were particularly important elements of the anti-bullying strategy that researchers felt needed to be emphasised.

A number of ways of achieving this were suggested, for example publicising the strategy through prisoner-induction programmes (Livingston et al. 1994), placing notices or posters detailing the strategy on all units (Brookes and Pratt 1996; Ireland 1999c, 1999f, 2000c; Ireland and Hill 2001), and providing leaflets to all prisoners that detail whom they should contact if they become the victims of bullying (Brookes et al. 1994). Brookes and Pratt (1996) also recommended the creation of 'How can you help?' sheets published for staff, and 'Are you being bullied?' and 'What to do if you are being bullied' handouts for prisoners. In addition, both Brookes and Pratt (1996) and Ireland and Hill (2001) suggested developing prison newsletters. Brookes and Pratt (1996) described how such newsletters could include articles on the anti-bullying strategy, with Ireland and Hill (2001) noting that they should avoid including specific incidents of bullying and focus more on the opinions of staff and prisoners about bullying. Crucially, the Prison Service now also recognises the importance of publicising the strategy in a number of relevant languages and of making it more accessible for prisoners with reading difficulties (Home Office Prison Service 1999).

The identification of a specific officer as responsible for collating information on actual and suspected incidents of bullying has also been identified as a useful strategy (Ireland and Hill 2001). Importantly, such officers should be trained in the anti-bullying policies and procedures and should represent an 'anti-bullying co-ordinator'. Many prisons already employ officers in this role. Generally, such co-ordinators are restricted to one prisoner unit, although it is recognised that their role could be emphasised if there was a co-ordinator placed on each prisoner unit within an establishment (Ireland and Hill 2001; Ireland 1998; Ireland 1999c). Employing a member of staff in this role acts to increase the profile of the strategy, represents an extra resource for staff wishing to report an incident of bullying (Ireland and Hill 2001), and is a contact point for other staff should they have any specific ideas, problems or queries concerning any area of bullying (Osiowy 1997). Making anti-bullying strategies high profile on all units through the use of such strategies may have a very positive effect in reducing the level of bullying behaviour (Ireland 1999c, 1999f, 2000c). Indeed, since the publication of the 1999 Prison Service Strategy (Home Office Prison Service 1999) it is now mandatory for all prisons to have an anti-bullying co-ordinator in place who is responsible for co-ordinating, developing, implementing and maintaining the strategy. It should be noted, however, that appointing an anti-bullying co-ordinator is not enough in itself, unless there is an acknowledgement that they have to be provided with sufficient time to carry out their role effectively.

Some researchers also suggested making the contents of any surveys into bullying available to all areas of the prison, including the hospital, education, chapel and gym, etc. (Ireland 1999c). Again, this ensures that all staff who work within the establishment have access to surveys, thus reinforcing the 'whole-prison approach' to bullying. The results could also be communicated to prisoners and a copy of the survey made available to them via the prison library (Ireland and Hill 2001). This latter point is certainly missing from the majority of prison strategies, yet it is an important one to consider. In the majority of cases it is prisoners who are completing the survey questionnaires and thus it is important to feed back to them, as participants, the results. The results of such surveys could be discussed with prisoners and would represent a good starting point for the discussions held in focus groups with prisoners (the use of which will be discussed in more detail on p. 164).

## Discussing bullying within the prison

Ten per cent of papers referred to a structure being set up within the prison that would allow for formal and informal discussions of bullying. This could take the form of anti-bullying committees, made up of staff from a range of disciplines, who would take responsibility for devising and updating anti-bullying strategies and procedures (Osiowy 1997). This is a strategy that has been adopted by the majority of prisons in the United Kingdom. It could also include committees made up of both prisoners and staff to discuss problems (Loucks 1998). The creation of a multi-disciplinary anti-bullying committee was seen as crucial by the 1999 Prison Service strategy (Home Office Prison Service 1999). It was suggested that their role should be one of monitoring and managing the anti-bullying strategy, and that they should be linked to other relevant committees such as those dealing with suicide awareness. Although it is important that there should be communication between all related committees, prisons should avoid merging them together. There have been instances in the past, for example, where joint 'suicide awareness and anti-bullying' meetings have been held in some establishments. By doing so there is a direct link made between self-harm as a consequence of bullying. Both, however, represent unique problems and as such should be considered separately. Although a link has been suggested between the two, the magnitude of this relationship is questionable and self-injurious behaviour should not be overemphasised: it represents one of many possible responses to bullying.

## Involving prisoners' families and visitors

Only two papers referred to the importance of providing information to prisoners' families and visitors. They suggested that families be informed about what can be done to prevent bullying, and that there should be a confidential contact point for the families of victims to report incidents to prison staff if they become aware that their family member is being bullied (Brookes et al. 1994; Brookes and Pratt 1996). In addition, all visitors could be given a notice on arrival to the prison that invites them to avoid encouraging or assisting bullying (Brookes and Pratt 1996).

It is important to include families and visitors in the anti-bullying strategy, particularly since they may become implicated in the bullying themselves: victims who are being pressured by bullies may ask their family or visitors to bring in or send them certain goods which they will then be forced to hand over to the bully. These goods can include illicit items such as drugs, or other desirable items such as batteries, toiletries or money that can be used to purchase goods from the canteen. Family members and visitors should be encouraged to monitor what they are being asked to bring in and to raise any suspicions or concerns that they may have either with the prisoner and/or staff. In addition, family members or visitors may also become involved since the prisoner may confide in them that they either have been bullied or are afraid that they may be (although it is acknowledged that prisoners may not inform their families to avoid worrying them). Informing families and visitors of the options available to them if they want to report bullying thus becomes important. This was highlighted in the 1999 Prison Service strategy (Home Office Prison Service 1999) which stated that the anti-bullying strategy should be communicated more effectively to prison visitors, and that visitors should be made aware of how they can contribute to the strategy. Specific suggestions included allowing visitors to complete questionnaires on which they could record their own observations of bullying, and making provisions for visitors to raise their concerns about bullying by providing a nominated person whom they could contact. Involving families and prison visitors in the strategy is crucial. In many instances they could represent the voice of a prisoner who is too scared to report their victimisation to staff. One could expect the risk of being labelled as a grass to be reduced if the responsibility for reporting the bullying is left to the family member or visitor and not the victim. This element is often neglected in anti-bullying strategies with resources channelled more towards prisoners and staff.

### Increasing prisoner involvement in the strategy

This theme has been touched upon in the other sections and is discussed here separately to reflect the importance of including prisoners as much as possible in the creation, maintenance and development of any anti-bullying strategy. Prisoners do have a significant contribution to make in reducing the level of bullying behaviour (O'Donnell and Edgar 1997), and they should be encouraged to take responsibility for this (Brookes *et al.* 1994; O'Donnell and Edgar 1997). Approximately one-third of papers recognised the importance of including prisoners as much as possible in the strategy.

The involvement that prisoners have can be as simple as encouraging them to create anti-bullying posters, leaflets or newsletters (Ireland 1998, 1999c, 2000c) or allowing them to have direct input into meetings where the anti-bullying strategy is discussed (Brookes *et al.* 1994; Willmot 1997). This latter point was also mentioned in the section on improving communication (p. 161) and is perhaps one of the most useful strategies to adopt. The exact form that this input takes is up to the discretion of the prison. It could include something as innocuous as a written report from a nominated prisoner, or prisoners, or an agenda item on the meeting set aside for prisoner views (a nominated prisoner could attend for this item without having to attend the whole meeting). The importance of fully representing the views of prisoners in such meetings was recognised by the 1999 Prison Service strategy that recommended 'prisoner representatives' be considered when anti-bullying staff committees are set up (Home Office Prison Service 1999). This could lead to the development of a prisoner anti-bullying committee, with prisoners selected for this committee (by other prisoners and staff) providing feedback to and from staff anti-bullying meetings (Ireland and Hill 2001). Aside from allowing prisoners to take part in formal meetings, informal meetings could also take place. This could include focus groups with prisoners where the effectiveness of the policy and how it could be improved could be discussed. Staff could act as facilitators in such meetings (Ireland 1999c). Such groups have been found to be very useful in terms of generating ideas for dealing with bullies and victims, and identifying problems with the strategy (Ireland and Hill 2001).

One role in which prisoners could be particularly proactive is that of education. Prisoners could be used as 'peer educators' (Ireland 1999c, 2000c) who, after being trained in the anti-bullying strategy, could educate other prisoners on the strategy and perhaps even be used to lead the focus groups described previously (Ireland and Hill 2001). These peer educators could also deliver an anti-bullying package as part of the prisoner induction programme (Ireland and Hill 2001). It is important, however, that such educators following a clear and consistent programme, possibly in the form of an 'anti-bullying strategy package' (Ireland 1999c). Such education could also be provided with members of staff acting as co-tutors with the prisoners, reinforcing the notion of the strategy being a collaborative effort between staff and prisoners.

Anti-bullying strategies devised and implemented without the direct involvement of prisoners are not likely to be very effective. Involving prisoners in anti-bullying strategies can only enhance their effectiveness. This is particularly important since the control that prisoners have over decisions about their care and management is limited and anti-authoritarian attitudes are encouraged by the prisoner subculture. Prisoners should be viewed very much as 'customers' of the anti-bullying strategy. In the same way that no company would market a product without first consulting its potential customers, anti-bullying programmes should not be implemented without consulting prisoners. If prisons are to be audited on the effectiveness of their anti-bullying strategy they need to acknowledge and accommodate the role of the prisoner. The 1999 Prison Service strategy does describe how prisoners should be included but this is limited to informing them of what the strategy includes and what is expected of them, perhaps allowing them to air their views through a prisoner representative at the staff anti-bullying committee meetings and considering allowing prisoners to come up with their own anti-bullying posters (Home Office Prison Service 1999). No mention is made of using prisoners in the creation and further development of the strategy. Prisoners should play an active role in the creation of these strategies, have the option to suggest changes to the strategy and be consulted when changes to the strategy are to take place.

Although the involvement of prisoners should be encouraged in all anti-bullying strategies, this does need to be carefully managed in terms of being clear about what they should and should not become involved in. Prisoners should certainly be involved in developing, maintaining and implementing the strategy, but their direct involvement in other aspects, such as protecting potential victims, should be considered with care. Some researchers, for example, have suggested setting up a 'chaperone' scheme whereby trustworthy and mature long-term prisoners could be encouraged, by means of suitable incentives, to look after potential victims of bullying (Brookes *et al.* 1994; Willmot 1997). There are two points of concern here. First, the onus is on staff to ensure that these 'trustworthy and mature' prisoners are not in fact bullies. In view of the lack of research addressing the actual characteristics of the different groups involved in bullying it can be very difficult to identify who the bullies are, particularly pure bullies who do not appear to stand out from their peers. In choosing a chaperone staff need to be very careful that they have not placed the victim at risk. The victim in this instance may find it difficult to report to staff that they are being bullied – who would believe the victim who tells staff that they are being bullied by a prisoner whom the staff have specifically chosen to protect them? Second, such schemes need to be carefully managed. If incentives are provided for these chaperones, then they are in effect being paid to 'protect' other prisoners. Even without being given an overt incentive, prisoners may be rewarded for protecting others in terms of accruing status among their peers. It is also worth noting that if similar chaperone schemes were developed solely by prisoners they could in some instances, where the original principles of the scheme became subverted, be described as 'protection rackets'. Such rackets would be condoned by the prison authorities and could be construed both as a form of bullying and as a potential threat to the management of the prison regime.

Authorities need to be careful that they are not seen to be legitimising such protection schemes. In view of these issues such 'chaperone' schemes should not be recommended.

### Assessment and monitoring

This theme refers to three main areas

1   predicting risk
2   managing the composition of the prisoner population
3   monitoring and evaluating the strategies that are in place.

Approximately half of all papers reviewed included reference to at least one of these areas.

#### Predicting risk

This element is similar to the one that recommends increased vigilance from staff. In this instance the focus is on trying to predict which prisoners may be at risk of becoming a victim and/or a bully before they have had much opportunity to mix with other prisoners. This includes designating one unit (or part of one unit) as an induction unit where prisoners could be located when they first arrive. The aim of this is to allow staff to get to know the prisoners and identify those individuals likely to become involved in bullying (Willmot 1997). Although induction units are common in prisons, their role as a method of assessing prisoners for potential bullying is not clear. In fact, a common method is to locate new prisoners on a totally separate induction unit and then move them into the main regime. Some prisoners report that being moved from the induction unit to a main unit can be a risky time for bullying, particularly if they are anxious about moving and mixing with other prisoners and their anxiety becomes apparent to other, more dominant, prisoners. Managing this transition thus becomes important. A more appropriate strategy may be to designate a number of cells near to the staff office as 'observation cells' where prisoners from induction units can be placed upon arrival at a main unit. Staff can observe them more closely over a set period of time while at the same time allowing the new prisoner to become adjusted to their new surroundings.

The 1999 Prison Service strategy also describes a 'cell allocation' policy that allows new people in custody to be placed in a cell adjacent to, or sharing a cell with, a more experienced prisoner (Home Office Prison Service 1999). Placing new prisoners with more experienced prisoners is not an ideal solution, particularly since experience, as measured by the total length of time that a prisoner has spent in custody, is actually a risk factor associated with bullying others. Prisoners who have managed to establish themselves in the prison will automatically possess a degree of power over newcomers. Thus, housing new prisoners with more experienced prisoners may actually place them at risk of being bullied. You may also be placing the potential victim in a situation that they may find difficult to escape from. If this experienced prisoner bullies them, the victim will find it difficult to report the abuse, not only because this would violate the inmate code of not informing on others but also because the bully is obviously a prisoner trusted by staff. Such bullies may be more likely to get away with it as the staff may be inclined not to believe the victim. Thus, housing new prisoners with experienced prisoners may inadvertently facilitate bullying.

## Managing the composition of the prisoner population

This refers to monitoring the composition of the prisoner populations on units, in terms of what types of prisoners are located there, and identifying if it is likely to increase the risk that bullying will occur. Livingston and colleagues (1994), for example, suggested monitoring the number of young prisoners housed on a unit as well as identifying those with a prior history of incarceration and/or with convictions for violent crime. This was based on the assumption that units housing large numbers of prisoners with these characteristics would have an increased level of bullying. Brookes and co-workers (1994) described recommendations from prisoners that included discouraging the formation of potentially subversive groupings within the prisoner population by separating co-accused, relatives and known associates, and ensuring that prisoners from the same area or ethnic background did not become too concentrated on any particular landing. In the same study staff recommended separating prisoners according to their sentence length, namely locating short- and long-term prisoners on separate landings. This suggestion was also made by Willmot (1997), and is based on the assumption that prisoners serving long sentences tended to bully those serving short sentences. Both staff and prisoners in Brookes and colleagues' (1994) study also recommended housing prisoners convicted of the same type of offence together. This latter point is based on the perception that violent offenders were likely to bully non-violent offenders, and that by housing them separately bullying could be reduced. Similarly, McGurk and McDougall (1986) suggested that prisoners thought to be 'unsuitable' for dormitories should be placed in single cells in order to reduce their opportunities for bullying others. It was suggested that this decision be based on the prior history of violence that prisoners presented with: any prisoner with a prior history of violence was viewed as 'at risk' of bullying others and thus not suitable for dormitory accommodation.

There are problems with using characteristics such as these to determine whether or not a prisoner is at risk of bullying others. Attempting to prevent and control bullying in this way may meet with only limited success. The assumption that characteristics such as age, offence type and sentence length are important is based largely on the perceptions that prisoners and staff have regarding which prisoners are likely to be bullies. To refer back to Chapter 5, the most distinguishing personal/descriptive characteristic between the different groups appeared to be the experience that they have had with prison life: bullies tended to be those who reported the most experience with prison life whereas victims were those with limited prison experience. The relationship between bullying and the other variables such as age and offence type is less clear.

Furthermore, focusing solely on the personal/descriptive character-istics of prisoners is not an advised preventative strategy and certainly should not be used to determine where prisoners should be located on a unit. Housing prisoners in accordance with their offence type or sentence length may have limited effect and, as I highlighted in Chapter 4, bullying is a product of an interaction between the individual and the environment. Separating prisoners according to the characteristics that they possess and expecting this to impact on the level of bullying fails to acknowledge the impact of the environment on their behaviour. Bullying can be expected to occur regardless of the control placed on the characteristics that prisoners bring with them to the environment.

## Monitoring and evaluating strategies

Recommendations relating to this area included monitoring the number of bullies on the unit and providing information about them that is readily accessible to staff (Brookes *et al.* 1994) and recording all incidents of bullying accurately (Ireland 1999f). With regard to this latter point, the emphasis here should be on recording the time and location of incidents, the types of bullying and the motives for bullying (O'Brien 1996; Ireland 1998). This would allow for bullying to be monitored and the locations and times where bullying is most likely to take place to be identified (O'Donnell and Edgar 1997). If these can be reliably identified, other strategies can then be put in place to reduce the opportunities that prisoners have to bully, for example CCTV cameras placed in areas where bullying is most likely to occur and/or changes in staff supervision at times of high risk. Such changes have been described in some detail in the section on making changes to the environment (pp. 148–155). Attention should also be given to how such information is obtained. Full use should be made of existing record systems such as wing observation logs, personal history sheets and security information reports (O'Donnell and Edgar 1997). In addition, staff should be encouraged to systematically document any suspicious behaviour that could indicate bullying or victimisation (O'Donnell and Edgar 1997), and to read wing occurrence books each time that they come on duty to familiarise themselves with any actual or suspected incidents of bullying that may have taken place (Brookes *et al.* 1994; Willmot 1997). The important point here is that existing record systems, if taken as a whole and used appropriately, can prove valuable resources for monitoring actual and suspected incidents of bullying, with the potential of highlighting when and where bullying is likely to take place.

Undoubtedly, an intrinsic part of any anti-bullying strategy is the importance of measuring the nature and extent of bullying in order to assess the type of approach that may be appropriate to that prison (Osiowy 1997). It is also important to monitor the nature and extent of bullying if some measure of the effectiveness of the anti-bullying strategy is to be obtained (Osiowy 1997). The general recommendation is that such surveys should be repeated on a 12- to 24-month basis (Ireland 1998; Bolt 1999; Ireland 1999c). Such surveys should not be restricted to an analysis of the nature and extent of bullying but should be expanded to include regular reviews and audits of the systems in place that could lead to the strategy being modified to improve its effectiveness (Marshall 1993; Ireland 1999f; Ireland and Hill 2001). Importantly, the more information that can be obtained about bullying, the more effective anti-bullying strategies will become at preventing bullying.

### Other strategies

This final theme relates to two main areas

1   the importance of tailoring the anti-bullying strategy to the prison and to the specific population that it is meant to serve
2   the importance of adopting a multidisciplinary approach.

Both areas are construed as preventative since incorporating each into an anti-bullying strategy should enhance its overall effectiveness.

Approximately one-third of all papers reviewed included reference to at least one of these areas.

## Tailoring strategies

Although anti-bullying strategies should be similar across different prisons (i.e. maximum-security through to low-security prisons) and populations (i.e. men, women, adults, young offenders and juveniles), there does need to be some recognition of the differences between them. These include differences in terms of why bullying occurs, which types of bullying are preferred, where and when bullying is likely to take place and what approach should be taken to deal with it. To refer back to Chapter 2, there is evidence for sex and developmental differences in the nature and extent of bullying: women appear to bully differently to men, and for adults indirect bullying seems to be the most dominant form of aggression. There is also some evidence for environmental differences, with the nature and extent of bullying reported dependent to some extent on the security classification of the establishment.

Such differences do need to be reflected in any anti-bullying strategy. This also highlights the importance of conducting research at a local level so that the findings can be incorporated into the strategy in order to develop it. The importance of tailoring a strategy to the individual needs of an establishment has been recognised by a number of researchers (e.g. Marshall 1993; Ireland and Archer 1996; O'Donnell and Edgar 1997; Ireland 1999c). The most comprehensive strategy is undoubtedly one that takes into account differences between both prisons and populations. It is important, however, that the aims, objectives and broad principles of anti-bullying strategies remain consistent across all prisons and populations. What is suggested here is the tailoring of the strategy once it is in place. Importantly, any tailoring that is done should be in accordance with research.

## Adopting a multidisciplinary approach to the problem

This is perhaps the most important element. Already discussed is the importance of including both staff and prisoners in the strategy, but equally important is the inclusion of all grades of staff, regardless of whether or not they will spend a great deal of time with prisoners. This is based very much on the recognition that in order to tackle bullying effectively there has to be a 'whole-prison approach' (Beck 1995; O'Donnell and Edgar 1996b; Osiowy 1997; Loucks 1998). Emphasising the strategy solely to officers and prisoners is not sufficient. Bullying is a product of the environment as much as it is a product of the individual and everyone who shares this environment needs to reinforce and take responsibility for the strategy and the message that it sends. This notion has been embraced by the Prison Service in the United Kingdom with the recent strategy recommending that staff anti-bullying committees should be multi-disciplinary (Home Office Prison Service 1999). In addition, O'Donnell and Edgar (1997) recognise the importance of developing strategies based on consultations with all groups within the prison. Osiowy (1997) develops this even further by suggesting area or national meetings in which representatives from different prisons can come together and discuss their approach to tackling the problem of bullying. This would give staff the opportunity to discuss their strategies and to collect ideas from others that could be implemented at their own establishment.

## What makes an effective strategy?

In this chapter I have described a number of elements that have already been included in some anti-bullying strategies and/or have been recommended in the literature. The focus here was on those elements that could be broadly described as preventative as opposed to reactive strategies. I will focus on these latter strategies in the following chapter when approaches to dealing with bullies and/or victims will be discussed. It is important, though, that this current chapter is read in conjunction with Chapter 8. There is a certain degree of overlap between preventative and reactive strategies, and their separation here was simply to aid interpretation. If interventions into bullying are to be effective, equal attention needs to be given to both.

### What should be included?

Based on the literature that I reviewed for the current chapter there appear to be a number of areas that a strategy should adhere to. These are presented in no particular order and all need to be emphasised if a strategy is to be effective.

1 Adopting a whole-prison approach and recognising that all grades of staff should be involved in developing, maintaining and taking responsibility for the strategy. This should be extended to include prisoners' families and visitors, where appropriate, and also

acknowledge the importance of adopting a multidisciplinary approach to preventing bullying.

2   Involving prisoners as much as possible in the strategy. Prisoners are unlikely to respond to a strategy that is imposed on them by staff. Involving them in the strategy highlights how they are all responsible for it.

3   Attempting to change the prison culture or climate. This is related to the idea of involving prisoners and the whole-prison approach. Although it is unlikely that prison culture will change enough to allow prisoners to report bullying to staff without violating the prisoner code of not informing, measures can be taken to develop a much more community-based approach to dealing with bullying. Including prisoners as much as possible in the strategy will allow them to view it more as a collaboration between themselves and the prison, and something that they can invest in. Ideally prisoners should be encouraged to view reporting incidents of bullying as positive self-protection measures and not as collusion with staff or the authorities (Brookes *et al.* 1994). It is recognised that expecting such change in prison culture may be somewhat idealistic. However, if change does occur, and prisoners do begin to see the act of bullying others as a violation of the prison code, it will take time. Prisons can take steps now to provide the groundwork for such change. Indeed, it could be speculated that bullying may occur to a lesser extent in prisons that operate as 'therapeutic communities'. Such regimes are based on the philosophy of empowering prisoners, encouraging support and tolerance of others and confrontation of their behaviour, where appropriate, with an emphasis on individual and collective responsibility (Cullen 1997: readers are referred to Cullen *et al.* 1997 for a further discussion of therapeutic communities in secure environments). The very fact that some prisons have been able to develop such communities suggests that cultural change within prisons may be possible.

4   Tailoring the strategy as much as possible to the prison and the specific population to which it is applied. Although the basic principles, aims and objectives of the strategy should be consistent across prisons, there should be recognition of the subtle differences between prisons and populations that should be reflected in the development of the strategy.

5   Basing strategies as much as possible on research conducted within prison (or other secure) environments. Incorporating school-based research, for example, will only be of limited value since the

environment and the population served by schools are distinct from prisons. The recent increase in prison-based research should allow for the development of appropriate strategies.

6   Acknowledging that although bullying is unlikely to be eradicated it can certainly be reduced. The focus of the strategy should be on preventative measures aimed at reducing the opportunities that prisoners have to bully others. It should also focus on recording and monitoring all incidents of bullying. The best strategies are those that acknowledge that bullying exists and are able to provide evidence of when it has occurred, where it happened, who was involved, why it happened and what action was taken. Prisons which claim to have no, or very little, bullying are likely to be measuring it using inadequate methods (see Chapter 2 where I discuss in more detail how the method used to measure bullying can impact on the nature and extent of bullying reported).

7   Communicating the strategy effectively, particularly by publicising it across the prison as a whole, by basing an anti-bullying co-ordinator on each unit and by allowing staff and prisoners access to any surveys into bullying conducted within the establishment.

8   Recognising the importance of carrying out research in order to develop the strategy that is in place. Ideally such research should be longitudinal and address any changes in bullying over time that could be used to evaluate the effectiveness of the strategy.

9   Ensuring that the anti-bullying strategy is understood by staff and prisoners and that it is applied consistently. Regular audits of strategies to ensure that policies are understood and procedures carried out correctly are essential.

10   Regular training or education for both staff and prisoners on bullying. Ideally, such training should be provided when staff or prisoners are new to the environment, and booster training should be provided to avoid complacency. Importantly, all training or education provided should be accurate and updated as knowledge about bullying increases. The specific elements that this should include were described previously in the section on education (pp. 155–159).

11   Making changes to the physical environment that will help limit the opportunities that prisoners have to bully others. These changes can be as simple as locating a CCTV camera in a location known to be a hotspot for bullying.

12   Considering ways of altering how prisoners are supervised. If supervision is made less predictable then this may make it harder for the bully to predict when an opportunity to bully others without being

caught will arise. In addition, bullying will be less likely to occur if increased supervision is provided at times known to be high risk.

13  Encouraging staff to attend to the symptoms of bullying. This includes being aware of how a victim may react to being bullied and also attending to evidence that a prisoner is bullying others, for example if they have accumulated more material goods than they have listed on their property card.

14  Ensuring that there are systems in place for controlling and monitoring the material goods that prisoners have access to. This should also include ways in which prisoners can avoid getting into debt.

15  Keeping prisoners occupied as much as possible and engaged in meaningful activity. The more prisoners are encouraged to invest in the regime the more they may feel they have to lose if they are caught bullying others.

16  Recognising that strategies need to be continually updated and improved as knowledge about bullying behaviour (based on research evidence) increases.

17  Making the anti-bullying strategy high profile across all parts of the prison.

18  Acknowledging that anti-bullying strategies need to be well resourced if they are to be implemented correctly, maintained and developed. This is perhaps the most important element of any strategy. Anti-bullying strategies should be viewed as a high priority in prisons and the clearest way of communicating a commitment to it is to ensure that it is well resourced.

## Summary

This chapter has described a range of strategies, broadly defined as preventative, which should be included in any anti-bullying strategy. The effectiveness of these strategies is not yet clear and there is a need for future research to address this issue, particularly that focusing on those elements that prove useful and those that do not. My aim here, however, was simply to provide guidance on what elements should, and more importantly should not, form part of the final strategy. It is also worth recognising that there are a number of incentives associated with bullying which act to encourage prisoners to engage in such behaviour. This, coupled with the environmental and individual characteristics that promote bullying, ensures that it becomes a very difficult behaviour to eradicate. This was highlighted at the start of the chapter when I stated that anti-bullying strategies should be aimed towards reducing bullying and not towards eradicating it completely. Attempting to eradicate bullying is an impossible task at which any strategy will fail. This should be recognised: bullying will adapt to whatever preventative strategies are put in place. Reducing an opportunity to bully by placing a CCTV camera in a high-risk area for bullying, for example, will simply encourage bullies to look for other locations where they can bully without detection. This is not to say, however, that prisons should not try and deal with bullying, rather it highlights the importance of setting realistic goals, recording all incidents of bullying and developing and adapting strategies. Primarily, strategies should aim to impact on the optimal conditions under which bullying takes place by making it harder for prisoners to bully by reducing the rewards for engaging in such behaviour and by making it easier to detect. Reaching this stage will take time thus illustrating how strategies should never be static, they should be continually evolving and adapting themselves to the changing behaviour of bullies. How the behaviour of bullies should be addressed, and how their victims should be supported, will be the focus of the following chapter.

# Chapter 8

# Strategies: 2 reacting to bullying

Reactive strategies are those strategies that should be put in place following an incident of bullying. They include the procedures that aid an investigation of bullying right through to challenging the behaviour of bullies and supporting victims. In the present chapter I aim to summarise the strategies that have been suggested in the research to date including those referred to in the 1993 and 1999 Prison Service anti-bullying strategies (Home Office Prison Service 1993, 1999).

In reviewing the research, a number of broad themes relating to reactive strategies emerged. These were

1  investigating incidents
2  dealing with prisoners who bully
3  dealing with prisoners who are bullied
4  encouraging good relationships between bullies and victims.

Each of these themes will be presented in turn. As for the preventative strategies described in Chapter 7, some of the interventions presented have already been implemented in prisons. This is not, however, always an indication of their appropriateness. Thus in the present chapter I will aim, where possible, to both describe and evaluate the interventions. I will also make suggestions regarding how intervention strategies should account for the different groups involved in bullying (pure bullies, bully/victims, etc.) and conclude with some guidelines that may prove useful when responding to bullying.

# Themes of intervention

## *Investigating bullying*

Approximately one-quarter of all papers reviewed made some reference to how incidents of suspected bullying should be investigated. Investigation should be one of the most important elements of any anti-bullying strategy and one that should be emphasised and implemented before any action is taken (Ireland and Hill 2001; Ireland 2002a). There are three main reasons for this.

1   To ensure that an incident of bullying has occurred. All incidents should be referred to as suspected until an investigation has taken place. Intermediate measures can be put in place until the investigation is completed. Prisoners suspected of bullying, for example, could be monitored more closely, suspected victims should be offered support and, depending on the type of bullying and the potential threat to victims, the prisoners involved could be separated until the investigation is completed. This latter course of action should be reserved for those incidents where it is believed that the potential threat to the victim(s) and/or other prisoners is severe enough to warrant such an action. Importantly, no other interventions should be put in place to address the behaviour of bullies until there is enough evidence against them. In view of the problems in measuring bullying accurately (see Chapter 2), extra care should be taken in deciding that an incident of bullying has taken place. Specific suggestions for conducting investigations will be described later.

2   To ascertain what actually happened during the incident, including who was involved, if the incident occurred on a single occasion or was related to other incidents, the motivation of the bully, the specific role that the bully took during the incident (were they a leader, assistant or follower bully?), and the effect on the victim(s) (Ireland 2002a). Intervention strategies should not be implemented without knowledge of these areas.

3   To identify what types of bullies and/or victims were involved. Intervention strategies should not be implemented without knowledge of what type of bully or victim is being dealt with. The type of bully or victim (pure bully, bully/victim, pure victim) should influence the strategy employed (Ireland 2002a). This will be addressed in more detail in the section on accounting for the different groups involved in bullying (pp. 200-203).

At present there are no set guidelines regarding how bullying incidents should be investigated, and this was not an area covered in the 1993 or 1999 Prison Service strategies, with neither strategy emphasising the importance of investigation (Home Office Prison Service 1993, 1999).

Anti-bullying strategies would be improved, however, if they were able to outline and standardise ways in which investigations should be conducted. Brookes and colleagues (1994), for example, recommended systematically interviewing suspected victims using a pre-designed questionnaire. Such questionnaires would certainly be useful in helping to standardise investigations and should be applied to all groups suspected of involvement. They should aim, however, to be non-threatening and (at least initially) avoid use of the term bullying. The term bullying is an emotive one and likely to produce a defensive reaction from individuals suspected of being a bully and/or a victim. Prisoners will also be reluctant to admit to a behaviour that they construe as childish, they may not have labelled their aggression towards others as bullying or wish to be labelled as either a bully or a victim of bullying (Ireland 2000a). Staff should instead concentrate on the discrete types of behaviours that prisoners may have displayed, for example asking them if they have been 'hit or kicked' or 'threatened' as opposed to asking them 'have you been bullied?'

In addition, investigations should aim to collect a range of evidence from different sources before a decision is made. In view of the problems in measuring bullying (see Chapter 2), extra care should be taken before a final decision is reached. Beck (1995), for example, highlights how self-reports of bullying need to be corroborated with information from other sources. Some assessment of the reliability of this source also needs to be obtained: identifying a prisoner as a bully based solely on the reports of others may not be sufficient, particularly if the source of this report is considered unreliable. Although it is acknowledged that bullying behaviour can be subtle, and at times hard to detect, there should still be some other evidence available that could help to corroborate self-reports. Some other avenues for gathering evidence are presented in Figure 8.1, where suggested guidelines regarding how incidents of bullying could be investigated are described.

### Dealing with prisoners who bully

Over half of all papers reviewed referred to ways in which prisoners who bullied others could be dealt with. These approaches were focused largely around challenging the bully and could be separated into punitive interventions, supervising bullies more closely, designated 'bully' units, positive approaches, group-based or individual interventions and other interventions. The majority of papers reviewed did not distinguish between the interventions that would be appropriate for pure bullies and those that would be appropriate for prisoners who reported both bullying others and being bullied themselves (i.e. bully/victims). Arguably, prisoners classified as bully/victims should be dealt with somewhat differently to those classified as pure bullies. The specific interventions that can be used with these two groups will be the focus of a later section. The purpose of the current section is simply to describe and evaluate the suggestions made by researchers, including those referred to in the current Prison Service anti-bullying strategy, that could potentially be applied to prisoners who bully.

## Punitive interventions

Approximately one-half of all papers reviewed recommended a punitive approach to dealing with bullies, with both prisoners and staff advocating severe measures against them (Ireland and Archer 1996; Loucks 1998; Power *et al.* 1997; McGurk and McDougall 1986; Willmot 1997). Such measures included reducing the number of privileges given to bullies (Brookes and Pratt 1996; Home Office Prison Service 1999), removing all privileges from them (Brookes *et al.* 1994), removing the bully from the wing (Brookes *et al.* 1994; Ireland and Archer 1996; Home Office Prison Service 1999), publicising what action was taken against them (Brookes and Pratt 1996), placing them on a governor's report (Brookes *et al.* 1994; Willmot 1997; Home Office Prison Service 1999) and imposing heavy penalties if the individual is found guilty, such as adding extra days on to their sentence (Brookes *et al.* 1994). Some researchers suggested that 'bully cells' be set up where bullies can be located, have their privileges restricted and not be allowed to associate with their peers (Willmot 1997). Also suggested was the segregation of bullies from other prisoners (Brookes and Pratt 1996; Loucks 1998; Power *et al.* 1997) or their transfer to other prisons, i.e. 'shipping them out' (Brookes *et al.* 1994; Brookes and Pratt 1996). Both these latter options are described in the Prison Service strategy although it is acknowledged that such actions depend on the severity of the incident (Home Office Prison Service 1999).

A more widely used approach to dealing with bullying is the development of 'stage systems' which were emphasised in the 1999 Prison Service strategy. Such systems use a series of procedures that are put in place each time a bullying incident occurs (Home Office Prison Service 1999). The specifics of these 'stage systems' are somewhat vague in the

An incident of suspected bullying is brought to the attention of staff. Regardless of how the incident was brought to the attention of staff the following steps should be taken.

1    An attempt should be made to obtain some initial information about the suspected incident from a *variety* of sources: peer reports, self-reports of victims, staff reports, observation. The information obtained should include what actually happened and who was involved, where the incident occurred, the motivation behind the bullying, what the immediate consequences were, the roles prisoners played in the incident, the effect on the victim(s) and an attempt to ascertain if the incident was a 'one-off' or related to other incidents (suspected or actual). Most of this information could be recorded on a Bullying Incident Report (BIR: see Chapter 2).

Based on step 1, some initial steps may be taken to protect and support the suspected victim(s). No direct intervention should be employed at this stage until the investigation is complete.

2    An attempt should be made to obtain other evidence that could corroborate the incident. This could include using information from pre-existing record systems (e.g. wing files, governor's reports, etc.) and attending to

- physical evidence of bullying (e.g. items missing from a prisoner's property card, a prisoner found in possession of another prisoner's property, physical cuts or bruises, copies of threatening letters). The evidence obtained will depend on the nature of the suspected bullying.
- behavioural evidence of bullying – this may be particularly useful when the suspected victim denies the bullying but staff feel that they are victims and may not be admitting to it for a range of reasons (e.g. fear of being seen as a 'grass', not wanting to cause trouble). Staff should attend to how the victim has been behaving and consider if any of these behaviours are symptoms of bullying (e.g. have they recently been on report for poor behaviour? are they spending a lot of time in their cell? have they recently requested a move?) (see Chapter 6 for more discussion of possible reactions).

3    Following steps 1 and 2, structured interviews should be conducted with *all* parties suspected of involvement (as either a bully and/or a victim). The purpose of the interview is to gather information and not to interrogate. Importantly this interview should avoid using the term bullying as much as possible and concentrate instead on the discrete behaviours that make up bullying (e.g. instead of asking a prisoner 'have you bullied?', this could be rephrased as 'have you been calling someone names and threatening them?' )The same approach

could be taken for those suspected of being a victim, e.g. 'have you been called names and threatened?' Any prisoner(s) who witnessed the suspected incident should also be interviewed.

4  A decision should be made as to whether there is enough evidence (based on steps 1 to 3) to conclude that an incident of bullying has actually taken place.

5  A decision should be made regarding the roles of prisoners in the incident(s), were they a leader bully, an assistant bully or a bully/victim?

6  An appropriate intervention and support strategy should be decided on for those involved as bullies and/or victims.

7  The results of the investigation should be recorded as well as details of the interventions used and support provided to the victim(s).

Ideally, steps 4 to 6 should be made in a multidisciplinary forum such as a 'case-conference' where the findings of the investigation can be considered and appropriate intervention and support strategies decided upon.

*Figure 8.1* Guidelines for investigating suspected incidents of bullying.

strategy and appear to relate to the creation of action plans where a series of graded targets are set for the bully. The targets set are determined by the type of bullying behaviour and the attitude of the bully. Such systems are already in place in some prisons although there is a great deal of variability among them in terms of what they include and how they are conducted. On the whole, they tend to advocate a different method of intervention based on the number of bullying incidents that a prisoner has been involved in, with the severity of the intervention increasing as the number of incidents increases. Figure 8.2 illustrates a system currently being run in a male young offenders' institution. There are four stages to this particular system. Each time that a prisoner is suspected of bullying others a Bullying Incident Report (BIR) is completed (see Chapter 2, Table 2.4 for a description of BIR forms). The number of forms completed denotes the stage that the prisoner is placed at (e.g. two BIRs = stage 2), and the intervention invoked.

The benefits of systems such as these are that they allow for a consistent staff response following an incident of bullying. It is also an open system which all prisoners have access to and knowledge of. Interestingly, the system described in Figure 8.2 also makes reference to including the family (at stage 2). As I mentioned in Chapter 7, this is an important intervention to consider: not only may family members be able to inform prison staff of why their family member may be behaving in such a way, based on their behaviour outside prison, but they may also be a useful source of intervention by discouraging the prisoner from bullying others. Prisoners may be more inclined to respond to a request from their family than from the prison authorities.

Such step-by-step systems, however, are not of use unless they are applied correctly and consistently by all staff and are fully understood. This highlights the need for such systems to be audited on a regular basis to ensure that they are being applied correctly. There are, however, problems with the structure of these systems in that bullies can seemingly bully on more than one occasion before a severe intervention is imposed (e.g. before his/her family are informed of their behaviour or before a formal governor's report is considered). Some systems, such as that described in Figure 8.2, also appear only to take into account the number of bullying incidents and not the type of bullying that has occurred, with an incident of physical bullying potentially being dealt with in the same way as verbal bullying.

Since such approaches are based on principles of punishment the limits of such an approach as a method of changing behaviour should be recognised. As highlighted by McGuire and Priestly (2000), in order to be effective punishment must fulfil a series of conditions

- it must be inevitable with the unwanted behaviour always being followed, without exception, by punishment
- it must be immediate and take place as soon as the behaviour has occurred
- it must be severe
- it must include alternative responses that the individual can engage in to replace the unwanted behaviour
- it must be comprehensible, with the individual able to understand the link between the unwanted behaviour and the consequences that follow.

Ensuring that all these conditions are met is difficult. Bullying is a subtle behaviour that can avoid detection for long periods of time and can often

**STAGE 1: Following an actual or suspected incident of bullying you should:**

a   Record information on Bullying Incident Report form
b   Isolate perpetrator for interview – remove him from his peers but not necessarily from the unit
c   Interview the suspected bully – do not directly accuse him of being a bully unless you have firm evidence
d   End interview by advising the (suspected) bully that staff will monitor his behaviour
e   Place completed Bullying Incident Report form in wing file. Allow prisoner to read report

**STAGE 2: If prisoner continues to bully:**

f   Repeat a) and b) as above
g   At interview have Senior Officer[a] present, advise prisoner of options open to staff, e.g. transfer out, risk of being placed on GOAD[b], advising his family of his behaviour

ACTION

h   Restrict the opportunity to bully by: loss of association (with peers), limiting work and leisure opportunities
i   Repeat e) as above

**STAGE 3: If prisoner *still* continues to bully:**

j   Repeat a) and b) as above
k   Interview with governor grade present

ACTION

l   i.   Decide whether GOAD will be applied by governor grade
    ii.  Send individual to separation and care unit[c] to have anti-social behaviour confronted
    iii. Inform the prisoner's family
m   Repeat e) as above
n   Return to residential unit after period in separation and care unit

**STAGE 4: If the prisoner still continues to bully:**

The Governor will keep the prisoner segregated for a longer period. If the evidence is overwhelming, it is important to persist, demonstrating a consistent discipline approach.

Stage 4 is also the stage at which transfer to another establishment is considered.

*Figure 8.2* Guidelines for action against suspected bullying.

Source: HMYOI/RC Lancaster Farms, *Anti-Bullying: Resource and Information Booklet*, HM Prison Service. Reproduced with permission of Governor David Thomas, HMYOI Lancaster Farms, Lancaster, UK. NB. This is an example of a form used with male young offenders.
a   Officer rank. In the prison system the officer grade ranks are (in ascending order) basic grade officer, senior officer, principal officer. The ranks are then followed by governor grades. Stage one of the system only requires the presence of a basic grade officer.
b   A governor's report resulting in a prison charge against the prisoner for behaving in such a way that contravenes 'Good Order And Discipline' (GOAD).
c   Segregation unit.

go unpunished as a result, thus ensuring that the conditions of inevitability and immediacy cannot be met. Even the time taken to investigate the incident fully, before employing punitive measures, ensures that the condition of immediacy will not be met. However, avoiding these problems is not possible: investigation is a crucial element of the process and no intervention can be employed before it has taken place. In view of this, it is important that if punitive interventions are employed, their limits in terms of effectiveness are recognised and that they form only part of a wider intervention programme that also includes some method of changing behaviour based on positive reinforcement. Trying to change behaviour based on the latter may prove to be more effective overall (McGuire and Priestly 2000).

There are also other problems associated with the use of punitive methods. For example, removing privileges from the bully, removing them from the wing and/or publicising the outcome of the incident, could potentially act to victimise the bullies themselves, particularly if the bully is a victim as well (i.e. a bully/victim). Employing such interventions with bully/victims may serve to continue their victimisation. Bully/victims have been conceptualised as prisoners who bully others in order to prevent their own victimisation. For this group, aggression is a way of communicating to other prisoners that they are not easy targets for bullies. As I described in Chapter 6, it has been suggested that bully/victims display aggression towards others in order to be removed to a safe environment, away from the prisoner or prisoners who are bullying them. Some of the punitive interventions suggested may actually reinforce this behaviour. For example, by creating 'bully cells' (another of the interventions suggested), the prison could be reinforcing their aggression by communicating to them that if they are aggressive they will be removed from their peers and hence those that are bullying them. Aggression for the bully/victim then becomes a method by which to obtain some respite from their aggressor. The same can be said for the four-stage system described in Figure 8.2 where stages 2 (restriction of association and activity time) and 4 (moving them out of the establishment) ensure that the bully/victim could avoid their bully without losing face in front of their peers. Importantly, bullying behaviour needs to be challenged in a constructive way that avoids the individual becoming entrenched in the problem behaviour (Home Office Prison Service 1999). It therefore becomes important to consider whether or not the suspected bully is actually a bully/victim before interventions are employed.

## Supervising bullies more closely

One-tenth of papers reviewed suggested supervising bullies more closely as an approach to reducing bullying, with officers responding to one survey stating that 'Staff should make a nuisance of themselves with suspected bullies, for instance by more frequent searching, extra attention' (Brookes *et al*. 1994: 6). A similar reaction was also reported by the prisoners in the same survey.

> Staff should watch the bully and let him know he is being watched and will be shipped out on the first sign of trouble . . . officers can make life harder for suspected bullies by applying rules more strictly, searching them regularly.
>
> (Brookes *et al*. 1994: 10)

Closer supervision of bullies was also implicated in the suggestion of Brookes and colleagues (1994) to send potential bullies for their meals, and to the prison shop, after the other prisoners, so as to avoid times when the opportunity to bully other prisoners is increased, and to randomly drug test possible bullies, to ascertain if one reason for their suspected bullying is to finance their illicit drug-taking activities. Strategies such as these, however, should be employed with caution. Although Brookes and colleagues (1994) refer to their use with *potential* bullies, it is perhaps more appropriate to restrict them to *proven* bullies. In addition, although increasing staff supervision may be appropriate in some circumstances, there needs to be a careful balance struck between observing bullies more closely and carrying this out to such an extent that staff are accused of harassing or victimising them. The extra supervision put in place should be subtle and not intrusive (Ireland 2002a). Staff could also consider making the supervision less predictable, as opposed to focusing wholly on increasing it. As I highlighted in Chapter 4, when discussing why bullying occurs in a prison, there are two aspects to supervision that are important – the amount and the predictability: bullying is likely to occur both when supervision is limited and also when the supervision occurs at predictable times and the bully knows when there are clear opportunities to bully. By making supervision unpredictable (e.g. by varying the times when prison officers patrol prisoner living areas), it becomes harder for the bully to predict when an opportunity will arise.

## Dedicated bully units

Approximately one-tenth of papers reviewed suggested separating bullies from victims and placing them onto separate bully units (Brookes *et al.* 1994; Loucks 1998). The units are discussed here separately since they represent a specific form of intervention that has been emphasised in some anti-bullying strategies. Although some of these units offer bullies 'treatment' during their stay, I would argue that they are primarily punitive approaches in that the bully is forcibly removed from their peers and has a number of restrictions placed on them. There are also a number of problems associated with bully units that undermine their use as an intervention.

1   Such units minimise the impact of the environment on an individual's behaviour and are based on the notion that a prisoner bullies solely because there is something intrinsically wrong with them. By removing the bully from their peers, 'treating' them and putting them back on normal location, it is expected that their behaviour will improve in some way (Ireland 2002a). Bullying does not, however, occur in isolation from the rest of the peer group. The bully may have some personal qualities that predispose them to engage in bullying others but whether or not they bully is dependent on a number of environmental conditions (see Chapter 4). Thus, if the behaviour of a bully is to be managed effectively attention needs to be given to altering aspects of the environment that promote bullying (see Chapter 7), and the behaviour of the bully needs to be managed within the environment in which the bullying took place (Ireland 2002a).

2   Bullying is pervasive and many bullies are also victims. Dedicated units would therefore only have a marginal impact (O'Donnell and Edgar 1996b). The overlap between bullies and victims is so great that such units cannot be sure to exclude victims (or vice versa on dedicated 'victim' units).

3   Bullying can continue on specialist units. Beck, for example, comments on how it is known that 'prisoners in so called protected units in a YOI[16] engage in bullying each other. This suggests that the categorisation of people as a bully or victim is a futile activity' (1992: 37). A further consequence of this may be that prisons will have to create two designated bully units: one for prisoners who have been found bullying when located on normal location in the prison and one for those who have been found bullying others while located on a bully unit.

4   O'Donnell and Edgar (1996b) make the important point that such specialist units create the potential for those who work on them to become an elite and for other staff to assume that the 'specialists' hold full responsibility for the problem of bullying throughout the prison. Obviously, this does not fit with a whole-prison approach to dealing with bullying.

5   Being known as a bully in prison carries with it a certain degree of status (Connell and Farrington 1996), whereas being a victim is stigmatising (Ireland and Archer 1996). Whereas moving a victim to a dedicated victim unit may add to their victimisation by stigmatising them even further, it is not unreasonable to expect bullies to view being moved to a dedicated bully unit as a positive consequence because of the status that goes with bullying. Indeed, this notion of clearly identifying bullies from their peers has previously been employed in prisons, for example by making bullies wear distinctive T-shirts in the hope of shaming them. These actions, however, served only to reinforce the bullies' status among their peers and obtaining a T-shirt became the goal of some prisoners.[17] In the same way, one could argue that dedicated units may also encourage competition among prisoners to get onto these units, regardless of the limited privileges available on them.

6   The existence of dedicated units may actually encourage bully/victims to continue to bully others. This was touched upon in the previous section, but to reiterate the point again: if a victim learns that by bullying others they will be moved to another environment away from the prisoner who is bullying them, then bullying others in order to obtain this respite from bullying becomes a valuable behaviour for the victim to engage in.

The use of dedicated units, however, has received some support from the Prison Service. Such an option is included in the 1999 Prison Service strategy (Home Office Prison Service 1999), although they suggest that a more neutral name be used to describe them. Indeed, a number of prisons do have independent bully units. Levenson (2000) describes one such unit at a young offenders' institution in which bullies are placed on a basic regime (i.e. with a minimum number of privileges) on the unit for a minimum of 4 weeks, with progress dependent on a points system. Prisoners are given points for the cleanliness of their cell, behaviour, appearance, relationship with staff and relationship with other prisoners. It is not clear, however, how the behaviour that is supposedly being improved relates to bullying (e.g. cleanliness of their cell and appearance).

This 'behaviour modification' is also occurring outside the environment in which the bullying first occurred and thus how generalisable it is to this environment is questionable.

Having such units, however, with dedicated staff allocated to work on them, undoubtedly sends out a message that the prison is seriously attempting to deal with bullying and, on a superficial level, may appear to be effective. If they are used, at the very least there need to be clear, consistently applied criteria for selecting who goes onto them. Location to such a unit should be governed by clear procedural safeguards and bullies should know what is expected of them before they can return to their normal location (O'Donnell and Edgar 1996b). Similarly, prisoners should only be placed on such units if they have a proven incident of bullying against them. Placing bully/victims on such units should be carefully considered in view of the suggestion that they are in fact a victim group and the prison cannot be seen to be continuing this victimisation and/or to place them at risk of further bullying. Regardless of this, however, the concerns raised in this summary alone suggest that the use of dedicated units as an intervention into bullying behaviour is ill conceived, of limited value and potentially damaging.

## Positive approaches

Approximately one-tenth of papers reviewed made some recommendation relating to rewarding bullies when they display appropriate behaviour. At present these 'rewards' have been limited to the use of praise. In a paper that I wrote in 1999, I suggested that prisoners who have been reported for bullying others and are not then reported again during the next 3 months should be verbally praised and that this should be recorded in their wing file (Ireland 1999c). Ideally such praise should be communicated to prisoners via a multidisciplinary format such as a sentence-planning board.[18] The important aspect of this approach is the recognition that any intervention should be followed up regularly, and bullies should be told when they have followed the rules as well as when they have not (Ireland 1999c). This is also a view voiced by prisoners, who felt that the improved behaviour of the bully should be reinforced, namely if they have not bullied for a while after being warned then this should be recognised (Ireland and Hill 2001). This element is often lacking from intervention programmes and receives no mention in the 1999 Prison Service strategy; the focus of this strategy is, instead, on identifying bullying when it takes place and challenging bullies constructively, based on principles of negative reinforcement. Rewarding them in the form of praise, however, when they have followed the rules, may be more likely to have an effect on their future behaviour, and acts to reinforce their good behaviour. Praise can be accommodated in intervention programmes relatively easily. To refer back to the section addressing punitive interventions, positive approaches to dealing with bullying may be more effective than punitive approaches. The challenge for future researchers is to address what methods of positive reinforcement, aside from praise, can be applied to effectively and consistently deal with the behaviour of bullies, and, importantly, what alternative responses bullies can be encouraged to engage in, in order to replace their motivation to bully.

### Group-based or individual interventions

One-quarter of papers reviewed recommended placing bullies on courses or giving them training to address their behaviour. Some papers did not identify the specific course that could be used (e.g. Osiowy 1997), whereas others did (e.g. Brookes *et al.* 1994; Loucks 1998; Beck 1995; Ireland 1999b). Programmes suggested included those aimed at improving the bully's cognitive skills, anger management, assertiveness, social skills, self-esteem and victim empathy. Similar suggestions for programmes were also made by the Prison Service (Home Office Prison Service 1993, 1999).

Taking a skills-based approach to addressing the behaviour of bullies and allowing them to improve skills in a group-based setting may be useful. Such programmes, however, as with the previously described dedicated bully units, are based on the principle that prisoners bully because there is something intrinsically wrong with them. Although it is expected that some prisoners do possess characteristics that may make it easier for them to bully others, this again fails to take into account the impact of the environment. Such programmes, as with dedicated units, send out the message that attendance on the programme is equal to treatment of the problem behaviour. Treating bullies in isolation from the wider environment, however, is not going to be successful. If used, the limits of such an approach should be recognised and it should form part of a wider intervention programme.

Problems with this approach also lie in the specific group of bullies that they are targeted towards and the lack of evaluation addressing their effectiveness as an intervention into bullying. To date no programmes implemented with bullies in a prison setting have been evaluated. Similarly, some of the programmes suggested may be addressing areas that have not actually been found to relate to bullying.

Assertiveness training, for example, may not be appropriate for pure bullies who have been found to be neither under- nor over-assertive (Ireland 2002c). Instead such programmes may be more appropriate for bully/victims who do present with a tendency to be over-assertive in some situations and under-assertive in others (Ireland 2002c). Similarly, anger-management programmes may not be appropriate for all bullies unless they actually display problems in this area. As I described in Chapter 1, bullying can represent either proactive or reactive aggression depending on the circumstances. Bullies who present as primarily proactive aggressors would not be appropriately placed on an anger-management course. Those who present primarily as reactive aggressors (i.e. bully/victims) may be more appropriate.

Programmes aimed at addressing self-esteem and/or social or cognitive skills should also be employed with caution. Considering self-esteem first: although based on the notion that bullies have low self-esteem and that they bully others in order to improve their self-esteem, the actual link between bullying and self-esteem is far from clear. Contrary to popular belief, research among children has generally not supported a link between bullying others and (high or low) self-esteem (e.g. Rigby and Slee 1991, 1993; Slee and Rigby 1993), and this has also been found among a prisoner sample (Ireland 2002b). With regard to social and cognitive-skills training, these are also based on the notion that bullies are in some way deficient in such skills. Such an assumption, however, may not be accurate and does not take into account the environment in which the behaviour is taking place. I touched on this briefly in Chapter 5 and readers are referred to this chapter for a further discussion of how social problem-solving skills relate to bullying. It is worth noting here, however, that it has been suggested that social cognitive skills may actually be required if a bully is to engage in indirect or physical bullying (e.g. Sutton *et al.* 1999b). Indeed, indirect bullying requires sophisticated social skills if it is to prove effective, and physical bullying requires a similar level of skill if the bully is able to maximise the harm to the victim and minimise the risk to themselves. Differences in social problem-solving skills between pure bullies and bully/victims have also been reported in a prisoner sample (Ireland 2001a), suggesting again that any intervention aimed towards prisoners who bully needs to take into account differences between groups. These are important areas to consider: by providing bullies with social-skills or cognitive-skills training you could potentially be improving their ability to bully others, and ultimately their ability to evade detection, by building on the skills that they already have. It could also be expected that the more socially skilled a bully becomes the more likely it is they will be able to convince prison authorities that the interventions applied to 'treat' their bullying have been 'successful', and that they no longer intend to bully when in fact they do.

Finally, the use of 'victim-empathy' training also needs to be carefully targeted. It has been suggested that women may respond to such training more than men because of their greater capacity for empathy (Ireland 1999b), although such interventions may actually be more important in targeting bullying among male prisoners. In one study I concluded that what appeared to be lacking in a male prison, unlike a female prison, was an ethos of support for the victims of bullying and an ability to empathise with the victim's plight (Ireland 1999b). However, if victim-empathy training is used it needs to be targeted towards a specific group of bullies: in the same study I reported differences in empathy between pure bullies and bully/victims and suggested that, unlike bully/victims, pure bullies may actually lack the capacity to empathise with others. This suggests that trying to get pure bullies to look at the victim's perspective may not be that effective since they appear to lack the actual ability to empathise with others. This contrasts with bully/victims who do appear to have an ability to empathise with others and may consequently respond well to an approach that encourages them to look at the victim's perspective.

## Other interventions

A number of further recommendations have been made by researchers. These have included exploring what is reinforcing and maintaining the bully's behaviour (Ireland 2000c, 2000d) and analysing what is maintaining the positive beliefs held by bullies regarding their use of aggression, such as the belief that aggression makes you feel better (Ireland and Archer 2002). Ireland and Archer (2002) speculate that one variable that helps to maintain these positive beliefs may be that aggression is viewed as an effective way of dealing with conflict in a prison setting, and can lead to social rewards in the form of status among their peers. In view of this, intervention should focus on searching for other effective ways of obtaining social rewards from the peer group, aside from the use of aggression.

## Dealing with prisoners who are bullied

Approximately half of all papers reviewed referred to ways in which prisoners who were victimised could be helped. The interventions suggested could be separated into group-based or individual interventions, designated victim units or cells, staff responses, involving victims in the process and supporting victims. The majority of papers reviewed did not, however, distinguish between pure victims (i.e. those who solely reported being bullied) and bully/victims (i.e. victims who *also* reported bullying others). The specific interventions that can be used with these different groups will be the focus of a later section. The purpose of the current section is simply to describe and evaluate the suggestions made by researchers, including those referred to in the 1999 Prison Service anti-bullying strategy, that could potentially be applied to prisoners who are victimised.

### Group-based or individual interventions

One-third of papers made reference to changing the victim's behaviour through some form of group or individual training. There were a number of similarities with the suggestions made for bullies, with anger management, self-esteem enhancement, assertiveness, social and cognitive training suggested for use with victims as well as bullies (Brookes *et al.* 1994; Beck 1995; Ireland and Archer 1996; Loucks 1998; Ireland and Hill 2001). Other suggestions included training victims in self-defence, weight training, money management (to help them to avoid getting into debt), training them to cope with conflict (Brookes *et al.* 1994; Willmot 1997) and encouraging them to take part in as many activities as possible (Ireland and Hill 2001).

By far, assertiveness courses were one of the most frequent suggestions made (Brookes *et al.* 1994; Ireland 1998; Beck 1995; Ireland 1999c; Ireland 2002c; Ireland and Hill 2001). There is empirical evidence that an individual's level of assertiveness does relate to the likelihood of their being bullied. In one study I found that pure victims reported lower overall assertiveness scores than other prisoners, with bully/victims tending to be under-assertive in some situations and over-assertive in others (Ireland 2002c). This reinforces the use of such interventions with victims and also highlights the importance of distinguishing between pure victims and bully/victims, since their specific skill deficits may be different. Such intervention should perhaps focus on how victims respond following an incident of bullying as well as aiming to teach them assertiveness skills that they can use either during the incident or to prevent an incident. This acknowledges the difficulty in dealing effectively with bullying in a prison, where even the most assertive prisoner can become a victim; words may not be an adequate means of defence and physical action may be necessary. For this reason self-defence training may not be wholly appropriate unless it also addresses non-physical ways in which the victim can deal with bullying. Indeed, teaching victims self-defence to respond in a physical way to bullying may lead to the incident escalating and increase the chance of physical injury both to the victim and the bully. Instead, avoidance or passive behaviours should be considered as appropriate strategies to deal with bullying, providing that victims are encouraged to employ them before a potential incident (in order to prevent it) or during the incident itself. For example, the victim who has assessed the risk of potential injury to themselves to be high is actually behaving appropriately if they respond passively during the incident. However, victims should not be encouraged to employ passive or avoidance strategies after an incident of bullying, for example they should not employ avoidance strategies such as completely isolating themselves from their peers. Instead, victims should be encouraged to use assertiveness skills after incidents, particularly when reporting incidents to staff. Assertiveness courses, however, should be considered as only one element of a wider intervention programme that addresses a range of social and cognitive skills that will ultimately help victims to deal with bullying. The specific content of these interventions will depend largely on the type of victim, and should be tailored to the specific needs of each.

As with the courses suggested for prisoners who bully others, it is important that any intervention employed is based on theory and takes into account the environment in which bullying is taking place. For example, no research has specifically looked at the relationship between anger and bullying behaviour, even though anger-management training is a suggested intervention. At the very least, the appropriateness of such interventions should be addressed on an individual basis. Based on what is known so far about the behaviour of bully/victims, early signs seem to suggest that anger-management training may be appropriate only for this particular victim group. Similarly, the suggestion of weight training (Willmot 1997) may imply that victims are of a smaller physical stature than bullies and that this may have contributed to their victimisation. Empirical research on this area among prisoners has found no link between size, weight and victim status (Falshaw 1993). Similar findings have been reported among samples of schoolchildren. Suggestions of weight training may have been born out of the apparent myth that the victim is always the physically weaker peer. It could also be argued that another purpose of weight training is to enhance the victim's self-esteem. Although such an approach may achieve this, it is likely to occur only for women and not men, with self-esteem and physical appearance closely related for women (Nolen-Hoeksema 1987). Even self-esteem enhancement, however, as a goal for interventions with victims should not be over-emphasised. Although research among children has tended to support the suggestion that victims have low self-esteem in comparison to other non-bullied children (Slee and Rigby 1993), the same findings have not been consistently reported among prisoners (Ireland 2002b). It is also not clear how self-esteem actually relates to an individual's status as a victim (e.g. is it a reason why the prisoner was bullied or was it a consequence of the abuse?).

All the interventions discussed in this section are based on the principle that prisoners are victimised because there is something intrinsically wrong with them or that they are different in some way to the rest of their peers. Victims, as we have seen, may well possess characteristics that make it easier for others to bully them. However, the environment also contributes to their victimisation and outside a prison setting they may not present as victims at all (Ireland 2002a). Thus, as with bullies, approaches with victims should not focus on removing them from their peers and 'treating' them, but instead on helping them to deal with the bullying in the environment in which it took place. Adopting an approach where victims are given access to a specific group-work programme designed solely for victims may have negative consequences. Such programmes will quickly become labelled by other prisoners in a derogatory fashion (e.g. as a 'muppet' or 'fraggle' group). If it is decided that a victim would benefit from a specific programme, it should be one that can be attended by non-victimised prisoners as well. The aim of such programmes would not be to deal with their status as a victim but rather to address one aspect of the victim that may have contributed to their victimisation, for example their tendency to be under-assertive. They would then be encouraged to practise the skills that they have been taught outside the group and in the environment in which the bullying took place. Ireland and Hill (2001) also suggest that the behaviour of victims should, and can, be addressed by encouraging them to interact in the same environment as other prisoners. Victims should be encouraged to take part in activities as much as possible, ideally in the form of small, supervised groups that are already present in the prison (e.g. workshops or education) where they could learn how to interact with others and to form friendships. Potentially, this could increase the support available to victims from their peers, with the number of friends that a prisoner has serving as a protective factor against the likelihood that they will be bullied, i.e. the more friends that they have the less likely they are to be bullied (Duckworth 1998).

## Designated victim units or cells

Such units were suggested by one-tenth of the papers reviewed; the papers proposed identifying potential or actual victims and placing them either in identified cells in designated areas of the wing, or on separate landings designated solely for use with victims (Brookes *et al.* 1994). It was hoped that prisoners on these units could be supervised more closely and generate some sort of mutual support (Willmot 1997). Brookes and colleagues (1994) suggested that the cells on these units be subjected to more regular searches with better recording of the property in them and any discrepancies noted to ensure that victims were not having property taken off them by bullies. The use of such units was not, however, included in either the 1993 or 1999 Prison Service strategies. Indeed, the 1993 strategy (Home Office Prison Service 1993) highlights the importance of keeping the victim on their normal location if possible. Removing the victim from the rest of their peers was seen as potentially damaging in that it could send the wrong signal to the bully and it would not help to protect the anonymity of the victim.

The problems posed by using such units or cells for victims, however, are the same in many respects as for dedicated bully units. For example, by dealing with bullying in this way, it is assumed that bullying occurs because of the individual and not as a result of an interaction between the victim and the environment. There is also a danger that inadvertently victims will be victimised further, in that they are separated from their peers and supervised much more closely. Similarly Brookes and colleagues (1994) talk about such procedures being used for potential victims. This raises the question of how potential victims are identified and how reliable these identifications are.

## Staff responses

This was suggested by approximately one-fifth of papers which focused on how staff should respond to victims immediately after an incident is reported, and how the role of staff is to provide advice, support and encouragement (O'Donnell and Edgar 1996b). How staff respond to a victim reporting an incident of bullying is critical: it is possible that the victim will have been bullied for a long time and that they have approached a member of staff as a last resort, because their previous attempts at preventing the bullying have been unsuccessful. By approaching staff they are also violating the inmate code by informing on others. Thus, it is not an easy task for a prisoner to approach staff with this sort of information and staff should remain aware of this. It is also likely that the victim will be unwilling to provide staff with the bully's name. Any victim approaching staff should not be placed under pressure to disclose the name of the person(s) bullying them. Such a response by a member of staff, unintentional or otherwise, is likely to place the victim under undue pressure (Ireland 1999c). This in turn will act to reinforce the victim's feelings of helplessness and victimisation. It also increases the possibility that the victim will not report any future victimisation to staff, and will have a knock-on effect for other prisoners who are being bullied (Ireland 1999c). If a victim discloses the name of the bully then it should be a purely voluntary admission.

Not only should staff respond in a supportive and non-challenging way to victims, but they should also show the victim that his or her concerns are being taken seriously, inform them that action will be taken and that the information provided by them will be treated in confidence (O'Donnell and Edgar 1996b). The importance of encouraging victims to report bullying to staff by assuring them that the information received will be treated with the strictest confidence was an element emphasised in the 1999 Prison Service strategy, with the strategy emphasising how it should not become gossip or discussed within the hearing of other prisoners (Home Office Prison Service 1999). If victims are not assured of their anonymity then they may not report victimisation for fear of their own personal safety (Ireland 2000c). It is also worth remembering that not only are prisoners who report being bullied acknowledging their status as a victim, which is in itself stigmatising, but they are also violating the prisoner code of not informing on others to staff, and in this way risking further victimisation by their peers. Their decision to inform staff, regardless of how vague their account of the incident is, should therefore be treated seriously and investigated accordingly.

### Involving victims in the process

Approximately one-tenth of papers indicated that victims should be involved in the anti-bullying strategy. In some cases there has been a tendency to obtain information from the victim about the bullying and then exclude them from the rest of the process. It is worth noting that the experience of victimisation for some may have left them with a sense of helplessness and powerlessness. Involving them as much as possible following the incident may be a way in which these feelings can be alleviated.

At the very least, victims should be kept informed of developments relating to their case (O'Donnell and Edgar 1996b; Ireland and Hill 2001), a recommendation also made in the 1999 Prison Service strategy (Home Office Prison Service 1999). Some researchers have suggested that victims should have more direct involvement than this. O'Donnell and Edgar, for example, argue that the victim should be given some say in how the situation is handled, stating how 'Demonstrating to victims that they can influence the course of events in the aftermath of an incident of victimisation, helps the victim to regain some sense of autonomy' (1997: 19), and Loucks (1998) suggested that the victim should decide on what is appropriate for the bully. This may not, however, be an appropriate level of involvement for the victim. The prison authorities should be seen to take responsibility for the incident of bullying and thus make decisions about how the bully is treated. In addition, this should not become an opportunity for the victim to seek revenge on the bully and as such engage in an act of indirect aggression towards them. The potential consequences for the victim should also be considered, particularly if the bully finds out that the victim has been involved in this decision and then retaliates against them. The overall aim of involving the victim is simply to try and empower them as much as possible in decisions made about their care which includes what support they would like (Ireland 2002a).

## Supporting victims

This intervention is perhaps one of the most important and was suggested by one-fifth of all papers reviewed. Anti-bullying strategies, however, do tend to emphasise the importance of identifying and challenging the bully in comparison to addressing how victims should be supported. Indeed, in the 1999 Prison Service strategy, although supporting the victims of bullying is emphasised as an intervention in its own right, the discussion given to this element is markedly less than that given to challenging bullying behaviour (Home Office Prison Service 1999). This is perhaps a reflection of the difficulties in identifying what can be provided for victims and what is actually meant by support. I would argue that 'support' is defined broadly and that one of the best ways of supporting victims is by limiting the opportunities that other prisoners have to bully them. This can be achieved by dealing with the behaviour of bullies and by helping victims to generate strategies by which they can deal with conflict (as well as using the preventative strategies described in Chapter 7). Other forms of support can include identifying victims through the symptoms that they show, including them more fully during investigations, not placing pressure on them to name the bullies and being seen to take a collaborative approach to the problem (Ireland 2002a). With regard to this last suggestion, the emphasis should be on joint working, with both the victim and staff taking responsibility for developing strategies to deal with the bullying. One of the best forums for this may be through the use of multidisciplinary case conferences where the victim can attend and play an equal role in any decisions made about their care. Thus, on the basis of this, it could be argued that all of the interventions presented in the current section (group-based or individual interventions, involving victims in the process, etc.) serve a supportive function for the victim.

Other suggestions for supporting victims have included using other prisoners. Using other prisoners in a supportive function may prove useful since they represent the prisoner's peers and may be able to empathise more readily with the victim's plight and the problems associated with reporting such behaviour. How this peer support is provided, however, needs to be carefully managed. Suggestions have included using prisoners who presently work as 'listeners' and who currently provide support for prisoners at risk of self-harm (Brookes *et al.* 1994; Ireland and Hill 2001), and developing a 'buddy' system where victims will share a cell or are looked after by trusted and more experienced prisoners (Brookes *et al.* 1994). Both these suggestions are present in the 1999 Prison Service strategy. There are problems associated with them, however. Staff, for example, may inadvertently place the victim at further risk of bullying if the buddy or listener actually turns out to be a bully. Once in this situation it then becomes very difficult for the victim to report the bullying (the problems in using listeners or buddies are the same as those associated with chaperone schemes that have been suggested as a way of preventing bullying and are discussed in Chapter 7).

Similarly, Brookes and colleagues (1994) also suggested that in the case of the victim who is being bullied by their cell-mate, one solution would be to move the victim to another cell with another prisoner who can be relied on not to bully them. Although this may look like a solution, with the victim possibly obtaining some support from their new cell-mate, it would not be a recommended one. First, not enough is known about the characteristics of bullies that would enable staff to reliably predict who will go on to bully others and who will not. Second, in all cases of bullying it should be the bully who is moved and not the victim. In the case described by Brookes and colleagues (1994), it should be the bully who is moved and placed in a single cell. Moving the victim can be construed as punishment for them and would certainly not serve a supportive function. Moving the victim should be done only in exceptional circumstances. It should be reserved for those instances where the victim wishes to be moved and it is felt that there will be a deterioration in their mental or physical health if this request is denied, or if staff feel that the risk of potential injury for the victim is higher if they are not moved.

Although both the 1993 and 1999 Prison Service strategies encourage prisons to support victims, no mention is made of the importance of documenting what support is given and of the importance of asking the victim what action they would like to be taken. There also appears to be a tendency, in both strategies, to focus on victims as individuals who have specific problems, whose victimisation is linked to their inability to cope in prison. The same sentiments are not, however, expressed for bullies, even though research suggests that some prisoners who display bullying behaviour, such as bully/victims, may also be experiencing difficulties in adjusting to prison and that their bullying behaviour is closely related to this. No mention is made, however, of offering support to this group which may be reflective of a tendency to view offering support to bullies, regardless of the motivation, as wrong.

In addition, there is no mention in either strategy of when support should be offered to the victim and what 'immediate support' should include. Arguably, any support or guidance offered to victims should occur soon after the incident and should be recorded along with a statement of how long after the incident it was provided (Ireland 1999f). There should also be a distinction between immediate support and longer-term support. Immediate support, for example, could come from the victim's personal officer, they could be offered the possibility of talking to other professionals and/or of having their family contacted. In extreme circumstances, where it is felt that the victim is at risk of injury from the suspected bully (although it is acknowledged that assessing this risk is difficult), the suspected bully could be moved prior to an investigation taking place. A longer-term support plan could include arranging regular case conferences which the victim attends and where the process of the investigation can be communicated and discussed with them, or encouraging them to interact more with their peers and recording their progress. This plan could also incorporate some of the suggestions outlined in the section on group-based or individual interventions (pp. 192–194) such as arranging for the victim to attend an appropriate course and to develop skills. Personal officers could also be asked to check on a regular basis that the victim has recovered from the incident and that they are not being subjected to any further bullying.

Importantly, staff should be encouraged to actively offer support to the victim since the victim may be reluctant to ask for it themselves. Any support offered, however, should be simply that – an offer. As mentioned previously, research has shown that victims can be quite unassertive in comparison to other prisoners and may thus lack the skills needed to decline offers of help should they want to and instead feel obliged to accept them. It is also possible that some victims may be coping quite well with the victimisation and staff should not encourage them to seek help by telling them that they need it: part of the process of trying to empower the victim begins immediately after the incident of bullying and includes allowing them to make the decision themselves about whether or not they require help. If the victim feels forced to accept help, staff may be inadvertently reinforcing the victim's feelings of victimisation and helplessness.

### Encouraging good relationships between bullies and victims

Two papers suggested dealing with incidents of bullying by providing a safe environment in which bullies and their victims could interact together. Both referred to using 'mediation meetings' between bullies and victims where the incident could be discussed (Loucks 1998; Ireland and Hill 2001). Such meetings would be mediated by staff, and could provide an opportunity where a positive relationship could be encouraged between bullies and their victims. Such meetings, however, would have to be carefully controlled and should not be used unless all parties consent.

## Accounting for the different groups involved in bullying

As mentioned previously, the majority of interventions suggested in the literature do not distinguish between the different groups involved in bullying. Instead, most operate on the principle that there are just two groups involved – bullies and victims – with no recognition of the third group – bully/victims. Although the existence of these three groups is now well established in the literature, this has been a fairly recent development which could explain the tendency for interventions to focus on just two groups. Suggestions about managing each of the three groups have been made, however, and some of these have been included in the sections on dealing with prisoners who bully (pp. 178–191) and dealing with prisoners who are bullied (pp. 191–200). More specific interventions that can be applied to each group are as follows (based on Ireland 2002a).

*Pure bully*   An emphasis is recommended on setting targets with pure bullies for appropriate behaviour (see the stage systems described earlier, Figure 8.2) which includes a behavioural contract individualised for each bully with an avenue for rewarding good behaviour. Exploring the motivation behind bullying is important with a focus on ascertaining what the costs and benefits related to bullying are and, where possible, teaching them more appropriate and prosocial ways of achieving their goals. It is recommended that staff complete a risk assessment of the bully's behaviour which looks at when, where and how they are likely to bully others. This should follow accepted frameworks for conducting risk assessments (see Towl and Crighton 1996), which includes assessing what conditions may help to increase the risk of the target behaviour occurring (in this case bullying), what may decrease the risk of its occurrence, how likely it is to occur and the consequences of the behaviour. If staff are able to assess the risk that the bully poses to others and predict the circumstances in which this is increased or decreased, it should be possible to put preventative strategies in place to reduce the likelihood of further bullying. This may be one of the most important aspects of managing the behaviour of pure bullies – if pure bullies cannot be encouraged to change their behaviour then limiting the opportunities that they have to bully others becomes critical and is the focus of intervention with them. It is also important that this risk assessment is updated if the bully adapts their bullying behaviour, i.e. if staff increase their supervision of bullies it could be expected that the bully will decrease the bullying behaviours that they know are being monitored and substitute them with more subtle behaviours. This needs to be accounted for in any risk assessment.

*Bully/victim*   Intervention with this group can include elements that are applied to pure bullies. There should be an increased emphasis here, however, on support. Bully/victims should be viewed primarily as a victim group and the support strategies applied to pure victims should also be considered for them. The focus with bully/victims should also be on recognising how they may present to staff in terms of the other behaviours that they display, and the function that these behaviours serve for them (e.g. their tendency to be aggressive and to display negative behaviour towards staff and prison rules, see Chapter 6). Intervention could also address ways of deterring them from using aggression towards others as a possible response to being bullied. Since bully/victims arguably retaliate against their own victimisation by bullying other members of their peer group (and not necessarily the bully), encouraging them to cope with their own victimisation in more prosocial ways is obviously important. Interventions with bully/victims could also consider victim empathy issues since their ability to empathise is not limited like that of pure bullies (Ireland 1999b); they could thus be expected to respond well to interventions encouraging them to look at the victim's perspective.

*Pure victims*   Intervention with this group should focus on providing support along the lines described in the section on supporting victims (pp. 197–200), i.e. by limiting the opportunities that other prisoners have to bully them, identifying them through the symptoms that they show, including them more fully in the investigations, being seen to take a collaborative approach to the problem, actively offering them support and not placing pressure on them to name bullies. Whereas the emphasis with bully/victims should be on both managing their aggressive behaviour in a similar way to pure bullies and providing support, the focus with pure victims should primarily be that of support (Ireland 2002a). As mentioned previously, this support should be conceptualised in broad terms and include all of the suggestions recommended in the section on dealing with prisoners who are being bullied (pp. 191–200).

Recognising the existence of these groups is important in helping to tailor strategies and highlights the importance of conducting full investigations before intervention strategies are employed. If a bully/victim is incorrectly identified as a pure bully, then the approach taken to address their behaviour cannot hope to be effective. It is also worth recognising, however, that 'being a bully' and 'being a victim' falls along a continuum of behaviour and prisoners can present at any point along this continuum. Research has yet to address how stable the classifications of pure bully, bully/victim and pure victim are and it could be expected that a prisoner's classification into these groups may change over time (Ireland 2002a). Thus it is important that any intervention strategy recognises this as a possibility and focuses on assessing the prisoner's most recent behaviour, and from this deciding how best it could be managed (Ireland 2002a).

Similarly, simply identifying an individual as a pure bully, for example, may not be enough. As described in Chapter 2, bullies may adopt different roles during bullying incidents (i.e. either leading the bullying or reinforcing or following the bully's behaviour: Sutton *et al.* 1999b). The roles that individuals adopt may be of particular interest in tackling bullying. It may be that different interventions need to be employed for those prisoners identified as leaders and those identified as reinforcers or followers. Until research has addressed the existence of such groups with a prison sample, intervention strategies pertaining to them cannot be suggested.

## What makes an effective strategy?

The present chapter has focused on those elements of an anti-bullying strategy that could broadly be described as reactive since they relate to what should be put in place following an incident of bullying. The strategies presented here should be read in conjunction with the preventative strategies described in Chapter 7, since an effective anti-bullying strategy needs to contain both preventative and reactive elements. Some of the reactive strategies that I have described in the present chapter have already been included in some anti-bullying strategies and/or have been recommended in the literature. As I mentioned at the start of the chapter, however, the inclusion of an intervention in a strategy is not necessarily an indication of its appropriateness. Whereas some of the interventions suggested are potentially useful, others may not be and are based upon poor evidence. Thus in the following section I aim to summarise the interventions described in the present chapter with a view to suggesting guidelines for the development of anti-bullying intervention programmes.

### What should be included in an anti-bullying strategy?

Based on the literature that I reviewed in the current chapter, there appear to be a number of elements that are important to include in any reactive component of an anti-bullying strategy. These are presented in no particular order and all need to be considered if a strategy is to be effective.

1   An emphasis on investigating suspected bullying incidents before any action is taken. The investigation should follow clear procedural guidelines with a focus on obtaining a full account of the circumstances surrounding the suspected incident and on obtaining collaborative evidence through the use of existing record systems. A decision regarding bullying, and importantly the interventions that should be employed, should only be made once the investigation is complete.
2   Careful consideration should be given to the use of punitive measures. Such measures were frequently suggested; they included removing privileges from the bully and increasing supervision of

their activities. The emphasis in the 1999 Prison Service strategy is on the development of stage systems to deal with bullying. Such systems are widely used in prisons and do have some benefits, for example they enable staff to be consistent in their response to bullying. They are not of use, however, unless they are applied correctly and consistently. The limits of adopting an approach aimed at changing an individual's behaviour based on principles of punishment should also be recognised. As highlighted previously, for such approaches to be effective they need to adhere to a number of criteria, for example the punishment must be consistently applied as soon as bullying takes place, and the bully should be provided with alternative responses. With bullying, these criteria are difficult to adhere to and thus it cannot be expected that punitive measures on their own will be effective. Other concerns include the possibility that applying such measures may serve to victimise prisoners, particularly those bullies who report being victims as well. The consequences of such an approach (i.e. removing a bully from a wing or restricting their activities) may actually reinforce the aggressive behaviour displayed by those prisoners who are both bullies and bullied. In view of this it is important that if punitive interventions are employed, they should form only part of a wider intervention programme that is tailored to the individual prisoner and includes some method of changing behaviour based on positive reinforcement.

3   One way of positively reinforcing changes in the behaviour of bullies that has been suggested relates to acknowledging and (verbally) praising them when they have shown an improvement in their behaviour. Ideally, this praise should be communicated to bullies via a multidisciplinary format.

4   Similarly, exploring alternative ways in which the bully can obtain their goals without the use of bullying may be a useful intervention. This can take the form of a cost–benefit analysis where the consequences of bullying for the prisoner are explored and, where possible, alternative and more prosocial ways of obtaining their goals suggested.

5   There needs to be recognition that group-based or individual interventions should be tailored to the specific skill deficits of the prisoners to whom they will be applied. Such interventions should form part of a wider strategy that acknowledges the importance of the environment. Attempting to treat bullies and/or victims in isolation from the environment in which the bullying takes place is unlikely to be

effective. For this reason (among others) the use of dedicated units for either bullies or victims is not recommended.

6  Based on the limited research available at present, a number of recommendations can be made about the use of specific group-based or individual programmes with bullies and/or victims. For example, programmes focusing on assertiveness, anger management, social skills, cognitive skills and victim empathy may not be appropriate for prisoners who report bullying others, particularly pure bullies. Research suggests that some bullies may actually be skilled in some of these areas already, particularly cognitive and social skills. Training them to improve their skills could inadvertently enhance their ability to bully others. There is some suggestion in the literature, however, that assertiveness, anger management and training focusing on victim empathy may be appropriate for prisoners who report both being bullied and bullying others. Courses focusing on enhancing the self-esteem of prisoners who bully others are not thought to be appropriate.

With regard to prisoners who report being bullied, assertiveness training may prove useful, particularly if it is part of an intervention programme that addresses a range of cognitive and social skills. Importantly such training should address how prisoners should respond before, during and after an incident of bullying. Training on how to respond following an incident of bullying, for example, can include using assertiveness skills to request help from staff. Importantly, training on how to respond during an incident should also acknowledge the value of passive strategies in circumstances where the risk of potential injury for the victim is deemed high. For this reason self-defence training for victims should only be used if it also addresses non-physical ways of avoiding conflicts. Similarly, the value of providing victims with weight training is unclear in that physical size is not actually related to victim status. If the aim of such training is to increase self-esteem, however, it should be acknowledged that although there is a relationship between self-esteem and victim status for children, the same has not been consistently found for prisoners.

7  A recognition that how staff respond to prisoners reporting that they have been bullied is important. The response of staff may determine whether or not the prisoner will report victimisation in the future and may affect how other victims feel about approaching staff. Staff need to be aware of the difficulties that victims face in reporting bullying to them: not only are they violating the prisoner code of not informing

but they are also acknowledging their status as a victim. Staff responses should be supportive and not challenging (i.e. not putting pressure on the victim to disclose the name of the bully or bullies) and they should communicate to victims that they are treating the matter seriously and sensitively.

8   Attempts should be made to involve victims in the process of investigation and resolution of the incident as much as possible with the aim of empowering them. At the very least, staff should keep victims informed of developments relating to their case. Any other direct involvement from victims (e.g. victims suggesting penalties for bullies) should be avoided and overall responsibility for the resolution of the incident should lie with staff.

9   Developing ways of supporting victims, attempting to empower the victim by asking them what support they require and documenting when support is given and what it includes, are all elements that a reactive strategy should include. With regard to this latter point, staff should be encouraged to offer support to victims but not to force it on them if they decline. Support should be defined broadly along the lines described in the section on supporting victims (pp. 197–200), and there should be a distinction between the immediate support that is offered to victims and that which should form part of a long-term support plan. Involving other prisoners in providing support to victims (e.g. using listeners or developing a buddy system) should be carefully managed and not used if there is any risk of placing the victim in further danger of being bullied. Finally, although there has been some suggestion of moving victims following an incident of bullying, as opposed to moving the bully, such an action needs to be carefully considered. Victims should be moved only under exceptional circumstances where they express a wish to be moved and where it is felt that their mental or physical health will deteriorate if they are not moved, or if staff feel that the victim will be at risk of further bullying if they stay.

10  'Mediation meetings' between victims and bullies where both parties can discuss the bullying incident(s) with staff acting as facilitators can also be considered. Such meetings should have clear aims and objectives in terms of what they hope to achieve and should form part of a wider intervention programme. They should only take place if all parties consent.

11  There needs to be a recognition that there are not just two groups involved in bullying (bullies and victims), but that there is also a third group (bully/victims). The group to which prisoners belong should

be taken into consideration when deciding which intervention should be employed with them. This is particularly true for bully/victims who have tended to be neglected by intervention strategies. The interventions suggested in the section on accounting for the different groups involved in bullying (pp. 200–203) should be considered once the prisoner has been identified as either a pure bully, a pure victim or a bully/victim. With pure bullies, the focus should be on managing their behaviour and limiting the opportunities that they have to bully others, with pure victims the focus should be on support and with bully/victims it should include a combination of both support and management.

12   A recognition that the stability of the classifications pure bully, bully/victim and pure victim remains unclear. It is suspected that a prisoner's classification in one of these groups may change over time. Intervention strategies need to take this into account and concentrate on the prisoner's most recent behaviour when developing specific interventions to manage them.

13   Connected to this, prison establishments need to demonstrate a commitment to improving their strategies for use with bullies and/or victims as knowledge about bullying behaviour increases. The need to evaluate the effectiveness of the intervention employed should form an integral part of the strategy.

14   A recognition that intervention strategies should be applied consistently if they are to be effective. If staff are inconsistent in their responses to bullies and/or victims, it cannot be hoped that the intervention will be effective.

15   A recognition that any intervention employed with bullies and/or victims needs to be tailored to their individual needs. Intervention with these groups also needs to form part of a programme where a range of different strategies are applied. Using a single strategy to try and deal with bullying (e.g. removing privileges from a bully and doing nothing else) is unlikely to be as effective as a strategy that includes a range of elements (e.g. a stage system, positive approaches, group-based intervention).

## Summary

This chapter has presented a number of reactive measures that could be employed following an incident of bullying. The importance of conducting thorough investigations prior to the implementation of direct strategies for either bullies and/or victims has been highlighted and suggestions offered regarding what reactive strategies should include if they hope to be effective. Undoubtedly, there is a great deal of overlap between the reactive strategies presented here and the preventative strategies presented in Chapter 7. Although they have been presented separately, this was simply for ease of interpretation and any strategy, if it is to be effective, should place equal emphasis on both reactive and preventative strategies. Ideally, each should inform the development of the other, for example the findings following an investigation into an incident of bullying should be used not only to inform what strategy should be taken to manage the behaviour of the bullies and to support the victims, but also to inform preventative strategies by highlighting where and when bullying is likely to take place.

I have also attempted to highlight the importance of the victim in anti-bullying strategies. At present there is a tendency for strategies to focus on challenging the behaviour of the bullies with less emphasis on how the victim forms part of the process. Whereas the focus on bullies should be on managing their behaviour, the focus on victims should be on supporting them (and a combination of both approaches if they are a bully/victim). Thus, the importance of supporting the victim, along with suggestions of what support can be put in place, should represent a major element of any strategy. With regard to bullies, I have attempted to highlight ways of dealing with them that do not emphasise the use of punishment, but include strategies designed to monitor and modify their behaviour, with the aim of either reducing the amount of bullying that they engage in and/or limiting the opportunities that they have to bully others. Importantly, it should be acknowledged that interventions for some bullies may not be about changing their behaviour, particularly if they are resistant to change, instead it may be more about limiting the opportunities that they have to bully others.

One of the most important points illustrated in the present chapter is the recognition that there are three groups involved in bullying – pure bullies, pure victims and bully/victims – and that if strategies are to be effective they need to recognise all of these groups and should be tailored accordingly. Although this chapter has focused on those directly involved in bullying, either as bullies and/or victims, intervention strategies also need to consider the behaviour of those prisoners who witness incidents of bullying and do nothing about it. This is perhaps a direction that future research could address. Little is known about the bystanders to incidents of bullying and, as highlighted in Chapter 7, involving the whole peer group in intervention strategies (not just those directly involved) is important since bullying is very much a product of the peer group.

Finally, there is a definite need for the interventions suggested to be evaluated and audited on a regular basis. This holds both for the reactive strategies presented here and the preventative strategies in Chapter 7. The question 'how do we know a strategy is being effective?' is not an easy one to answer in terms of what prisons should be looking for as evidence of 'effectiveness'. As mentioned previously, since bullying is a product of many factors, some of which are outside the control of prison authorities, the goal of intervention strategies should be the reduction of bullying and not the eradication of it since this is an unobtainable goal. Indeed, prisons that claim to have no, or very little, bullying are unlikely to be measuring it accurately. Thus, although reducing bullying should be a primary measure of effectiveness, it should not be the only measure. I would suggest the following as indicators of effectiveness as well.

1   Evidence that the strategy is being applied by all staff consistently, i.e. that all incidents of bullying are investigated thoroughly in accordance with specified guidelines and that the reactive strategies put in place for bullies and/or victims are tailored to their individual needs.

2   Evidence that information obtained during investigations is being used both to develop and inform reactive and preventative strategies. If the investigation highlights a particular area in the prison where bullying is likely to occur, for example, preventative strategies can be put in place to reduce it. A measure of effectiveness in this instance would include a reduced number of bullying incidents associated with this location.

3   Evidence that all staff (and prisoners) show a commitment to the anti-bullying strategy, consider it to be a high-profile issue and recognise their personal responsibility towards ensuring that it is adhered to.

4   Evidence that both prisoners and staff are supportive of victims and disapproving of bullies. Attitudes of indifference towards bullying and those that condone the use of bullying or act to stigmatise victims should be viewed as evidence that the strategy is having limited success. Staff attitudes are as important as those held by prisoners. Evidence of inappropriate staff attitudes include derogatory comments being made about certain types of offenders (e.g. sex offenders), victims being made fun of (e.g. being called 'herbets' or 'fraggles'), prisoners being encouraged to deal with problems themselves and not to seek the help of staff, and prisoners who appear withdrawn and are not being engaged with.

5   Evidence that all staff present with a good understanding and working

knowledge of the policies and procedures that should be put in place following a suspected incident of bullying. The same should be true for prisoners: all prisoners should have a good understanding of the overall strategy and not just those who have had direct experience of it (i.e. as a bully and/or victim).

# Notes

1   This reference does not appear in Table 1.1 since the majority of the results from this research were published separately.

2   Ireland (1997) was an MSc thesis that was later published as Ireland (1999a). The specific results presented here are unique to the thesis.

3–6  These results appear in Ireland (1997), an MSc thesis on which Ireland (1999a) was based.

7   Although it should be noted that Feld is commenting here on male prisoners, the extent to which this applies to women is unclear, as the social and cultural background of women prisoners is a neglected area of research.

8   These accounts were recorded as part of the data collected by Ireland (2002d) but did not appear in the published paper.

9   Some of these results can be found in Ireland (2000b), a PhD thesis on which Ireland (2001a) was based.

10  BIRs were raised by staff on prisoners if they were identified either as a bully or as a victim, or if they were suspected of bullying others or of being bullied themselves.

11  These accounts were recorded as part of the data collected by Ireland (2002d) but did not appear in the published paper.

12  These latter results appear in Ireland (1997), an MSc thesis on which Ireland (1999a) was based.

13  Importantly, Livingston and Chapman (1997) note how this is not a euphemism for 'manipulation', stating how the idea that self-injury is in some way manipulative (and therefore of limited concern) is a flawed and potentially dangerous misconception.

14  The majority of prisoners in the UK *do* now have access to televisions either in their dormitories or cells.

15  Programmes in which all prisoners new to an establishment will attend in order to familiarise them with the rules and regulations of that particular prison.

16  Young Offenders' Institution.

17  Interestingly the 1999 Prison Service strategy specifically stated that 'special clothing' should not be used to identify bullies.

18  A multidisciplinary board that meets to discuss how individual prisoners are progressing through their sentence with the aim of setting goals and targets for them to achieve.

# Bibliography

Adams, A. (1992) *Bullying at Work: How to Confront and Overcome It*. London: Virago Press.

Adams, A. (1997) Bullying at work. *Journal of Community and Applied Social Psychology* 7: 177–180.

Ahmad, Y. and Smith, P. K. (1994) Bullying in schools and the issue of sex differences, in J. Archer (ed.) *Male Violence*. London: Routledge.

Archer, J. (1970) Effects of population density on behaviour in rodents, in J. H. Crook (ed.) *Social Behaviour in Birds and Mammals*. London: Academic Press.

Archer, J. (2000) Sex differences in physical aggression to partners: a reply to commentaries. *Psychological Bulletin* 126: 697–702.

Archer, J., Monks, S. and Connors, L. (1997) Comments on SP0409: A. Campbell, M. Sapochnik and S. Muncer's Sex differences in aggression: does social representation mediate forms? BJSP, 1997, 36: 161–171. *British Journal of Social Psychology* 36: 603–606.

Askew, S. (1989) Aggressive behaviour in boys: to what extent is it institutionalised? in D. P. Tattum. and D. A. Lane (eds) *Bullying in Schools*. Stoke-on-Trent: Trentham Books.

Baer, J. (1976) *How to be an Assertive (not Aggressive) Woman in Life, Love, and on the Job: a Total Guide to Self-assertiveness*. New York: New American Library.

Bartollas, C., Miller, S. J. and Dinitz, S. (1974) The Booty-Bandit: a social role in a juvenile institution. *Journal of Homosexuality* 1: 203–212.

Beck, G. (1992) *Bullying Among Incarcerated Young Offenders*. Unpublished MSc thesis, Birkbeck University, London, UK.

Beck, G. (1995) Bullying among young offenders in custody. *Issues in Criminological and Legal Psychology* 22: 54–70.

Beck, G. and Ireland, J. (1997) Measuring bullying in prisons. *Inside Psychology* 3: 71–77.

Beck, G. and Smith, P. K (1997) An alternative assessment of the prevalence of bullying among young offenders, in G. Beck. and J. L. Ireland Measuring bullying in prisons. *Inside Psychology* 3: 71–77.

Beck. G. and Smith, P. K. (1999) A longitudinal study of young offenders' conduct and experiences in prison, in J. L. Ireland., S. Jarvis., G. Beck. and S. Osiowy Bullying in prison: a review of recent research. *Forensic Update* January, 56: 4–9.

Besag, V. (1993) *Bullies and Victims in Schools: a Guide to Understanding and Management*. Cambridge, UK: Open University Press.

Biggam, F. H. and Power, K. G. (1998) A comparison of the problem-solving abilities and psychological distress of suicidal, bullied, and protected prisoners. *Criminal Justice and Behavior* 25: 177–197.

Birkett, D. (1998) In defence of the bully. *Guardian Weekend* April 25: 24–33.

Björkqvist, K. (1992) Preface, in K. Björkqvist and P. Niemelä (eds) *Of Mice and Women: Aspects of Female Aggression*. San Diego, CA: Academic Press.

Björkqvist, K. (1994) Sex differences in physical, verbal, and indirect aggression: a review of recent research. *Sex Roles* 30: 177–188.

Björkqvist, K. and Niemelä, P. (1992) New trends in the study of female aggression, in K. Björkqvist and P. Niemelä (eds) *Of Mice and Women: Aspects of Female Aggression*. San Diego, CA: Academic Press.

Björkqvist, K., Lagerspetz, K. M. J. and Kaukiainen, A. (1992a) Do girls manipulate and girls fight? *Aggressive Behavior* 18: 117–127.

Björkqvist, K., Österman, K. and Kaukiainen, A. (1992b) The development of direct and indirect aggressive strategies in males and females, in K. Björkqvist and P. Niemelä, (eds) *Of Mice and Women: Aspects of Female Aggression*. San Diego, CA: Academic Press.

Björkqvist K., Österman, K. and Hjelt-Bäck, M. (1994a) Aggression among university employees. *Aggressive Behavior* 20: 173–184.

Björkqvist, K., Österman, K. and Lagerspetz, K. M. J. (1994b) Sex differences in covert aggression among adults. *Aggressive Behavior* 20: 27–33.

Blackburn, R. (2000) Treatment or incapacitation? Implications of research on personality disorders for the management of dangerous offenders. *Legal and Criminological Psychology* 5: 1–21.

Blud, L. (1999) Cognitive skills programmes, in G. J. Towl and C. McDougall (eds) *What do Forensic Psychologists do? Current and Future Directions in the Prison and Probation Services*. Issues in Forensic Psychology, 1, Division of Forensic Psychology, Leicester: British Psychological Society.

Blyth, D. and Traeger, C. (1983) The self-concept of self-esteem in early adolescents. *Theory into Practice* 22: 91–97.

Bolt, C. (1999) *A Questionnaire Survey to Establish the Incidence and Nature of Bullying at HMP Holme House*. Unpublished report, Psychology Department, HMP Holme House, UK.

Boulton, M. J. and Hawker, D. S. (1997) Non-physical forms of bullying among school pupils: a cause for concern. *Health Education* 2: 61–64.

Bowker, L. (1983) An essay on prison violence. *The Prison Journal* 62: 24–31. Cited in R. J. Mutchnick and M. R. Fawcett (1990) Violence in juvenile corrections: correlates of victimization in group homes. *International Journal of Offender Therapy and Comparative Criminology* 43: 43–57.

Brookes, M. (1993) *Reducing Bullying At HMP Ranby*. Unpublished report, Psychology Research Report, 8, East Midlands, UK.

Brookes, M. and Pratt, M. (1996) An anti-bullying strategy in a category C prison (HMP Ranby). *Issues in Criminological and Legal Psychology* 25: 10–16.

Brookes, M., Cooper, R., Trivette, E. and Willmot, P. (1994) *Bullying Survey at HMP Lincoln*. Unpublished report, Psychology Research Report, 19, East Midlands, UK.

Bushman, B. J. and Anderson, C. A. (1998) Methodology in the study of aggression: integrating experimental and non-experimental findings, in R. G. Geen and E. Donnerstein (eds) *Human Aggression: Theories, Research and Implications for Social Policy*. San Diego, CA: Academic Press.

Calhoun, G. and Morse, W. (1977) Self-concept and self-esteem: another perspective. *Psychology in the Schools* 14: 318–322.

Campbell, A., Sapochnik, M. and Muncer, S. (1997) Sex differences in aggression: does social representation mediate forms of aggression? *British Journal of Social Psychology* 36: 161–171.

Connell, A. and Farrington, D. (1996) 'Bullying among incarcerated young offenders: developing an interview schedule and some preliminary results. *Journal of Adolescence* 19: 75–93.

Connell, A. and Farrington, D. (1997) The reliability and validity of resident, staff and peer reports of bullying in young offender institutions. *Psychology, Crime and Law* 3: 1–11.

Cooke, D. J. (1991) Violence in prisons: the influence of regime factors. *The Howard Journal* 30: 95–109.

Cooley, D. (1993) Criminal victimization in male federal prisons. *Canadian Journal of Criminology* 4: 479–495.

Crick, N. R. and Grotpeter, J. K. (1995) Relational aggression, gender, and social-psychological adjustment. *Child Development* 66: 710–722.

Cullen, E. (1997) Can a prison be a therapeutic community? The Grendon Template, in E. Cullen, L. Jones and R. Woodward (eds) *Therapeutic Communities for Offenders*. London: John Wiley & Sons.

Cullen, E., Jones, L. and Woodward, R. (eds) (1997) *Therapeutic Communities for Offenders*. London: John Wiley & Sons.

Davis, M. (1980) A multidimensional approach to individual differences in empathy. *JSAS Catalogue of Selected Documents in Psychology* 10: 85.

Davis, M. H. (1983) Measuring individual differences in empathy: evidence for a multidimensional approach. *Journal of Personality and Social Psychology* 44: 113–126.

Dodge, K. A. (1986) A social information processing model of social competence in children, in M. Perlmutter (ed.) *Eighteenth Annual Minnesota Symposium on Child Psychology*. Hillsdale, NJ: Erlbaum.

Dodge, K. A. (1991) The structure and function of reactive and proactive aggression, in D. J. Pepler and K. H. Rubin (eds) *The Development and Treatment of Childhood Aggression*. Hillsdale, NJ: Erlbaum.

Dodge, K. A. and Coie, J. D. (1987) Social information-processing factors in reactive and proactive aggression in children's playgroups. *Journal of Personality and Social Psychology* 53: 1146–1158.

Donaldson, S. (1984) *Rape of Males: a Preliminary Look at the Scope of the Problem.* Unpublished thesis, cited by R. W. Dumond (1992) The sexual assault of male prisoners in incarcerated settings. *International Journal of the Sociology of Law* 20: 135–157.

Duckworth, N. (1998) *Can Young People in a Secure Environment be Identified as Potential Victims of Bullying by their Behaviour within the Secure Centre Environment?* Unpublished MSc thesis, University of Birmingham, Birmingham: UK.

Dyson, G. P., Power, K. G. and Wozniak, E. (1997) Problems with using official records from young offender institutions as indices of bullying. *International Journal of Offender Therapy and Comparative Criminology* 41: 121–138.

Ekland-Olson, S. (1986) Crowding, social-control, and prison violence: evidence from the post-Ruiz years in Texas. *Law and Society Review* 20: 389–421.

Ellis, D., Grasmick, H. G. and Gilman, B. (1974) Violence in prisons: a sociological analysis. *American Journal of Sociology* 80: 16–43.

Falshaw, L. (1993) *Why Me? Can Incarcerated Young Offenders be Identified as Potential Victims of Bullying by their Behaviour within the Penal Environment?* Unpublished BSc thesis, Aston University, UK.

Farrington, D. P. (1993) Understanding and preventing bullying, in M. Tonry (ed.) *Crime and Justice: a Review of Research.* Chicago: University of Chicago Press.

Farrington, D. P. and Nuttall, C. P. (1980) Prison size, overcrowding, prison violence and recidivism. *Journal of Criminal Justice* 8: 221–231.

Feld, B. C. (1981) A comparative analysis of organisational structure and inmate subcultures in institutions for juvenile offenders. *Journal of Crime and Delinquency* 27: 336–363.

Fuller, D. A. and Orsagh, T. (1977) Violence and victimisation within a state prison system. *Criminal Justice Review* 2: 35–55.

Gaes, G. G. and McGuire, W. J. (1985) Prison violence: the contribution of crowding versus other determinates of prison assault rates. *Journal of Research into Crime and Delinquency* 22: 41–65.

Galassi, M. D. and Galassi, J. P. (1978) Assertion: a critical review. *Psychotherapy: Theory, Research and Practice* 15: 16–29.

Geen, R. G. (1998) Processes and personal variables in affective aggression, in R. G. Geen and E. Donnerstein (eds) *Human Aggression: Theories, Research and Implications for Social Policy.* San Diego, CA: Academic Press.

Gilbert, P. (1994) Male violence: towards an integration, in J. Archer (ed.) *Male Violence.* London and New York: Routledge.

Grant, K. (1999) Survey of the extent and nature of bullying among female prisoners and its relationship with fear and precautionary behaviours. *Prison Research and Development Bulletin* April: 5–6.

Green, L. R., Richardson, D. R. and Lago, T. (1996) How do friendship, indirect and direct aggression relate? *Aggressive Behavior* 22: 81–86.

Hancock, S. and Sharp, S. (1985) Educational achievement and self-esteem in a maximum security prison program. *Journal of Offender Rehabilitation* 20: 21–33.

Hare, R. D. (1991) *The Hare Psychopathy Checklist – Revised*. Toronto: Multi-Health Systems.

Hare, R. D. (1998) The Hare PCL-R: some issues concerning its use and misuse. *Legal and Criminological Psychology* 3: 99–119.

Harter, S. (1993) Causes and consequences of low self-esteem in children and adolescents, in R. F. Baumeister (ed.) *Self-esteem: the Puzzle of Low Self-regard*. New York: Plenum Press.

HM Inspectorate (1999) *Suicide is Everyone's Concern: a Thematic Review by HM Chief Inspector of Prisons for England and Wales*. London: Tactica Solutions.

Hoel, H., Rayner, C. L. and Cooper, C. (1999) Workplace bullying, in C. L. Cooper and I. T. Robertson (eds) *International Review of Industrial and Occupational Psychology*. London: John Wiley & Sons.

Home Office Prison Service (1993) *Bullying in Prison: a Strategy to Beat It*. London: HMSO.

Home Office Prison Service (1999) *Anti-bullying Strategy*. Prison Service Order 1702.

Home Office Prison Service (2001) *PINphones project*. Prisoner Administration Group Newsletter 1, March, London, UK.

Hutt, C. and Vaizey, M. J. (1966) Differential effects of group density on social behaviour. *Nature* 209(30): 1371–1372.

Ireland, C. A. (1998) *An Analysis of the Nature and Extent of Bullying at HMP Frankland*. Unpublished report, Research, Development and Psychological Services, HMP Frankland, UK. A summary of this report was later published in Ireland and Ireland (2000).

Ireland, C. A. (2000) Development and evaluation of a bullying awareness training package for staff. *Forensic Update* 61: 15–18.

Ireland, C. A. and Ireland, J. L. (2000) Descriptive analysis of the nature and extent of bullying behaviour in a maximum-security prison. *Aggressive Behavior* 26: 213–233.

Ireland, J. L. (1995) *Descriptive Analysis of Bullying in Male and Female Adult Prisons*. Unpublished BSc thesis, University of Central Lancashire, Preston, UK. A version of this thesis was later published in Ireland and Archer (1996).

Ireland J. L. (1997) *Bullying Amongst Prisoners: a Study of Gender Differences, Provictim Attitudes and Empathy*. Unpublished MSc thesis, Manchester Metropolitan University, Manchester, UK. Elements of this thesis were later published in Ireland (1999a, 1999b).

Ireland, J. L. (1998a) *Styles of Bullying Amongst Incarcerated Female Offenders*. Paper presented at the International Society for Research into Aggression XXVth Conference, July, Ramapo College, NJ, USA.

Ireland J. L. (1998b) *Direct and Indirect Prisoner Behaviour Checklist (DIPC)*. Unpublished report, University of Central Lancashire, Preston, UK.

Ireland, J. L. (1999a) Bullying among prisoners: a study of adults and young offenders. *Aggressive Behavior* 25: 162–178.

Ireland, J. L. (1999b) Provictim attitudes and empathy in relation to bullying behaviour among prisoners. *Legal and Criminological Psychology* 4: 51–66.

Ireland, J. L. (1999c) A recent bullying survey: results and recommendations for intervention. *Prison Service Journal* 123: 27–30.

Ireland, J. L. (1999d) *Identifying the Victims of Bullying in a Prison Environment*. Paper presented at the Division of Forensic Psychology Annual Conference, September, Cambridge University, Cambridge, UK.

Ireland, J. L. (1999e) Bullying in Prisons, in G. J. Towl and C. McDougall (eds) *What do Forensic Psychologists do? Current and Future Directions in the Prison and Probation Services*. Issues in Forensic Psychology 1, Division of Forensic Psychology, Leicester: British Psychological Society.

Ireland, J. L. (1999f) *Brief Report on Bullying Incident Reports Recorded January 1998 – February 1999*. Unpublished report, Psychology Department, HMYOI Lancaster Farms, Lancaster, UK. A version of this report was later published in Ireland (2002d).

Ireland, J. L. (2000a) Bullying among prisoners: a review of research. *Aggression and Violent Behaviour: A Review Journal* 5: 201–215.

Ireland J. L. (2000b) *Bullying Among Prisoners*. Unpublished PhD thesis, University of Central Lancashire, Preston, UK. Elements of this thesis were later published in Ireland (2001a, 2001c, 2002b, 2002c) and Ireland and Archer (2002).

Ireland, J. L. (2000c) *Bullying Behaviour at HMYOI Lancaster Farms*. Unpublished report, Psychology Department, HMYOI Lancaster Farms, Lancaster, UK. A version of this report was later published in Ireland (2002e).

Ireland, J. L. (2000d) *The Relationship Between Social Problem Solving and Bullying Behaviour Among Male and Female Adult Prisoners*. Paper presented at the International Society for Research into Aggression (ISRA), July, University of Valencia, Valencia, Spain.

Ireland, J. L. (2001a) The relationship between social problem solving and bullying among male and female adult prisoners. *Aggressive Behavior* 27: 297–312.

Ireland, J. L. (2001b) Bullying amongst female prisoners: a brief review of research, in F. Columbus (ed.) *Advances in Psychology Research* vol. II. New York: Nova Science Publishers.

Ireland, J. L. (2001c) 'Bullying behaviour among male and female adult prisoners: a study of perpetrator and victim characteristics. *Legal and Criminological Psychology* 6: 229–246.

Ireland, J. L. (2002a) Working with bullies and victims, in G. Towl (ed.) *The Handbook of Psychology in HM Prison Service*. In press.

Ireland, J. L. (2002b) Social self-esteem and bullying behaviour among adult prisoners. *Aggressive Behavior* 28: 184–197.

Ireland, J. L. (2002c) How does assertiveness relate to bullying behaviour among prisoners? *Legal and Criminological Psychology* 7: 87–100.

Ireland, J. L. (2002d) Official records of bullying incidents among young offenders: what can they tell us and how useful are they? *Journal of Adolescence*: in press.

Ireland, J. L. (2002e) Do juveniles bully more than young offenders? *Journal of Adolescence*: in press.

Ireland, J. L. (2002f) Bullying behaviour among prisoners. *The Psychologist* 15(3): 130–133.

Ireland, J. L. and Archer, J. (1996) Descriptive analysis of bullying in male and female adult prisoners. *Journal of Community and Applied Social Psychology* 6: 35–47.

Ireland, J. L. and Archer, J. (2002) The perceived consequences of responding to bullying with aggression: a study of male and female adult prisoners. *Aggressive Behavior*: in press.

Ireland, J. L. and Hill, C. (2001) Anti-bullying focus groups with prisoners at HMYOI Lancaster Farms. *Prison Service Journal* 133: 40–42.

Ireland, J. L., Beck, G. B. and Smith, P. K. (1998) *Bullying in Prison: a Study of Adults and Young Offenders*. Poster Presentation, Developmental Psychology Conference, September, Lancaster University, Lancaster, UK.

Ireland, J. L., Jarvis, S., Beck, G. and Osiowy, S. (1999) Recent research into bullying in prison. *Forensic Update* 56: 4–9.

Jackson, G. (1970) *Soledad Brother*. New York: Bantam.

Johnson, R. (1978) Youth in crisis: dimensions of self-destructive conduct among adolescent prisoners. *Adolescence* 13: 461–482.

Johnson, R. (1987) *Hard Time: Understanding and Reforming the Prison*. Monterey, CA: Brooks/Cole.

Lagerspetz, K. M. J., Björkqvist, K. and Peltonen, T. (1988) Is indirect aggression typical of females? Gender differences in aggressiveness in 11 to 12-year-old children. *Aggressive Behavior* 14: 403–414.

Lerner, M. J. (1980) *Belief in a Just World: a Fundamental Decision*. New York: Plenum Press.

Levenson, J. (2000) Beating the bullies? The prison service's anti-bullying strategy. *Monitoring Prison Regimes*, London: Prison Reform Trust.

Leymann, H. (1990) Mobbing and psychological terror at workplaces. *Violence and Victims* 5: 119–126.

Liebling, A. (1995) Vulnerability and prison suicide. *The British Journal of Criminology* 35: 173–187.

Liebling, A. and Krarup, H. (1994) Suicide attempts in male prisons. *Research Bulletin* 36: 38–43.

Livingston, M. (1994) *Self-injurious Behaviour in Prisoners*. Unpublished PhD thesis, University of Leeds, Leeds, UK.

Livingston, M. (1997) A review of the literature on self-injurious behaviour amongst prisoners, in G. J. Towl (ed.) *Suicide and Self-Injury in Prisons*.

Issues in Criminological and Legal Psychology, 28, Leicester: British Psychological Society.

Livingston, M. and Beck, G. (1997) A cognitive-behaviour model of self-injury and bullying among imprisoned young offenders, in G. J. Towl (ed.) *Suicide and Self-Injury in Prisons*. Issues in Criminological and Legal Psychology, 28, Leicester: British Psychological Society.

Livingston, M. and Chapman, A. J. (1997) Bullying and self-injurious behaviour in young offenders. *Journal of Prison Service Psychology* 3: 78–81.

Livingston, M., Jones, V. and Hussain, S. (1994) *The Extent of Bullying Amongst Adult Prisoners at HMP/YOI Moorland*. Unpublished report, Psychology Research Report, 20, East Midlands, UK.

Lockwood, D. (1980) *Prison Sexual Violence*. New York: Elsevier.

Loucks, N. (1998) *HMPI Corton Vale: Research into Drugs and Alcohol, Violence and Bullying, Suicides and Self-injury, and Backgrounds of Abuse*. Occasional Papers 1, Scottish Prison Service.

MacDonald, K. B. (1988) *Social and Personality Development: an Evolutionary Synthesis*. New York: Plenum Press.

McCorkle, R. C. (1992) Personal precautions to violence in prison. *Criminal Justice and Behavior* 19: 160–173.

McGuire, J. and Priestly, P. (2000) Reviewing 'what works': past, present and future, in J. McGuire (ed.) *What Works, Reducing Re-offending: Guidelines from Research and Practice*. London: John Wiley & Sons.

McGurk, B. J. and McDougall, C. (1986) *The Prevention of Bullying Among Incarcerated Delinquents*. Directorate of Psychological Services Report 2, London: HMSO. Later published as McGurk and McDougall (1991).

McGurk, B. J. and McDougall, C. (1991) The prevention of bullying among incarcerated delinquents, in D. Thompson and P. K. Smith (eds) *Practical Approaches to Bullying*. London: David Fulton.

Marshall, R. E. (1993) The application of psychological principles to the problems of bullying amongst young offenders: a multi-disciplinary approach. *Journal of Prison Service Psychology* 1: 8–16.

Masden, K. M. (1997) *Differing Perceptions of Bullying*. Unpublished PhD thesis, University of Sheffield, Sheffield, UK.

Mealey, L. (1995) The sociobiology of sociopathy: an integrated evolutionary model. *Behavioural and Brain Sciences* 18: 523–599.

Megargee, E. I. (1976) Population density and disruptive behaviour in a prison setting, in A. K. Cohen, A. F. Cole and R. G. Bailey (eds) *Prison Violence*. Lexington, MA: D.C. Heath.

Megargee, E. I. (1977) The association of population density, reduced space and uncomfortable temperatures with misconduct in a prison community. *American Journal of Community Psychology* 5: 289–298.

Mellor, A. (1998) cited by D. Birkett, In defence of the bully. *Guardian Weekend* April 25: 24–33.

Millon, T., Simonsen, E., Birket-Smith, M. and Davis, R. D. (eds) (1998) *Psychopathy: Antisocial, Criminal and Violent Behavior*. New York: Guilford Press.

Mosson, L. (1998) A survey of bullying at HMP/YOI New Hall. *Prison Research and Development Bulletin* 6: 23–24.

Mutchnick, R. J. and Fawcett, M. R. (1990) Violence in juvenile corrections: correlates of victimization in group homes. *International Journal of Offender Therapy and Comparative Criminology* 43: 43–57.

Nacci, P. L., Teitelbaum, H. E. and Prather, J. (1977) Population density and inmate misconduct rates in the federal prison system. *Federal Probation* 41: 26–31.

Nolen–Hoeksema, S. (1987) Sex differences in unipolar depression: evidence and theory. *Psychological Bulletin* 101: 259–282.

O'Brien, M. (1996) *Bullying Information Report: Initial Report.* Unpublished report, Psychology Department, HMYOI Lancaster Farms, Lancaster, UK.

O'Donnell, I. and Edgar, K. (1996a) *The Extent and Dynamics of Victimization in Prisons (revised report).* Unpublished research paper, Centre for Criminological Research, University of Oxford, UK.

O'Donnell, I. and Edgar, K. (1996b) Victimisation in prisons. *Research Findings, Home Office Research and Statistics Directorate* 37: 1–4.

O'Donnell, I. and Edgar, K. (1997) Responding to victimisation: victimisation and safety in prisons and young offender institutions. *Prison Service Journal* 109: 15–19.

Olweus, D. (1978) *Aggression in Schools: Bullies and Whipping Boys.* Washington, DC: Hemisphere.

Olweus, D. (1989) Bully/victim problems among school children: basic facts and effects of a school based intervention programme, in K. Rubin and D. Peplar (eds) (1991) *The Development and Treatment of Childhood Aggression.* Hillsdale, NJ: Erlbaum.

Olweus, D. (1992) Victimisation by peers: antecedents and long-term outcomes, in K. H. Rubin. and J. B. Asendorf (eds) *Social Withdrawal, Inhibition and Shyness in Childhood.* Hillsdale, NJ: Erlbaum.

Olweus, D. (1996) Bully/victim problems in school. *Prospects* 26: 331–359.

O'Moore, A. M. and Hillery, B. (1991) What do teachers need to know? in *Bullying: a Practical Guide for Coping for Schools.* Harlow: Longman Group.

Osiowy, S. (1997) *Anti-bullying Strategies in Adult Prisons.* Unpublished MSc thesis, Loughborough University, Loughborough, UK.

Owens, L. D., Shute, R. and Slee, P. T. (2000) Guess what I just heard!: indirect aggression among teenage girls in Australia. *Aggressive Behavior* 26: 67–83.

Perry, D. G., Perry, L. C. and Kennedy, E. (1992) Conflict and the development of antisocial behaviour, in C. U. Shantz and W. W. Hartup (eds) *Conflict in Child and Adolescent Development.* London: Cambridge University Press.

Power, K. G. and Spencer, A. P (1987) Parasuicidal behaviour of detained Scottish young offenders. *International Journal of Offender Therapy and Comparative Criminology* 31: 227–235.

Power, K. G., Dyson, G. P. and Wozniak, E. (1997) Bullying among Scottish young offenders: prisoners' self-reported attitudes and behaviour. *Journal of Community and Applied Social Psychology* 7: 209–218.

Ramanaiah, N. V. and Deniston, W. M. (1993) NEO personality inventory profiles of assertive and nonassertive persons. *Psychological Reports* 73: 336–338.

Randall, P. (1997) *Adult Bullying: Perpetrators and Victims*. London: Routledge.

Rathus, S. A. (1973) A 30-item schedule for assessing assertive behaviour. *Behaviour Therapy* 4: 398–406.

Richard, B. A. and Dodge, K. A (1982) Social maladjustment and problem solving in school-aged children. *Journal of Consulting and Clinical Psychology* 50: 226–233.

Richardson, D. R. and Green, L. R. (1999) Social sanction and threat explanations of gender effects on direct and indirect aggression. *Aggressive Behavior* 25: 425–434.

Rigby, K. and Slee, P. T. (1991) Bullying among Australian school children: reported behaviour and attitudes towards victims. *Journal of Social Psychology* 131: 615–627.

Rigby, K. and Slee, P. T. (1993) Dimensions of interpersonal relations among Australian children and implications for psychological well-being. *Journal of Social Psychology* 133: 33–42.

Rivers, I. and Smith, P. K. (1994) Types of bullying behaviour and their correlates. *Aggressive Behavior* 20: 359–368.

Rubin, K. H. and Krasnor, L. R. (1986) Social cognitive and social behavioral perspectives on problem solving, in M. Perlmutter (ed.) *Eighteenth Annual Minnesota Symposium on Child Psychology*. Hillsdale, NJ: Erlbaum.

Ruchkin, V. V., Eisemann, M. and Hagglof, B. (1998) Juvenile male rape victims: is the level of post-traumatic stress related to personality and parenting? *Child Abuse and Neglect* 22: 889–899.

Sagarin, E. (1976) Prison homosexuality and its effect on post-prison sexual behavior. *Psychiatry* 39: 245–257.

Salmivalli, C. (1998) Intelligent, attractive, well-behaving, unhappy: the structure of adolescents' self-concept and its relations to their social behaviour. *Journal of Research on Adolescence* 8: 333–354.

Salmivalli, C., Lagerspetz, K., Björkqvist, K., Österman, K. and Kaukiainen, A. (1996) Bullying as a group process: participant roles and their relations to social status within the group. *Aggressive Behavior* 22: 1–15.

Shields, I. W. and Simourd, D. J. (1991) Predicting predatory behaviour in a population of incarcerated young offenders. *Criminal Justice and Behaviour* 18: 180–194.

Simonsen, E. and Birkett-Smith, R. D. (1998) Preface, in T. Millon, E. Simonsen, M. Birket-Smith and R. D. Davis (eds) *Psychopathy: Antisocial, Criminal and Violent Behavior*. New York: Guilford Press.

Slee, P. T. and Rigby, K. (1993) The relationship of Eysenck's personality factors and self-esteem to bully–victim behaviour in Australian schoolboys. *Personality and Individual Differences* 14: 371–373.

Smith, P. K. (1991) The silent nightmare: bullying and victimization in school peer groups. *The Psychologist* 4: 243–248.

Smith, P. K. (1994) What can we do to prevent bullying in school? *The Therapist* 2: 12–15.

Smith, P. K. (2002) Bullying and harassment in schools and the rights of children. *Children and Society*: in press.

Smith, P. K. and Brain, P. (2000) Bullying in schools: lessons from two decades of research. *Aggressive Behavior* 26: 1–9.

Smith, P. K. and Sharpe, S. (1994) *School Bullying: Insights and Perspectives*. London: Routledge.

Stephenson, P. and Smith, D. (1989) Bullying in the junior school, in D. P. Tattum and D. A. Lane (eds) *Bullying in Schools*. Stoke-on-Trent: Trentham Books.

Sutton, J. and Smith, P. K. (1999) Bullying as a group process: an adaptation of the participant role approach. *Aggressive Behavior* 25: 97–111.

Sutton, J., Smith, P. K. and Swettenhem, J. (1996) *Bullying: Perspectives from Social Cognition*. Paper presented at the British Psychological Society Annual Conference, April, London, UK.

Sutton, J., Smith, P. K. and Swettenhem, J. (1999a) Bullying and 'theory of mind': a critique of the 'social skills deficit' view of anti-social behaviour. *Social Development* 8: 117–127.

Sutton, J., Smith, P. K. and Swettenhem, J. (1999b) Social cognition and bullying: social inadequates or skilled manipulators? *British Journal of Developmental Psychology* 17: 435–450.

Swift, J. (1995) *Results of an Investigation into Bullying at HMYOI Deerbolt*. Unpublished report, Psychology Department, HMP Frankland, UK.

Tattum, D. P. (1989) Violence and aggression in schools, in D. P. Tattum and D. A. Lane (eds) *Bullying in Schools*. Stoke-on-Trent: Trentham Books.

Thomas, C. W. (1977) Theoretical perspectives on prisonisation: a comparison of the importation and deprivation models. *Journal of Criminal Law and Criminology* March: 135–145.

Tittle, C. R. (1969) Inmate organisation: sex differentiation and the influence of criminal subcultures. *American Sociological Review* 34: 492–505.

Toch, H. (1978) Social climate and prison violence. *Federal Probation* 42: 21–25.

Toch, H. (1992) *Living in Prison: the Ecology of Survival*. Washington, DC: American Psychological Association.

Towl, G. J. and Crighton, D. A. (1996) *The Handbook of Psychology for Forensic Practitioners*. London: Routledge.

Turner, J. C. (1987) *Rediscovering the Social Group: a Self-Categorisation Theory*. Oxford: Blackwell.

Tversky, A. and Kahnmann, D. (1974) Judgement under uncertainty: heuristics and biases. *Science* 185: 1124–1131.

Weisfeld, G. E. (1994) Aggression and dominance in the social world of boys, in J. Archer (ed.) *Male Violence*. London: Routledge.

Willmot, P. (1997) The development of an anti-bullying strategy at HMP Lincoln. *Journal of Prison Service Psychology* 3: 81–86.

Wright, K. N. (1991) The violent and victimised in the male prison. *Journal of Offender Rehabilitation* 16: 1–25.

# Index

Note: page numbers in *italics* refer to figures/tables.